JACOB BOEHME:
His Life and Thought

JACOB BOEHME:

His Life and Thought

JOHN JOSEPH STOUDT

Foreword by Paul Tillich

Wipf & Stock
PUBLISHERS
Eugene, Oregon

Wipf and Stock Publishers
199 W 8th Ave, Suite 3
Eugene, OR 97401

Jacob Boehme
His Life and Thought
By Stoudt, John J.
ISBN: 1-59244-933-6
Publication date 10/8/2004
Previously published by Seabury Press, 1957

TO MOTHER

FOREWORD

AN EXTENSIVE, scholarly, and readable book on Jacob Boehme in English has been long overdue. It has now been provided by John Stoudt in *Sunrise to Eternity*. For many years his interest was centered around the life and the work of the mystical and philosophical shoemaker and shoetrader of Görlitz in eastern Germany. As a result of the author's work, we have a concrete and vivid picture, not only of the personal affairs of his hero, but also of the spiritual and cultural situation of Protestant Germany in the early sixteenth century. One of the achievements of the book is that it reports in an interesting way the destruction of the Boehme "legend," which has dramatized, as well as distorted, the unique figure of Boehme in the traditional view.

But the main purpose of the book is an analysis of the development and structure of the philosophy and theology of Boehme. This is not an easy task, for although Boehme's thoughts have changed during his writings from a stage of crudity to a stage of comparative clarity, they are always expressed in a language which mirrors speculative vision, mystical experience, psychological insight, and alchemist traditions. It is often difficult to uncover the rational element in this mixture, but it is there and it had an astonishing influence on the history of Western philosophy. One need only mention Schelling's famous book on human freedom which is thoroughly dependent on Boehme's vision of the genesis of God, world, and man. From here, Boehme's indirect influence reaches Hegel and Schopenhauer, Nietzsche and Hartmann, Bergson and Heidegger. He also was a power in the speculative theology of the nineteenth century, especially through his ideas concerning creation and evil. If Protestant theology wants to penetrate the ontological implications of the Christian symbols, it would do well to use the ideas of Boehme more than those of Aristotle. In contrast to the *actus purus* of Aristotle, Boehme tried to describe in metaphysical-psychological symbols the *living* God in whom the roots of every life must be sought.

John Stoudt's book will be a help to all philosophers and theologians who desire an introduction to one of the most profound and strangest systems of Western thought—strange in comparison to the prevailing method of modern philosophy —profound in comparison with much theism in modern theology.

PAUL TILLICH

Harvard University

CONTENTS

ACKNOWLEDGMENTS

Dr. Rufus M. Jones first lighted our Boehme candle in our years at Haverford College and we are in increasing debt to him.

Dr. Will-Erich Peuckert led us to the newly discovered biographical materials, thus enabling us to shake off the dust of old legends.

Dr. Ernst Benz gave valuable help in clarifying several points.

Dr. Hugh Watt and Dr. John Baillie aided in structural arrangement.

The Schwenkfelder Historical Library, Pennsburg, Pennsylvania, allowed use of extensive Silesian materials.

The British Museum gave many favors during the trying war years.

Dr. Alexander Koyré's book proved provocative.

Dr. Howard Brinton and Dr. Anna Brinton shared our Boehme "concern."

Mr. Geoffry Watkins enabled us to acquire the older Boehme editions.

Dr. Paul Tillich, with graciousness, helped us relive Boehme's spirit.

ABBREVIATIONS

THE German text herein used and cited is that of the 1730 edition, edited by Johann Wilhelm Ueberfeld and published in ten volumes under the over-all title of *Theosophia Revelata.* All references to Boehme's works are given within the text itself. The abbreviations are the standard ones adopted by the early editors. The *Epistles* are numbered and so cited as in the 1730 edition which offers the largest number of letters.

There follows a list of Boehme's writings in the probable order of their composition with German title and standard abbreviation of each:

Die Morgenröthe im Aufgang	*Aurora*
Von den drei Principien Göttlichen Wesens	*Princ.*
Vom Dreyfachen Leben des Menschen	*Dreyfach*
Vierzig Fragen von der Seele	*Seel. Frag.*
Von der Menschwerdung Jesu Christi	*Menschw.*
Von Sechs Puncten, or *Sechs Theosophische Punkte*	*Theos. Punkt.*
Eine Kurze Erklärung or *Sechs Mystische Punkte*	*Myst. Punkt.*
Vom Irdischen und Himmlischen Mysterium	*Ird. u. himl. Myst.*
Unterricht von den Letzten Zeiten I	*Letzte Zeit I*
Unterricht von den Letzten Zeiten II	*Letzte Zeit II*
Erste Schutzschrift gegen Balthasar Tilke	*I Apol. Tilke*
Von vier Complexionen	*Complex*
Bedenken über Esaias Stiefels Buchlein	*Bedenk. Stief.*
Zweite Schutzschrift gegen Balthasar Tilke	*II Apol. Tilke*
Von der Geburt und Bezeichnung aller Wesen	*Sig. Rer.*
Erklärung über Stiefels Auslegung	*Irrth. Stief.*
Von Wahre Busse	*Busse*
Von der Wahren Wiedergeburt	*Wiedergeburt*
Von der Wahren Gelassenheit	*Gelassen.*

15

Vom Uebersinnlichen Leben	Uebersinn. Leb.
Von Gottlicher Beschaulichkeit	Beschau.
Von der Gnadenwahl	Gnad.
Schlüssel zum Verstand Gottlicher Geheimnisse	Busse II
Erklärung über das Erste Buch Mosis	Myst. Mag.
Tafel Göttlicher Offenbarung der Dreyen Welten	Taf.
Von Christi Testamenten	Test.
Tafel der Drey Principien	Tab. Princ.
An eine Hungrige und Durstige Seele, or Gespräch einer Erleucht- und Unerleuchteten Seele	Gespräch 2er Seel.
Schlüssel der Vornehmsten Punkte	Clav.
Schutzrede gegen Gregor Richter	Apol. Richt.
Ein Gebet Buchlein	Gebet
Von 177 Theosophischen Fragen	Theos. Frag.

Abbreviations of the standard biographical and critical works used in this work:

Francis Okeley: *Memoirs of the Life, Death, Burial, and Wonderful Writings of Jacob Behmen* . . ., Northampton, 1780; (translations of the early biographical materials)

Okeley: *Memoirs*

Richard Jecht: *Jakob Böhme, Gedenkgabe der Stadt Görlitz*, Görlitz, 1924; (Publication of newly discovered biographical materials)

Jecht: *Böhme*

Will-Erich Peuckert: *Das Leben Jakob Böhmes*, Jena, 1924; (The one usable, standard modern biography)

Peuckert: *Böhme*

Alexander Koyré: *La Philosophie de Jacob Boehme*, Paris, 1929; (The standard work of exposition)

Koyré: *Boehme*

Werner Buddecke: *Verzeichnis von Jakob Böhmes Handschrifften;* (The critical analysis of the newly discovered manuscripts)

Buddecke: *Verzeichnis*

Ernst Benz: *Der vollkommene Mensch nach Jakob Böhme*, Stuttgart, 1937; (The sharpest modern insight into Boehme)

Benz: *Böhme*

Im Innern ist ein Universum auch
Daher der Völcker löblicher Gebrauch,
Das Jeglicher das Beste, was er kennt,
Er Gott, ja seinen Gott benennt,
Ihn Himmel und Erden übergibt,
Ihn fürchtet, und wo möglich liebt.
  —GOETHE: *Sprüche in Reimen*

AUTHOR'S PREFACE

THE TURBULENT SEVENTEENTH CENTURY saw the birth of the modern world, for when Francis Bacon destroyed ancient, stubborn idols, trusted experiment, and established the empirical method our technical civilization arose on the debris of medieval culture. It gained impetus—this scientific world of ours—from René Descartes who, though skeptical, was discovering new certainty in a mathematically grounded rationalism which even then was enriching Scholastic systems with Galilean methods of research. For modern science was being born in a world which was seeking the unity of spirit, a sunrise to eternity, and this longed-for cohesion of man's knowledge was expressed by Descartes in these words of his *Principes de la Philosophie:*

The whole of philosophy is like a tree, the roots of which are metaphysics, the trunk is the science of physics; and the branches shooting from that trunk are all the sciences.[1]

And the road here laid out goes straight from Descartes to Einstein—a highway which more lately passed through Hiroshima, Nagasaki, and Bikini too!

Several years before Descartes had likened the sciences to a branching tree, Jacob Boehme, known as the German philosopher, had employed the same metaphor, but in a far different connotation. Boehme had said:

I liken . . . philosophy to a precious tree which grows in a lovely garden. Now the earth in which the tree stands continually gives sap to the tree from which the tree gets its living quality. But in itself the tree grows from the earth's sap, increases, and broadens out with its branches. Now, just as the earth works on the tree with its vital force so that it grows and increases, so also the tree continually works with its branches . . . ever to produce much good fruit. (*Aurora*, Preface, 1, 2, 3)

Descartes' tree is metaphorical, expressing the sought-for rational unity of technical civilization; Boehme's tree, however, is symbolic, asserting the inner connection between the order of being and the content of theological discussion. For Boehme, philosophical theology is not *like* a tree—it *is* a living, vital, fruit-bearing organism!

Here with Jacob Boehme, then, we come to grips with a theological and philosophical—and perhaps even a religious —tradition different from that which now dominates within Western culture. It is a philosophical theology which subjugates the tables and formulae of the scientist to life's vital force. For with Jacob Boehme the philosophy of life (*Lebensphilosophie*) reasserted its ancient, compelling claims against Western culture's dominant rationalism. He stressed once again those feelings for life's primitive vigor which the Renaissance had cherished and which then were pouring forth—no, bursting out—into new and broader channels. He expressed these intuitions not by orderly exposition but through a fragmentary vision which was at once the vital as well as logical center of his thought. His exposition lent itself to flashes of genius, to aphorism, to cryptic insight, and to bold and far from meaningless symbolism.

Much has been written on Boehme. His place in Western culture's history has become obscured by the exalted reputation some have given him and by the Faustian quackery associated with his name. The extravagant praise heaped upon him has led to wild claims and to wilder writing; he has been called "God-taught," "God-illuminated," the "man who walked with God," and "our blessed Jacob." Indeed, Boehme's obviously meaningful religious experiences have been dismissed as gossamer and fancy while Descartes' visionary bout with the German stove is allowed the substance of truth! Already in the first generation of men after Boehme's death—and to some degree while he was yet alive—there were those, like Abraham von Franckenberg, his first editor, who surrounded his name with hagiographical adoration, ascribing to him an authority which he, in humility, would have been the first to deny. Indeed, a Boehme "folklore" has arisen which suggests "amazing private visions and direct heavenly dictation"—myths which careful reading of Boehme's writings dispels.

Some of this confusion comes from Boehme's way of writing. He was no word-artist. His vocabulary was sometimes barbaric—at least in his earlier and best-known works. On the whole, though, he developed a German which became an adequate instrument for conveying his meaning, even rising at times to high cadence, developed rhythm and outer ear-quality. Yet language obscurities render his thought so opaque that Émile Boutroux, himself an admirer of Boehme's achievement, confessed that he found his language

a mixture of abstruse theology, speculations on the indiscernible and the incomprehensible, fantastic poetry and mystic confusion; in fact, a dazzling chaos.[2]

Gerhard Tersteegen, devout eighteenth-century mystical poet, wrote:

I cannot say that I understood, but I read [Boehme] until I was filled with strange fears and bewilderments. . . . At last I took the books to their owners, and it was like a weight lifted off my heart.[3]

John Wesley, founder of Methodism, was somewhat more emphatic, saying that Boehme's writings were the

most sublime nonsense, inimitable bombast, fustian not to be paralleled.[4]

However ill Boehme's spirit may have been communicated by his words, nonetheless, it has become a force and field of influence within Western culture, even spilling over to the

East. Hegel consecrated an elegiac although not always accurate chapter to him in his *Vorlesungen über die Geschichte der Philosophie,* considering him father to German philosophy.[5] Schelling, much moved by Boehme's spirit, believed that he was a miracle in human history,[6] and Boehme's influence on Romantics like Coleridge, Tieck, and Novalis is obvious.[7] Boehme's philosophical impulses, as his view of the "original craving" and his anticipation of the modern view of existence, became influential for modern philosophy, mediated by Schelling, Kierkegaard, Nietzsche, and Bergson to Heidegger and Jaspers.[8] While historians seem to agree that in Boehme's speculations

religious thought is carried to a limit, a limit which no subsequent attempt of a similar kind has succeeded in transcending,[9]

there is by no means agreement on the exact element or on the nature of that significance. Hegel believed that Boehme was a pantheist-idealist.[10] Franz von Baader believed that Boehme's realism earned him his reputation as *the* Christian philosopher.[11] Baur reproached Boehme for his gnostic Manicheanism.[12] Bréhier links Boehme with Weigel in introducing his chapter on Leibnitz.[13] Lord Russell does not mention Boehme in the index of his *History of Western Philosophy.*[14] While somehow agreeing that Boehme is significant, historians of philosophy read their own systems in him [15] and so, anomalously, Boehme remains vaguely significant in the history of Western thought.

However, if philosophers agree at least that Boehme is somehow significant, churchmen, more confident, have violently disagreed. Gottfried Arnold, prince of Pietist historians, gave Boehme large place, but then Arnold's penchant for heresy made his historiographical principles unique.[16] Mosheim lumped Boehme together with chemists, *Rosenkreutzer,* fanatics, fire-philosophers and other venom.[17] The Commission of the Churches of Berne, February 8, 1699, condemned Boehme's works as enthusiastic and fanatical books.[18] Dorner saw in Boehme only fermenting speculative chaos.[19] Max Göbel gave Boehme place in the Rhineland's spiritual history even though detailed analysis lay beyond his scope.[20] Ritschl opposed Boehme because he believed that the shoemaker had presumed to oppose evil in the Lutheran churches and Ritschl argued that Boehme's *The Way to Christ* was used as a foil to parry established Lutheranism's thrusts—as it was —and he concluded that it was impossible to know Boehme's meaning because his writings were not clear.[21] R. Seeberg mentions Boehme but twice in his two volumes on Protestant doctrine.[22] The Quaker, Rufus M. Jones, however, claimed that Boehme's influence on the radical left-wing groups was strong and he saw in Boehme a man of towering stature.

We propose now to add another book on Boehme—to confound the confusion, if that be possible—by turning iconoclast and breaking the traditional image of venerated sainthood in a heretical eternity which his well-meaning but misguided admirers have formed. Moreover, we propose to give Boehme his rightful place, as we see it, within the history of Western culture by an objective exposition of his mature doctrine. Nor do we propose to walk a middle road, for we know that he who walks down the middle of the road gets shot at from both sides! We are seeking facts and, although positivism is now old-fashioned in historical scholarship, it may prove feasible to present what is surely known. Who was he? What did he write, and in what order? What were the lines of his growth? What did he really mean to say? For we are seeking neither a heaven-blessed saint nor a baroque Faust but a man who saw the sunrise to eternity.

Two basic problems appear and our book's two parts are attempts to answer these problems: first, Boehme's life, age, region, and spiritual growth; and second, his mature religious thought.

Charting Boehme's intellectual development rests on what we can learn from external source materials combined with informed reading of his works. Before 1924 our knowledge of Boehme's life depended upon the biographical materials gathered together by Abraham von Franckenberg and other early admirers. These documents are not always reliable. Discovery of new biographical matter by Jecht and Peuckert, rediscovery of the original manuscripts by Buddecke, new knowledge of the background, and careful reading of

Boehme's letters in their proper chronological order, allows a new picture of Boehme, the prosperous merchant, to supplant that of the simple, stuttering cobbler who dreamed doctrines from vision-stuff. We propose to try to paint this new portrait on the basis of the evidence now available, one which may, perhaps, project Boehme as the proponent of a theology which stresses feeling and intuition instead of reason and intellect.

Expounding Boehme's doctrine, which is our second task, remains hopeless as long as we are so naive as to accept everything that he wrote, at every stage of his life, as of equal value; for no hope seems to exist for us if we do not see his astonishing capacity for growth. His was a restless mind which never really found a static, stable, "systematic" point of view; his thought was ever mobile and alive; and he grew from what he himself called a "childlike beginning" to deep maturity. We have chosen 1623, the last full year of his life, during which he wrote *Gnad.* and *Myst. Mag.*, as his finest mature period. His works of 1624, some of which remained incomplete, presaged a still higher synthesis yet to come and he died just as his profoundest thought was emerging in clearly expressed ideas. His promise was great. Our exposition of his views, then, is an attempted cross-section of his thought during the year 1623 which is, we believe, his finest period. Astute scholars will be able to discover passages in his earlier works which seem to contradict our exposition; but, we believe, these contradictions were ultimately resolved in his last synthesis.

Moreover, Boehme's doctrine, never fully systematized, emerges from matter which may, perhaps, defy rational order. His earlier periods were the least lucid, marked by efforts to adopt terms and symbols foreign to his thought which were being urged on him by his friends. The Pietist Spener wanted someone to wade through the swamp of Boehme's terms to the dry land of clear ideas. Boehme did this himself; he threw off the foolish jargon of alchemy and the Cabala as he matured, and, while ideas from such sources continued to influence his doctrine, their terms were being rejected by Boehme himself as he wrote to Christian Bernhard:

I am sorry that you find my writings so difficult in some points, and I wish I could impart my soul to you so that you may grasp my meaning . . . for I understand that it deals with the deepest points where I have used some Latin words; but my sense rests in truth, more in the natural language than in the Latin. . . . (*Epist.* iv, 25, 26)

Slowly he gained courage to reject the foreign terminology which his friends urged on him and the works of his maturity are as clear as they need be.

Boehme's mature system—if such it be—was not Spinoza's: tight, logical, orderly, and static. His expressed words emerged from what may be called mystical vision—and we have sought to reconstruct that vision of the sunrise to eternity from his own accounts—for he sought to expose the mystical analogue. Moreover, he was part poet, enamored of metaphor, and we must not confuse poets' words with theological substance. He was prophet, too, and we ought not to mistake prophetic passion for religious insight.

Untrained in the schools, free as only Renaissance men were free, unhindered by the past yet with a sense of history, Jacob Boehme approached old, old problems with a new sincerity. Like Clement of Alexandria Boehme was driven by an individualizing freedom which places him, with Bacon and Descartes, as one of the founders of modern culture. The scientists, who with formula and tables have split the atom, have only proved in the laboratory what Jacob Boehme saw in that fire-flaming quarter of an hour—his sunrise to eternity —that in Yes and No all *things* consist!

JOHN JOSEPH STOUDT

Norristown, Pennsylvania
Nineteen Fifty-Six

NOTES TO PREFACE

1. As quoted by Lucien Lévy-Bruhl, *A History of Modern Philosophy in France*, Chicago, 1924, p. 8.

2. *Historical Studies in Philosophy,* London, 1912, p. 171.
3. Quoted by H. E. Gowan, *Life of Gerhard Tersteegen,* London, 1898, p. 42.
4. Quoted by G. C. Cell, *The Rediscovery of John Wesley,* New York, 1935, p. 117.
5. *Vide: Werke,* xv, Berlin, 1936, p. 297, *et passim.* In 1809 Van-Ghert, the Dutch philosopher, presented Hegel with a "beautiful edition of Jacob Boehme's writings in two volumes." This was doubtless the 1715 edition. Cf. *G. W. Fr. Hegels Lebensbeschreibung durch Karl Rosenkranz,* Berlin, 1844, p. 284.
6. *Philosophie der Offenbarung,* in *Werke,* II, iii, Stuttgart, 1858, p. 123.
7. O. Walzel, *German Romanticism,* New York, 1932, pp. 6, 66ff, 86, 98ff, and 92.
8. Cf. Paul Tillich, "Existential Philosophy," in *Journal of the History of Ideas,* January, 1944, I, pp. 44ff.
9. H. Höffding, *A History of Modern Philosophy,* tr. Meyer, London, 1924, I, p. 78.
10. *Werke,* xv, pp. 301ff.
11. *Vorlesungen über J. B. Theologumena und Philosophie,* in *Werke,* III, Leipzig, 1853, p. 357.
12. *Die Christliche Gnosis,* Tübingen, 1835, pp. 586, 591.
13. Émile Bréhier, *Histoire de la Philosophie,* II, i, pp. 231ff.
14. *A History of Western Philosophy,* New York, 1945.
15. A Koyré, *La Philosophie de Jacob Boehme,* Paris, 1929, pp. ixff.
16. Gottfried Arnold, *Unpartheyischen Kirchen- und Ketzer Historei,* Franckfurt, 1579, pp. 1130–1155a. *Vide:* Erich Seeberg, *Gottfried Arnold, Die Wissenschaft und Mystik seiner Zeit,* Meerane, 1923, pp. 35ff.
17. *Vollständige Kirchengeschichte,* Heilbronn, 1780, IV, pp. 67–69.
18. Hadorn, *Geschichte des Pietismus in dem schweitzerischen Reformirten Kirchen,* Konstanz, 1901, p. 82.
19. *History of Protestant Theology,* Edinburgh, 1871, II, p. 184.
20. *Geschichte des Christlichen Lebens in der rheinisch-westphälischen Kirche,* II, Coblenz, 1852, pp. 608ff.
21. *Geschichte des Pietismus,* I, Bonn, 1880, p. 96, and II, Bonn, 1894, pp. 301 and 902.
22. *Lehrbuch der Dogmengeschichte,* IV, i, Leipzig, 1917, and IV, ii, Leipzig, 1920.

JACOB BOEHME:
His Life and Thought

*Write the things which thou hast
seen, and the things which are,
and the things which shall be
hereafter.*

—THE REVELATION OF ST. JOHN, i, 19

HISTORICAL
INTRODUCTION

IF IN his experience which was for him a sunrise to eternity
Jacob Boehme saw good and evil, Yes and No, in all things;
if his mystical knowledge embraced dialectic, then he was his
age's sensitive son reflecting in his vision the bitter factional
disputations of the age of the religious wars.

Already in 1528 Caspar Schwenkfeld had written that a
new world was arising.[1] Scholasticism, chivalry, feudalism,
monkish asceticism, other-worldliness, courtly love were passing. The bourgeoisie, like Boehme himself, were arriving with
their wide-eyed interest in this world's wonders. A new life
was waiting, a new birth portending. But of what?[2] Even in
its first meaning, Renaissance had embraced Joachim of
Flora's religious hopes, dreams more sharply defined by Fran-
ciscan spirituals and Dominican mystics[3] as combining new
birth with cultural regeneration. This desire for renewal was
in accord with the Renaissance veneration of classical form,
for Renaissance man found himself attracted by ancient culture's incomparable simplicity and purity, by its precision of
expression and conceiving, by its easy, natural ways of
thought.

Saint Francis had sought renewal by restoration of apostolic living, a new birth which was for history as well as for
individual man. Both a new world and a new man were
waiting to be born in the purest of Apollonian forms.

Life was no longer simple and violent, centered in the next
world. Medieval brusqueness had given place to endless

searching. This led to science. Even humanist Erasmus and theologian Melanchthon had searched the skies to know the future. This was significant because the medieval mind had been incapable of imagining spirit as spirit inhabiting this world. But the men of the Renaissance trusted their own experience, relied on their own minds, disciplined their fantasies by study of nature, and supplemented the upsurging medieval gothic with the ideas of a single natural scheme and with a this-world culture.

So the Renaissance world view began with man, thus sharply contrasting with medieval theocentrism. Instead of conceptions the men of the Renaissance demanded things:

instead of artificially constructed words, the language of the cultivated world, instead of subtle proofs and distinctions, a tasteful exposition that could speak to the imagination and heart of living man.[4]

Scripture and nature were twin sources of revelation: one told of the macrocosm, the other of the microcosm. The idea of God thus retained a point of unity for the diverging branches of science, spiritual and secular.[5]

During the early years of the sixteenth century, Theophrastus Paracelsus von Hohenheim had melted Renaissance impulses into one fused system of thought [6] and transmitted it to German minds. He had been a lone genius, a compassionate, devout physician of original ideas, a man whom Sebastian Franck called a "strangely wonderful man." [7] He was humanist, reformer, original thinker, but above all consecrated physician and healer. By birth a Swabian physician's son, he had traveled to Italy, France, Russia, Egypt, Arabia, and Asia before settling down.[8] Speculative problems interested him because he wanted to heal and to do so he had to know the causes of disease.[9] He found Hippocrates and Galen unsatisfactory and he sought a new master in nature. He said that life must be based on Scripture and on Christ's teachings, and that there were three corner stones: prayer, faith, and imagination: [10]

In consciousness we come to God, in faith to Jesus Christ, and through the imagination we receive the Holy Spirit.[11]

To heal, Paracelsus believed, the physician must enter into his heart, know the origin of disease, and experience the cure. Nature breeds disease; nature cures, too. How do health and disease exist together? How are they cured?

First the physician must know heaven and earth in their material, species, and essence, and when he is educated into this, then he is one who may practice medicine, for in such experience, knowledge, and art medicine begins.[12]

Here is yet another motive to study nature. The Florentine Platonists had sought God within nature; the alchemists had sought by knowledge to control nature; Paracelsus sought to cure disease by knowing nature.

Paracelsus' light of nature, as he named it, brought the physician more knowledge than he needed to heal for the more he knew of nature the deeper his faith in God became. This was a different way to knowledge of God than the Thomistic and Neoplatonic way of negation—the notion that God is known by negating the world.[13] Rather, in Paracelsus' words,

He who understands and knows much of nature's work is high in faith, for the Creator is his teacher. What sanctified Peter but Christ's works which made him believe? What [sanctifies] nature? The activities of the plants. The greatest one is he who knows, learns, and experiences natural wonders. Each believer should be such a philosopher, or have a neighbor who is such, so that he knows what maintains the health of his life. . . . He should know what it is that he eats and drinks. . . . He should know all the impressions so that he may know how it is possible to make something out of nothing. . . . He should know about the earth, what grows on it, of the sea and sky, so that he knows the Creator of all things . . . Then is he wealthy, for he knows Him through His works, and believes from them to Him.[14]

God is hidden in nature and to find Him therein is man's task.

Paracelsus also transformed Jewish Cabalism, accepting, however, its profound theology. If Jews were looking for God's own esoteric name, then Paracelsus boldly proclaimed it—*Jesus!* He accepted Jewish mysticism's epistemological insights but believed, as also did Boehme, that the hidden God has stepped out from anonymity in the word *Jesus.* Cabalism is possible only where the incarnation is denied and Jewish mysticism therefore could not reap the full harvest of its own profound religious insights. Paracelsus incorporated medieval Jewish mysticism into Christian nature philosophy and so deepened the traditional Logos doctrine.

The sixteenth century had also been the time of Martin Luther, a Roman monk who had met mysticism in all its characteristic forms—Dionysian, Augustinian, Bernardine; Tauler, the nameless Franckfurter who wrote the *Theologia Germanica,* Thomas à Kempis, and the Vicar Staupitz. Luther had met God face to face and then he wrote:

> *Come, Holy Spirit, God and Lord!*
> *Be all Thy graces now outpoured*
> *On the believer's mind and soul,*
> *To strengthen, save, and make us whole. . . .*

Now! Not later! Not in heaven! For Luther wanted no secure berth in heaven and he knew that no penny-pinching Johann Tetzel could control the Holy Spirit's coming and going. This was the same German lay mysticism and piety which during the fourteenth and fifteenth centuries had worked in broad and increasing circles, infecting the towns with an independent, anti-ecclesiastical Christianity, freed from hierarchies, the main points of which were personal religious experience, inwardness, ethical regeneration, religious reformation, and social change.[15] Staupitz too had taught that God's love was in man prior to man's love for God. This lay mysticism had leavened the lump [16] and Luther's break signified the coming of a new, though perhaps only revived, religious ideal.[17] With the northern Renaissance and the Reformation older ideas of an inward spirituality again made themselves felt: Sebastian Brandt had written:

> *Gott hat uns darum nicht geschaffen*
> *Dass wir Mönche werden oder Paffen;*
> *Und zumal, dass wir sollten entschlagen*
> *Der welt.*[18]

Ulrich von Hutten had written:

Mut, Landsleute, gefasset! Ermannen wir uns zu dem Glauben,
Dass wir das göttlichen Reich durch redliches Leben erwerben.[19]

More important for Boehme, who had not read these writers, was the expression of such universal theism and the new religious ideal in the sixteenth century's popular art and poetry.[20] Pictorializations of the dance of death portraying man as controlled by dark powers were supplanted by Dürer, the Holbeins, and the Cranachs.[21] And the sweet singing of the German *Minnesänger* had infected German poetry with allegorical images from Canticles describing the soul's relation to God in erotic terms.[22]

This revolution in religious thought was symbolized by the Lutheran battle doctrine of justification by faith,[23] a protective argument for a precious religious insight—the Pauline view that in Christ all things become new. Luther wanted no voluntary contempt of self such as classical mystics assumed, for their forced humility masked pride, the chief sin. As early as 1513 Luther had asserted that hell's torments were the despair man feels in the conflict of penitence.[24] But he did not then also claim that man's joyous love for God was possible in this world. Only after 1517, after meeting Tauler and the *Theologia Germanica*, and only after 1518 when Staupitz had taught him the meaning of *simul iustus et peccator*, did he assert future blessedness to be a present good; however, it should be confessed that in *De Libertate* he still regarded monkish cathartic as necessary for spiritual growth.[25] For Luther, faith meant resignation and repentance, a conflict of penitence in which God becomes justified *in* us. Here Luther's basic dialectical idea appears, namely, that with God's justification in us our own justification in God takes place.[26] This mystical heart of Luther's doctrine of justification implies resignation, repentance, humility here in this world, for with Luther as with Eckhart and German mysticism one act of faith unfolds itself both as man's justification by God and God's justification in man.

If God and man become justified through man's faith Christ's work is less a satisfaction and more a struggle of penitence (*Busskampf*).[27] Luther's atonement formed a whole with the remainder of his doctrine, and it was not tucked away in inaccessible works but was present in his catechisms and hymns.[28]

> *Christ Jesus lay in death's strong hands*
> *For our offences given;*
> *But now at God's right hand He stands*
> *And brings us life from heaven* . . .
>
> *It was a strange and dreadful strife,*
> *When life and death contended;*
> *The victory remained with life.* . . .

Translating Notker's *Mitten wir im Leben sind* Luther added the new note of struggle; and during the seventeenth century this hymn was believed to have magical powers; Boehme quoted it in his *Aurora:*

> *In the midst of life the jaws*
> *Of hell against us gape*
> *Who from this peril dire as this*
> *Openeth us escape?*
> *'Tis thou, O Lord, alone!*

These Lutheran hymns were contained in a hymnal printed in 1611 by Georg Rhambaw in Görlitz and used in Saint Peter and Saint Paul Church where Boehme worshiped: *Harmonia Ecclesiae et Scholae Gorlicensis.* For Görlitz was Lutheran, the Reformation having come quietly between 1520 and 1530 although final victory was delayed until 1550. The first Lutheran had been the industrious and temperate Pastor Martin Faber, successor to the boisterous priest, Johann Boehme, who was, as the records put it, *ein Zanker, und dem Rath viel zu schaffen machte,*[29] instigator of many beer brawls. Lutheran tracts were being circulated, sent home by the young men studying at Wittenberg and Leipzig.[30] On April 11, 1518, the Sunday after Easter, Faber announced the religious reform,[31] and after his death in 1520 came a line of Lutheran pastors who were zealous for reform: Rupertus, Rüdel, and Press.[32] Görlitz was secured for Lutheranism by the sacrifices of the pastors during the plague of 1521.[33] Schwenkfeld's followers were probably in Görlitz as early as 1520. Small in number but influential, they consisted of three related families: Schütze, Hoffmann, and Ender.[34] Schwenkfeld was a guest of the Schützes between 1527 and 1529. Here the congregation, led by Franz Leidel, met around the year 1544. The neighboring nobility, related by marriage to these patrician families, were also associated with it.[35] In 1560 the Görlitz Lutherans refused Christian burial to Schütz's daughter Ursula, wife of Hans Hoffmann, patrician Lord of nearby Hennersdorf. The bell ringer dared not toll her passing but the municipal fathers intervened, even in the face of protests by Pastor Wirthwein. In 1565 and 1566 the Senate forbade booksellers to trade in Schwenkfelder books,[36] and the Senate ordered Schwenkfelder families to become converted or to accept banishment. Several "conversions" followed; in 1569 old Sebastian Schütze received Lutheran absolution on his deathbed.[37] In 1575 when Georg Hoffmann died, the Görlitz pastors refused to give a eulogy or to accompany his remains to the churchyard. The magistrates ordered the bells tolled and the school children to march in procession.[38] Michael von Ender von Sercha, Hoffmann's brother-in-law and later Boehme's patron, took the complaint to the Emperor who, being Catholic, sided with the Schwenkfelders.[39] The Lausatian nobility generally were sympathetic to Schwenkfelders, being loyal to their nobleman neighbor's ideas.[40] Pastor Mohr of Boehme's native village, Seidenberg, told of a Schwenkfelder in his congregation as late as 1608, ten years after Boehme had left the village, who had not taken communion for twenty-nine years.[41]

Anabaptists were in the Görlitz area in 1525 and 1529 when they were banished from Franckenstein and Schweidnitz.[42] In 1539 Johann Ender was preaching Thomas Münzer's doctrines in and about Görlitz and he gathered many followers on the Görlitz heath. They were ruthlessly suppressed. In 1549 the Senate forbade further Anabaptist controversy. Several re-baptizers were burned, others banished.[43]

In 1565 a Meister David married a tailor's daughter and then misguidedly became an Anabaptist.[44]

Görlitz became a center of Crypto-Calvinism. The first three rectors of the Gymnasium Augustum studied with Melanchthon at Wittenberg.[45] In 1563 Pastor Rauch was banished for preaching Calvinist sermons.[46] In 1591, after the Prince Elector's death, Philippists and Crypto-Calvinists were chased from Saxony[47] and Wittenberg was "cleansed."[48] In the same year both Catholics and Lutherans took the offensive against the Calvinists who were led by Nestlein.[49] The parties battled in the streets. Broadsides appeared; the authorities were perturbed; no one trusted his neighbor.[50] Görlitz sent a delegation to the Prince Elector to plead the city's orthodoxy and one of its members was Gregory Richter, later chief pastor and Boehme's persecutor. Others were Burgomaster Scultetus, Johann Weiss, Elias Dietrich, and Martin Chilius.[51] Philippism found adherents in eastern Germany: Breslau held to the *Corpus Philippicum;* Brieg and Liegnitz used these works as texts until 1601.[52] Martin Moller, Boehme's pastor and deep friend, became involved in controversy with Solomon Gessner, Lutheran champion of orthodoxy at Wittenberg.[53] At the beginning of the Bohemian war John Christian, Duke of Brieg, espoused Calvinism and Breslau adopted the Reformed worship.[54]

Görlitz was also the home of humanists, scholars, men of learning, and physicians.[55] After 1550 the sons of Görlitz had gone to Basel, Wittenberg, and Leipzig to study. Basel was then the center of northern humanism and the seat of Paracelsian studies. Chief among these young men was Bartholomäus Scultetus, who became the Burgomaster between 1592 and 1614,[56] and who with Johann Huser edited the works of Paracelsus between the years 1589 and 1590.[57] Also, there were Tobias Kober and Boehme's friend and physician, Dr. Michael Kurtz, who wrote a eulogy on Boehme.[58] In Görlitz also there was the scholarly Staudt family, especially Daniel (1566–1616), doctor of laws, who placed one thousand marks at the disposal of needy scholars and put his fine library to their use.[59]

But Martin Luther's reform had not proven final and the hatreds it had bred did not easily die. The Peasant's Revolt, although suppressed with unnecessary ruthlessness, only increased the discontent. The shoe—and Boehme was to become a master shoemaker—still was symbol of Jacquerie and Apocalypsis. Across the mountains in Bohemia the Taborites and the Adamites were holding bold social ideas which spread into Swabia and the *Oberpfalz*. Indeed, the countryside was alive with groups like the Evangelical Brethren, and the destruction of the Swabian League, May 25, 1525, had merely postponed the peasants' hope of liberation. Restless, expectant, certain of final change in their status, longing for basic religious reform, the peasants were waiting for their deliverer—perhaps even another Hans Boehme! And the nobles, faced with the disintegration of feudalism, were groping for certainty.

Long-faced Jeremiahs appeared to proclaim the coming judgment. With declining economics chiliastic dreams appeared in the Rhineland and in Silesia.[60] Landowners were hated for their grand ways, for gourmandizing, carousing, dissipating. The peasants toiled, hungered, dreamed of liberation. All the apocalyptic of the suppressed and dispossessed was molded into a dream of re-birth, culminating in an ultimately decisive day. Near the end of the sixteenth century Michael Niedermayer, a Bavarian farm hand, had predicted the world's end and in Sagan one day in 1575 he had told how the Lord was commanding him to preach repentance.[61] At Harpersdorf two prophets, Georg Rischmann and Hans Neuchel, based their prophecies on the apocalypses of Saint John and Saint Matthew.[62] Rischmann foretold famine, war, and divine judgment, all of which did follow in the Thirty Years' War.[63] In Görlitz there appeared the eccentric tanner, Christoph Kotter, who saw angels as he trudged along and who foretold the destruction of Babel, the founding of the true church, and the soon-coming Youngest Day.[64]

Luther's doctrine allowing the punitive sword to civil magistrates began to bear its logical fruit—the wars of religion. The treaties of Passau (1552) and Augsburg (1555) brought no peace because they were made by equally stubborn parties who sought only brief armistices. Creed followed creed, book answered book, dispute succeeded dispute. The Saxon Elector opposed toleration of Calvinists and united with the

Papists, whom he hated, to suppress them. The dissensions following the *Variata* and the various treaties and alliances continued the factions, and exclusion of the Reformed from religious settlements made peace almost impossible:

Deutschland soll von dreien Glauben nunmehr behalten
    einen;
Christus meint, wann er wird kummen, dürft er alsdann
    finden keinen.[65]

In Boehme's time it seemed as if pen and speech were anticipating the coming decision by sword, for like Platonic, Scholastic, and early Renaissance epochs, this time was marked by intense but unnatural intellectuality.[66] Mysticism was being rocked in the Reformation cradle but soon the cradle became too small. Rationalized dogma ended in stifling theological wrangling:

Lutherisch, päpstisch, und Calvinisch, diese Glauben alle
    drei
Sind vorhanden, doch ist Zweifel, wo das Christenthum denn
    sey.[67]

The age was indeed enamored of religious controversy. Lutheran and Calvinist both became stiff, violently opposing one another. Each became divided internally: the Lutherans between orthodox and Philippists; the Reformed regionally. Famous controversies attracted attention: Hoë von Hohenegg denounced Scultetus, the Reformed theologian.[68]

This fussing was not inconsequential and it naturally went deep at one important point—the Lord's Supper.[69] The rational change which the theologians had made was not yet popularly understood. In 1562 a broadside appeared, entitled *Von Grawlichen Misgeburten*, expressing discontent with all disputation. It said that all which Luther, the third Elias, had foretold would not come to pass because of the increase of Papists, Epicureans, Sodomites, *Schwärmgeister*. Blasphemy, cursing, vice, adultery, oppression were increasing. The trumpet call would soon be heard!

Unrest seethed. Each new star brought new fears. When a new one flashed across the heavens between 1604 and 1606,

Boehme's own pastor, Martin Moller, said that it was more tragic than a comet because it surpassed comets in magnitude.[70] The movement for calendar reform did not alleviate the unrest; Protestants suspected the Catholic insistence on reform.

Superstition, magic, witchcraft, crimes of magic were rife. The princes had delusions: Christian of Denmark ranted, Johann Friedrich of Weimar raved.[71] Personal life degenerated: intemperance in eating and drinking, extravagant dressing, exorbitant usury, sexual vice, raucous living, plundering by soldiers, barbarous manners, violent deeds,[72] became usual. Then the infidel Turk's lengthening shadow was cast over eastern Europe with grim foreboding.

And the Jesuits! Frightening legends circulated: Spanish gold from Peru and Pegu would finance his most Catholic majesty's war for world domination. The pope prayed publicly for increase in power and planned to reconvert Luther's Germany. Princes betrayed one another; government was by assassination. Holland was bleeding and the Huguenots were deserting France.[73]

With Protestant union under Frederick IV of the Palatinate at Anhausen in 1608 and with alliance of Catholic princes under Maximilian of Bavaria in 1609, Europe's unrest became crystallized into a clear Yes and No. Anxiety grew, sides were chosen, and the question of succession to the Duchies of Cleves and Jülich electrified the air. To the common man one thing was clear: his world was breaking in two. Old medieval apocalypses were being revived. Joachim of Flora had seen the third Elias coming in 1260.[74] But his reckoning was wrong for he should have begun to count from A.D. 325, from Nicea. Three twenty-five and twelve hundred and sixty gave 1585:

> Wer im '85 Jahr nit wird verderben
> Und im '86 nit thut sterben
> Und im '87 nit wird erschlagen
> Und im '88 nit wird vergraben
> Der mag wohl im '89 Jahr von guten Tagen sagen.[75]

Heinrich Rätel of Sagan, following Daniel, said that 1591 was the year:

> *Dies Königreich, Herr Jesu Christ,*
> *Dass dein und keinens andern ist,*
> *Wollst du anbrechen lassen bald.*
> *Inmittler Weil dein Reich erhalt.*
> *Gott sei gelobt in Ewigkeit!*
> *1591.*[76]

Johannes Hilthemis said that 1606 would bring the final struggle between God and Magog, the ultimate Yes and No. Others, following the Elias calculations which allowed six thousand years, brought in Saint Matthew's "except those days be shortened. . . ." [77]

Blue prints of the new age were common. More's *Utopia,* Bacon's *New Atlantis,* the strange and wonderful visions of Christian Rosenkrantz! Here was a tense and expectant age and the people were waiting for the time when the desert should bloom like the rose, or, as Boehme said, when a lily should bloom in all the ends of the earth.

Gottfried Arnold, who was close to this time, has written of this mood of despair and of hope spawned in that bifurcating world.[78] Yes and No were clearly apparent and the schizoid threat was real, not only to individual men but to their world as well. But the solution was also apparent to some:

> The one ground . . . is that we love Christ in us, and love one another as Christ loved us. (*Gnad.* xiii, 23)

These words of Jacob Boehme point to the resolution of the polarites of his experience in a point of coincidence where Yes and No meet.

NOTES TO HISTORICAL INTRODUCTION

1. H. Ecke, *C. Schwenkfeld, Luther und die Gedanke einer apostolischen Reformation,* Berlin, 1911, p. 100.
2. *Vide:* Konrad Burdach, *Reformation, Renaissance, Humanismus—Zwei Abhandlungen über die Grundlagen moderner Bildung und Sprachkunst,* Berlin, 1926, *passim.*

3. E. Benz. *Ecclesia Spiritualis, Kirchenidee und Geschichtstheologie der Franziskanischen Reformation*, Stuttgart, 1924, *passim;* and Burdach, *op. cit.*, p. 19.
4. Windelband, *History of Philosophy*, tr. Tufts, New York, 1938, p. 353.
5. *Ibid.*, p. 367.
6. Some Paracelsian materials are found in G. Arnold, *Kirchen- und Ketzer Historei* and a sound monograph is Walterhausen, *Paracelsus am Eingang deutschen Bildungsgeschichte*, Leipzig, 1935. Also, C. G. Jung, *Paracelsica. Zwei Vorlesungen über den Arzt und Philosophen Theophrastus*, Zürich, 1942.
7. *Chronica oder Zeitbuch*, 1521.
8. Arnold, *op. cit.*, I, 778a.
9. Paracelsus was also interested in the Cabala, writing a *Theologia Cabalistica de perfecto homine in C. Jesu* which was printed in Huser's 1618 edition and so known to Boehme.
10. Arnold, *op. cit.*, I, 779a.
11. *Ibid.*
12. Paracelsus in *Paragranum*, 2, 106, in Vol. viii of the 1924 Munich edition.
13. Peuckert, *Pansophia*, Stuttgart, 1936, p. 210.
14. Paracelsus in *Prologus in die Bücher Meteorum*, 8, pp. 280ff, quoted by Peuckert, *op. cit.*, p. 202.
15. R. Seeberg, *Dogmengeschichte*, III, i, 9.
16. R. M. Jones, *The Flowering of Mysticism*, New York, 1939.
17. Augustine's earnestness, his passionate longing for redemption, and his personal faith notwithstanding.
18. Quoted by Dilthey, *Weltanschauung und Analysis des Menschen seit Renaissance und Reformation*, Berlin-Leipzig, 1923, p. 48. "God has not created us to be monks or priests, or further, that we should forsake the world."
19. *Ibid.* "Come, comrades, be prepared! Let us take courage in the Gospel! So by upright living we may win the Kingdom of God!"
20. *Vide: Das Knaben Wunderhorn*, Berlin, 1857, and *Mystische Dichtungen aus sieben Jahrhunderten*, Leipzig, 1925.
21. H. Höhn, *Deutsche Holzschnitte*, Leipzig, 1925, and Hannah Closs, *Art and Life*, Oxford, 1936. This latter work gives the relation between ideas, life, and artistic form. For a study of the relation of folk art, or peasant art, to mystical imagery, *vide* Stoudt, *Pennsylvania Folk Art*, Allentown, 1948. Boehme's imagery was much used by folk artists.
22. August Closs, *The Genius of the German Lyric*, London, 1938.

23. E. Seeberg, *Christus: Urbild und Wirklichkeit*, Stuttgart, 1937, *passim*.
24. H. Boehmer, *Luther in the Light of Modern Research*, London, 1931, p. 75.
25. E. Seeberg, *op. cit.*, p. 148.
26. G. Aulen, *Christus Victor*, London, 1940, p. 117.
27. *Ibid.*, p. 119f.
28. Cf. Johannes Meyer, *Luthers Kleiner Katechismus*, Bonn, 1913, and also *Die Deutsche Litaney* of Luther.
29. F. G. Müller, *Versuch einer Oberlausitzischer Reformazions-geschichte*, Görlitz, 1701, p. 318.
30. Neumann, *Geschichte von Görlitz*, Görlitz, 1850, p. 275.
31. Müller, *op. cit.*, p. 318.
32. *Ibid.*, pp. 324–326.
33. *Ibid.*, pp. 326–327.
34. R. Jecht, *Böhme*, p. 16.
35. *Ibid.*, p. 86.
36. *Ex memorabili Domini Eliae Metlzeri, Senat Görlitz*, Anno 1565, as quoted in Jecht, *Böhme*, p. 61.
37. Koyré, *Boehme*, p. 4.
38. *Ibid.*
39. *Ibid.*
40. The Schwenkfelder nobility consisted of Carl von Ender, Michael von Ender, Hans von Salze, David von Schweidnitz. Cf. G. Hoffmann, *Geschichte der Religionsbewegungen in Schlesien*, Breslau, 1880. Other materials in the Schwenkfelde Historical Library, Pennsburg, Pa.
41. Knauthe Ms: *Historia Crypt. in Lausitz*, in Görlitz Archives.
42. Peuckert, *Die Rosenkreutzer*, Jena 1923, p. 243.
43. *Ibid.*, p. 35.
44. *Ibid.*
45. Knauthe ms cited above.
46. Jecht, *Böhme*, p. 86.
47. Koyré, *Boehme*, p. 5.
48. *Ibid.*
49. *Ibid.*
50. *Ibid.*
51. Arnold, *op. cit.*, II, xvii, 5.
52. Moller, *History of the Christian Church*, New York, 1902, iv, p. 311.
53. Boehme was himself drawn into the Crypto-Calvinist controversy.
54. Moller, *op. cit.*, p. 331.

55. *Vide:* Neumann, *Geschichte von Görlitz*, p. 361. Scultetus was astronomer, friend of Tycho Bache and co-editor of the *Diarum Humanitatis Christi*, published at Frankfurt-Oder in 1600. Cf. M. Lipensius, *Bibliotheca Realis Theologica*, Frankfurt, 1685, I, 577b.

56. Jecht, *Böhme*, p. 60.

57. *Ibid.*

58. Material from the family records of the Staudt-Stoudt-Stout family, care of Don Ricardo W. Staudt, Buenos Aires.

59. Peuckert, *Böhme*, p. 1. Cf. also Corrodi, *Kritische Geschichte des Chiliasmus*, Frankfurt, 1781–1788.

60. Peuckert, *Böhme*, p. 3.

61. Peuckert, *Rosenkreutzer*, p. 296ff.

62. Hensel, *Beschreibung der Stadt Hirschberg*, 1799, p. 323ff.

63. Peuckert, *Schlesische Sagen*, Leipzig, 1924, p. 72ff.

64. Born, 1583; died, 1647. Cf. his *Zwey Wundertractätlein*, 1732.

65. Peuckert, *Rosenkreutzer*, p. 3. "Of three faiths Germany shall have but one. Christ intends when He returns to maintain but one."

66. T. R. Hughes, *The Philosophic Basis of Mysticism*, Edinburgh, 1931, pp. 41–42.

67. Peuckert, *Rosenkreutzer*, p. 3. "Lutheran, Papist, Calvinist—these three faiths are extant, still there is doubt where Christianity is."

68. J. G. Walch, *Einleitung in die Religions-Streitigkeiten*, Jena, 1734, *passim.*

69. Grünhagen, *Geschichte Schlesiens*, Gotha, 1886, p. 99.

70. Peuckert, *Rosenkreutzer*, p. 12.

71. *Cambridge Modern History*, IV, p. 17.

72. *Ibid.*, pp. 8–11, *et passim.*

73. Peuckert, *Rosenkreutzer*, pp. 16ff. Also, B. Duhr, *Jesuiten Fabeln*, Freiburg, 1904.

74. Peuckert, *Rosenkreutzer*, pp. 10ff.

75. *Ibid.*, p. 11. "He who does not rot in '85, and who does not die in '86, and who is not killed in '87, and who is not buried in '88, he may surely speak of good times in '89."

76. Peuckert, *Rosenkreutzer*, p. 13. "The Kingdom, Lord Jesus Christ, which is Thine and none others, do Thou permit to be established soon, since it embraces Thy Church. Let God be praised in Eternity! 1591."

77. Boehme quotes this in *Letzte Zeit*, i, 30.

78. I, pp. 609–656.

PART ONE

THE UNFOLDING OF
BOEHME'S THEOLOGY

Jacob Boehme's religious knowledge began in mystical vision and realized itself in mature rational expression through living. The irrational Unconditioned became Logos through existential demands, emerging both initially as insight and finally as theology as the product and perhaps even as the reflection of his life in his Lausitz homeland. The Yes and No came from his life; their resolution, empirically as well as speculatively, however, was the result of mysticism, a final reworking of the insight he received in the quarter-of-an-hour dawning to eternity. From this he received his precious pearl which was so often cast before swine and wordlings.

Slowly, as he matured, vision and life were fused in an all-comprehending dialectical theology which was both the reflection of his environment and the projection of his mystical knowledge. He both reflected and transcended his age.

Ich lebe noch in dieser Welt
Und bin doch schon zum Himmel aufgehoben,
Ich trag ein Joch das mir gefällt,
Ich bin ein Engel, und kan Gott doch loben.
                                    —GOTTFRIED ARNOLD

CHAPTER ONE

BOEHME'S LIFE: 1575–1600

J ACOB BOEHME [1] was born in the Upper Lusatian village of
Old Seidenberg, situated on a hillside south of Görlitz near
the Bohemian border, on or just before April 24, 1575.[2]
    He was the fourth child of Jakob Boehme who died in 1618
and of his wife Ursula whose family name is not known.[3] The
parents were solid and perhaps even well-to-do [4] farmers, "of
the good German stamp," [5] and in spite of the surname's foreign connotation the family was natively German, as pure
Germans had lived beside Czech and Moravians in Lusatia
since the thirteenth century and the Boehmes were in Seidenberg already in the fifteenth century.[6]
    The theologian's great-grandfather was also Jakob, farmer
in Old Seidenberg in 1558, seventeen years before the theologian's birth. His sons were Michael, Andreas, Ambrosius, and
Georg.[7]
    Ambrosius, the theologian's grandfather, inherited the fam-
ily lands instead of the younger brother Georg, who died at
an early age. Ambrosius became well-established in the com-
munity, being freed from feudal obligations. He was elder
in the Seidenberg church and magistrate in the local court.[8]
He had the following children: Hans, Martin, Ambrosius,
Anna, Margaretha, Jakob, and Dorothea. He died in 1563 and
his land passed to his youngest son, Jakob, as was the custom.
    Jakob Boehme, the theologian's father, bought the land
rights from his brothers and sisters for six hundred marks, on
Martinmas, 1563.[9] Like his father he too was a church elder

and local magistrate.[10] He married twice. His first wife bore
him five children, among them the theologian; his second wife
bore him three daughters.[11] His first wife died in 1611; the
second in 1634. On the father's death in 1618, Michael,
the youngest son, purchased the land rights from his brothers
and sisters for six hundred marks.[12] An interesting but uncon-
firmed tradition suggests that Jakob Boehme, the father, had
"enthusiastic" tendencies.[13]

Little is known of the theologian's boyhood. Farm he could
not inasmuch as he was sickly, small, and underdeveloped;
furthermore, having a younger brother, he was not to inherit
the right to the family lands. But, as with farm boys generally,
he minded the cattle and so made himself useful at home.
Franckenberg, the first editor, tells a story of his boyhood:

During the time of his being a herd-boy, he met with a
curious and remarkable occurrence. Having one day, about
noon, been rambling to a great distance from the other lads,
and climbing up alone by himself on an adjacent mountain
called *Landeskrone,* being arrived at the summit . . . he
espied amongst the great red stones a kind of aperture or entrance, overgrown with bushes, and enclosed in a manner not
much unlike a doorcase or passage. This in his simplicity he
penetrated into, and there descried a large portable vessel
. . . full of money, and he made the very best of his way out
again, without taking so much as a single piece. . . . Tho' he
had frequently climbed up to the same place afterwards, in
company with other herd-boys, yet he could never hit upon
the aperture again.

Franckenberg confessed to see in this an

emblematic omen of his future spiritual admission to the sight
of the hidden treasury of wisdom and mysteries of God in
nature.[14]

Franckenberg's symbolism does not convince. The *Landeskrone* is a good eight English miles from Seidenberg and a
"grotto legend" has long been associated with it. However,
Lusatian herd-boys did wander long distances to graze their
herds.

Next, Franckenberg says that Jacob Boehme's parents,

having observed that the son . . . gave proof of an excellent, good, and sprightly genius, kept him to school, where together with daily prayers and good behavior, both at table and in his family, he learned to read tolerably well and a little writing.[15]

Between 1580 and 1590 the Seidenberg school was taught by Johann Leder of Schneidsburg, instruction being based on Scripture and Luther's Smaller Catechism.[16] Leder also was *Vorsinger* in the local congregation. Jacob stayed in school until his fourteenth year, learning, as has been said, to read, write, and cipher, as well as a few scraps of Latin.[17] The existence of a school in Old Seidenberg during this period has not been established.[18]

The Boehmes were prominent in the affairs of Old Seidenberg. They owned most of the village land and the theologian's father was village leader.[19] As *Kirchenvater* the father surely took his family to the Seidenberg church and sent his children to the Pastor to be catechized. This, then, was Jacob Boehme's first contact with established religion.

The Seidenberg church, like those of neighboring villages, was soundly Protestant.[20] Its first Lutheran Pastor was Johann Schneider whose ministry began in 1542 [21] and continued into the lifetime of the theologian's father. In 1535 the Seidenberg estates and their municipal and ecclesiastical administration passed to Friedrich von Räder, an ardent Protestant,[22] who shared management with his brother until 1591 when he became the sole administrator. In this same year, possibly urged by the Prince Elector, he began reform of church matters, summoned his Pastors to Friedhof, his seat, and said that he wanted the remnants of superstition purged from worship and insisted that preaching be based on the Prophets, Apostles, Symbolic documents, and the Augsburg Confession. He formulated a standard form of purified worship and appointed Martin Nüssler superintendent.[23]

During these years Jakob Boehme, the father, was vestryman, his name appearing among the *tutores et nutrices ecclesiae*.[24] If more were known about von Räder and the local

Pastors, the meaning of these events for Boehme's theology might be gauged.[25] In 1624, the year the theologian died, the Seidenberg church again became Catholic.

During these years Jacob Boehme was in Seidenberg, for in 1589 when the lad was fourteen his father had taken him to the village shoemaker to learn the trade of cobbling. Apprenticeship was for three years, so Boehme began his journeyman travels in 1592. Franckenberg spins another yarn about Boehme in these trade-learning days:

It fell out that . . . during his apprenticeship a stranger . . . comes to the shop, and asks to buy a pair of shoes; but as neither Master nor Mistress were within, he, Jacob Boehme, . . . would not venture to sell them, till the stranger . . . insisted upon his letting him have them; now, then, he, having more of a mind to put the buyer off than to sell the shoes, set a somewhat enormous price upon them. The man, however, paid down the money demanded . . . and, taking up the shoes, went away. But being arrived at some distance . . . and then stopping short, he called out with an audible and serious tone of voice: 'Jacob, come out hither to me.' An address like this from a person unknown . . . startled the boy; but . . . he got up and went into the street to meet him. The man, then, whose mien was serious and loving, with sparkling eyes, taking him by the hand, and looking him full in the face, said: 'Jacob, you are small, but you shall become great, and a man so different from the common cast, that you shall be the wonder of the world. Be therefore a good lad; fear God, and reverence His Word. Let it especially be your delight to read the Holy Scriptures, wherein you are furnished with comfort and instruction; for you shall be obliged to suffer a great deal of affliction, poverty, and persecution also; nevertheless be of good comfort, and firmly persevere, for God loves you, and He is gracious to you.' Upon which the man, after squeezing him by the hand and looking him full in the face, went his way.[26]

Such instruction, typical of Franckenberg's interest in the strange and mysterious, was aimed at keeping young Boehme from straying into heresy and nonorthodoxy; indeed, Franckenberg adds that Boehme was led to renewed seriousness and interest in his work. But the whole incident is colored by the effort to plead for Boehme's remarkable yet safe eccentricity.[27]

Boehme's journeyman travels were in a land torn by dissension, party strife, and religious unrest. Upper Lusatia was then the scene of social conflict and religious controversy, which in some instances were joined, especially between feudal barons and the rising bourgeoisie, between established and nonestablished religions; indeed, so bitter had the strife been that in 1592, the year Boehme's travels began, Rudolf of Saxony ordered a thoroughgoing religious purge.[28]

Franckenberg, to whom we are indebted for so much imaginative biography which seems to miss the truth, claims that at this time Boehme experienced his first "illumination." There is no evidence in Boehme's writings to support this statement. Indeed, Franckenberg's account is vague and indefinite in all but one point:

> Whereas now, Jacob Boehme . . . had . . . walked from his youth up in the fear of God, and had taken pleasure in attending sermons,[29] he, . . . was awakened in his own heart, and through the multiplicity of controversy and scholastic wrangling about religion . . . he set himself upon fervently and incessantly praying, seeking, and knocking, until, being at that time with his master on his travels, he . . . was . . . translated into the Holy Sabbath and glorious day of rest in the soul; and thus . . . had his rest granted him here (to use the words of his own Confession) "surrounded with the divine light for the space of seven days successively," he stood possessed of the highest beatific vision of God, and in the ecstatic joys of his Kingdom.[30]

This passage from "his . . . confession" cannot be located in Boehme's known writings, although the work in which it is said to appear may be lost. That religious wrangling gave Boehme his discontent and doubt is clear enough; the seven-day ecstasy is dubious, to say the least. Boehme never mentioned it. Surely Boehme was melancholy, serious, and even stern; and Franckenberg continues that he laid

aside the trifling lusts of youth, and kept constantly to his church, together with reading the Holy Bible, a regular at-

tendance upon the Word preached, and participation in the
Holy Sacraments, a zeal of God moved him so that he was
not able to bear, or to endure, foolish conversation and least
of all blasphemous expressions and curses; nay, he could not
refrain from checking and rebuking them in his own master.
. . . Moreover, his love of godliness and virtue made him
addict himself to a modest and retired life, bidding adieu to
and shaking off the wantonness and bad company, which being a turn of course drew ridicule and reproach upon him;
and at length he was, by the very master he wrought with
(unable to brook a family prophet like this), discharged and
sent about his business elsewhere.[31]

Where Boehme served out the rest of his apprenticeship it is
not clear; but as shoemakers were then scarce in Seidenberg
and in Görlitz he may have gone to the larger town to finish
his training.

So, around 1594 and 1595, perhaps even before his journeyman days were over, Boehme made his way to Görlitz,
there to pursue his handicraft and to maintain himself "with
the labor of his hands and the sweat of his brow." [32] Görlitz
then was an important city in eastern Germany, one of the
few German towns which had had an indigenous culture
even during the medieval period.[33] Nonfeudal and bour-
geois, it was typical of the new societies then arising out of
the debris of medievalism and its baroque architecture externally expresses the age of its greatest prosperity. It was the
home of merchant princes like Georg Emmerich and Johannes Haas who, while not as famous as the Augsburg Fug-
gers, were still known as the "kings" of Görlitz.[34] It was indeed a center of trade, a place where men and ideas met, a
crossroads for the conflicting philosophies and religious impulses of the age.[35]

Little is known of Boehme's early years in Görlitz. If he
was apprenticed at fourteen then at twenty he was free to
set up his own shop. Few cobblers were able to start in business for themselves so it may be assumed that around 1595
Boehme began to work for another master shoemaker, probably for Valentin Lange. On April 24, 1599, Boehme purchased a "bench" from Lange, his future brother-in-law, for
the sum of two hundred marks.[36] On May 10th he was made

a citizen of the town and also became the husband of Catharina Kuntzschmann, daughter of a Görlitz butcher. For these privileges he paid three crowns.[37] Catharina's mother had been a Bartsch and one of her uncles was the influential butcher, Elias Bartsch, city alderman between 1604 and 1616. Catharina had three brothers and a sister, Sarah, wife of the Valentin Lange from whom Boehme bought the shoemaker's bench. Inasmuch as a shocmakers' guild statute of March 23, 1573, stated that when "a journeyman becomes a master he shall marry within half a year" it may be assumed that Boehme had become master shoemaker just before his marriage.[38] Catharina probably brought Jacob a substantial dowry, for on August 29, 1599, he bought a house in the Rabengasse from Paul Adam for three hundred marks.[39] Jacob and Catharina had the following children: Jacob, baptized, January 27, 1600 [40]; Michael, baptized, January 8, 1602 [41]; Tobias, baptized September 11, 1603 [42]; and "little Elias," baptized September 14, 1611.[43] The two girls with the surname Boehme baptized during this period were children of another Jacob Boehme in Görlitz, by trade a tanner.[44]

Christopher Knauthe (died, 1784), pastor at Friedhof, seat of the von Raders during the eighteenth century, has left an important reference about Boehme's early days in Görlitz.[45] He wrote that Martin Moller became chief pastor in 1600, that many conversions followed, that among these was Jacob Boehme who because of his awakened condition associated with like-minded persons in the conventicles Moller had organized.[46] Glusing, editor of the 1715 edition of Boehme's writings, also said that Moller was the instrument which awakened Boehme's spirit.[47]

This was indeed a fateful year. Even the weather was erratic. On Easter a great snow came down and the cold lingered long into the spring. It was only a week before Whitsunday that the cattle could be taken from their stalls into the open fields and the trees still had no leaves. The cherry trees were not in bloom until Trinity Sunday.[48] In this remarkable setting the shoemaker had his "second illumination," as Franckenberg called it, for his spirit

was . . . enraptured with the astral spirit of the soul by

means of an instantaneous glance . . . cast upon a bright pewter dish . . . introduced into the innermost ground or center of the . . . hidden nature.[49]

The pewter dish is psychologically suggestive and may have been the immediate stimulus, but it is more likely that the ultimate origin was Martin Moller's bright and shining spirit. Martin Moller had been born at Liessnitz, son of a mason. He had attended school at Wittenberg and at the Görlitz gymnasium, but poverty prevented him from hearing lectures in the university. Nonetheless he was appointed cantor at Löwenberg, and in April, 1572, he was ordained to the ministry in Kesseldorf. In the autumn he became deacon at Löwenberg and in 1575 the pastor at Sprottau. In July, 1600, he became the chief pastor in Görlitz where he organized the "Conventicle of God's Real Servants," a group in the true German mystical tradition to which Jacob Boehme belonged.[50]

Moller wrote much. Already in 1584, 1590, and 1591 he had published volumes of religious poetry. The first, *Meditationes sanctorum patrum durch Martin Mollerum,* appeared in Görlitz.[51] It consisted of prose and poetry from Augustine, Tauler, and other devotional and mystical writers. In it Moller's translation of Bernard of Clairvaux' *Jesus dulcia memoria* appeared, later a favorite of the Pietists and included by Johann Arndt in his *Paradiesgärtlein,* his book of prayers. The first stanza is still precious:

> *O Jesu süss, wer dein gedenkt,*
> *Dess Hertz mit Freud wird überschwemmt,*
> *Noch süsser aber alles ist,*
> *Wo du, O Jesu, selber bist.*[52]

The second part of this work shows Moller's chiliastic ideas [53] as the hymn which begins, *Der letzte Tag nu kommen wird.* In 1595, while still at Sprottau, he had published a little mystical work [54] in which union was seen in erotic imagery as union of the believer with the inner church, saying that the individual's life should be a pattern for congregational living.[55] In 1601, having been chief pastor in Görlitz for a year, he published his sermons on the pericopes, *Praxis Evangelio-rum*,[56] sermons doubtlessly preached with Boehme in the pew. Dr. Peuckert, who has investigated these materials in detail, has found numerous verbal passages of parallel character between this work and Boehme's first work, the *Aurora*,[57] passages which not only prove Moller's spiritual influence on Boehme but his literary dominance during these years. This work of Moller was challenged by the orthodox Solomon Gessner of Wittenberg.[58] Moller's devotional tracts continued to appear: *Manuale Mortis* which went through many editions; *Schedia Regia*, 1605, et cetera. Even after Moller's death on March 2, 1606, his writings were in demand.[59]

When Martin Moller had come to Görlitz in 1600 Boehme had been a young, pious shoemaker of twenty-five with enthusiastic tendencies. Newly married, beginning his career as a prospering workman, with restless mind, and moved in his heart by the tensions of the age, he had attended Moller's conventicles where he met similarly minded people: noblemen, physicians, peasants, burghers, fellow craftsmen.[60] Surely it was this spirit which Martin Moller communicated, rather than the pewter dish or other fanciful objects, which brought to the young Boehme a deep interest in the devotional life. For Boehme was not yet a philosopher.[61] His interests were in the deepest that Christianity had to offer, for Moller was surely a lover of Apostolic Christianity, a "pure" witness, the translator of the martyred Ignatius' letters, of Theodoretus' dialogues, and of other patristic literature.[62] Moller also knew Tauler, and he culled excerpts from Augustine, Bernard of Clairvaux, the Victorines, Ruysbroeck, Suso, and Thomas à Kempis.[63] Here Boehme was brought face to face with Christian mysticism at its medieval best and Dr. Peuckert's comparison of the parallel passages in Moller and Boehme's *Aurora* establishes that Moller's spirit worked on Boehme much as that of Thomas à Kempis and Arndt.[64] Ritschl, no friend of Pietism, said that Moller's soteriology had stressed regeneration instead of justification.[65] For Moller and for Boehme it was Christ *in* us rather than Christ for us. So Martin Moller was the first and perhaps the continuingly deepest influence on Boehme, bringing to the shoemaker the rich imagery of bride mysticism, a tempered chiliasm, and an ideal of a pure Christianity.

One of Moller's prayers [66] has survived within German devotional literature, a sacramental prayer of the indwelling spirit: [67]

Thou dost unite Thyself so deeply within me that Thou dost abide in me all of the time, quickening me through Thy Spirit, never wanting to depart therefrom again. . . . [68]

Four of Moller's hymns have become part of German hymnody, [69] and they show the depth of his spirit:

> Ach Gott! Wie manches Herzeleid
> Begegnet mir zu dieser Zeit . . .

Both Boehme and Moller designate man as a worm, Boehme in *Busse* i, 6, and Moller thus:

> Hier lieg ich armes Würmelein,
> Kan regen weder Arm noch Bein
> Für Angst mein Hertz in Leib zerspringt,
> Mein Leben mit den Tode ringt,
> Vernunfft und alle Sinn sind matt. . . .

Here Moller, dead and blind, poured out his suffering soul: life was at war with death, reason was inadequate and vitality much too weak.

So, Martin Moller was the first and perhaps the dominant influence on Jacob Boehme. Boehme's silence about him is surprising and perhaps even logical—surprising in that Moller meant so much to him, logical because Boehme cherished the memory of Moller preciously during the days of his persecution by Moller's successor, Gregory Richter. Only once does Boehme even mention the name and that is in 1624 when he sends his greetings to the pastor's son from Dresden (*Epist.* lxiii, 12), showing that the friendship endured to the end.

NOTES TO CHAPTER ONE

1. The name is variously spelled even in the old records. German scholars use Jakob Böhme; the British Museum uses Jacob Boehme.

2. The date is gotten: a) the year, from Franckenberg's *De Vita et Scriptis*, #1, and by calculating back from Boehme's death; b) the day and month, from the implication in the *Görlitzer Bürgerbuch*, 24 April, 1592.
3. Jecht, *Böhme*, p. 15.
4. *Ibid.*, p. 16, where property holdings of the Boehmes in Old Seidenberg are given.
5. Franckenberg, *De Vita* . . . #32.
6. Oldest reference to a Boehme in Seidenberg is October 23, 1416, when Hans buys land. Cf. Jecht, *Böhme*, p. 19.
7. *Ibid.*
8. Cf. Fechner, *Sketch of the Life of Jacob Boehme*, trans. in Earl's *De Electione Gratiae*, London, 1930, pp. xivff.
9. Jecht, *Böhme*, p. xiv.
10. Fechner, *op. cit.*, p. xiv.
11. Elizabeth, Dorothea, Maria.
12. Fechner, *op. cit.*, p. xiv.
13. Fechner suggests the father's evangelical leanings.
14. Franckenberg, *De Vita* . . . , #6. Legends about the holy grotto are common in European folklore.
15. Franckenberg, *op. cit.*, #6.
16. Fechner, *op. cit.*, p. xiv.
17. Neumann, *Geschichte von Görlitz*, p. 365.
18. Jecht, *Böhme*, p. 20.
19. Neumann, *op. cit.*, p. 367.
20. The Reformation *Graf* was Matthias von Bieberstein whose two sons were at Wittenberg when Luther nailed his theses to the door. Cf. Müller, *Versuch einer Oberlausitzischen Reformazionsgeschichte*, pp. 353ff.
21. Müller, *op. cit.*, p. 562.
22. *Ibid.*
23. *Ibid.*, p. 563.
24. Jecht, *Böhme*, pp. 20–21.
25. Müller, *op. cit.*, p. 563.
26. Franckenberg, *De Vita* . . . #5, #9.
27. *Ibid.*, #7.
28. Peuckert, *Böhme*, p. 14.
29. Franckenberg takes pains to protest Boehme's orthodoxy, seeking to vindicate Boehme from the suspicion of heresy.
30. Franckenberg, *op. cit.*, #7.
31. *Ibid.*, #10.
32. *Ibid.*
33. Jecht, *Böhme*, p. 84.

34. For a list of chronicles and other sources of Görlitz history, *vide* Jecht, *Quellen zur Geschichte der Stadt Görlitz*, Görlitz, 1909.
35. Müller, *Oberlautzischen Reformazionsgeschichte*, p. 318.
36. *Görlitzer Kaufbuch*, 1598ff., Bl. 77, Cf. Jecht, *Böhme*, p. 10.
37. *Görlitzer Traubuch*, 10 May 1599, Cf. Jecht, *Böhme*, p. 10.
38. Koyré, *Boehme*, p. 11. Peuckert, *Böhme*, p. 12.
39. *Görlitzer Kaufbuch*, 1598ff., Bl. 77. Cf. Jecht, *Böhme*, p. 10.
40. *Görlitzer Kirchenbuch*, #29, 1600.
41. *Ibid.*
42. *Ibid.*, 11 September, 1603.
43. *Ibid.*, 9 September, 1611.
44. Jecht, *Böhme*, p. 18.
45. *Historia Cryptocalvinismi in Lausat.*, *suc.*, in Görlitz Archives, Annales, 255ff.
46. *Neues Lausitzischen Magazin*, Vol. 94, 1918, pp. 48ff.
47. *Mehrere Merckwürdigkeiten*, #8 (in the biographical materials in Volume X of the 1730 edition).
48. Max Kwiecinski, *Das Wichtigste aus der Stadt Görlitz*, 1902, p. 170.
49. Franckenberg, *De Vita* . . . #11.
50. Jecht, *Böhme*, p. 27 and Koch, *Geschichte des Deutschen Kirchenlieds*, Stuttgart, 1852, I, pp. 178–180.
51. Wackernagel, *Das Deutsche Kirchenlied*, Leipzig, 1877, II, p. 34ff.
52. This hymn became quite popular.
53. Wackernagel, *op. cit.*, #55.
54. The title, *Mysterium Magnum*, was later adopted by Boehme as the title of his main work.
55. Ritschl, *Geschichte des Pietismus*, II, 27.
56. Peuckert, *Böhme*, p. 24.
57. There are at least four major parallel passages.
58. The controversy lasted several years. Moller was being accused of Calvinism.
59. The posthumous works were reprints.
60. Heckel, *Geschichte der deutschen Literatur in Schlesien*, Breslau, 1929, I, p. 164.
61. Bornkamm, *Luther und Böhme*, p. 75.
62. *Mehrere Merckwürdigkeiten*, #8.
63. Ritschl, *Pietismus*, II, p. 57.
64. Peuckert, *Die Rosenkreutzer*, pp. 259–260.
65. Ritschl was incapable of understanding Moller's theology.
66. *Vide*: F. Heiler, *Das Gebet*, München, 1923, pp. 284–386.

67. *Vide: Versuch eines allgemeinen evangelischen Gesang- und Gebetsbuch zum Kirchen und Hausgebrauche,* Hamburg, 1833, pp. 722ff.

68. Koch, *op. cit.,* I, p. 179.

69. *Geistliches Gesangbuch,* Gotha, 1738, p. 350, p. 620, p. 727, and p. 1756.

Sponsae cultum aemulantes,
Sponsae vultum speculantes,
Sponsae cultu sociemur,
Sponsae vultu satiemur.

—DE BEATA MARIA SEQUENTIA

CHAPTER TWO

SUNRISE TO ETERNITY: 1600

SOMETIME in the spring of the year 1600 Jacob Boehme, the young Görlitz shoemaker who was under the spiritual influence of Martin Moller, had a shattering mystical experience which became the vital center of his life and thought, the stimulus to a remarkable literary and theological career, and the dawn of a new life of the spirit—a true sunrise to eternal life.

This experience has been much misunderstood and it needs to be reconstructed from the three accounts which Boehme has left in which he tries to piece together what happened with tolerable precision: the famous nineteenth chapter of the *Aurora*, which was written in 1612; portions of the preface to *I Apol. Tilke* which were written towards the beginning of 1621; and an Epistle to Caspar Linder, written on May 10, 1622. Speaking of this watershed experience, Boehme said,

It unfolded itself within me from time to time. . . . I went around pregnant with it for twelve years, and a hefty impulse arose in me before I could bring it to external form. (*Epist.* xii, 10)

As his first writing was probably in 1612 the experience then took place in that year when the cold lingered so long and just after the pious and devout Martin Moller had come to Görlitz as chief pastor. So these three accounts record a mellowing but still vital memory of an astonishing conflict of ideas and of the still more astonishing resolution which followed. They are not, like Pascal's directly snatched record, the cryptic accounts of a vision caught in passing but the lingering tones of a melody once played but remembered with fervency of spirit.

Franckenberg, with his penchant for the occult and strange, claimed that the reflected light from a pewter dish set Boehme's spirit to moving in the deep subconsciousness, but Boehme himself is much more precise and sensible:

The right heaven . . . has until now been tightly concealed from human children and there have been many explanations of it.

The learned also have scratched around it with many queer writings, and fallen into each others' hair with calumny and disgrace . . .

People have always believed that heaven is many hundreds or thousands of miles from this earth, and that God only lives in that heaven; some physicists have even tried to measure this height and have brought forth quite strange things.

Indeed, before this my knowledge and revelation, I myself believed this to be the right heaven which extends above the stars in a round light-blue sphere. . . .

This was indeed the usual medieval view which was then being questioned by the worldly immanentism of the Renaissance.

When this had given me many a hard blow . . . I finally fell into deep melancholy and sadness when I contemplated the great deep of this world . . . and considered in my spirit all the world's creation.

Then I found evil and good, love and wrath in all things, in irrational creatures, in wood, stones, earth, and elements as well as in men and beasts. (*Aurora* xix, 1–6)

Here Boehme had felt the confusion of his times and he rebelled against the upward surging of medieval thought, against the soaring gothic which was the goal of medievalism. Renaissance natural philosophy and man's new interest

in this world had dimmed high heaven's light for him and
brought good into the world. He continues,

> But after I found a strong contradiction within me . . . I
> put myself so hard against the serpent's seed that I thought
> I should overcome and destroy the in-born evil will and
> propensity and join myself to God's Love in Christ . . . so
> that God's spirit might rule, drive, and lead me. (*I Apol.
> Tilke*, preface, 21)
>
> In addition I contemplated man's little spark (*Füncklein*),
> what it should be valued before God along side of this great
> work of heaven and earth.
>
> As I found that evil and good were in all things . . . and
> that it went as well in this world with the impious as with
> the pious, also that the barbarous people possessed the best
> lands and that they had more good fortune than the pious . . .
>
> I therefore became very melancholy and highly troubled.
> No Scripture could comfort me, though I was quite well
> versed in it . . .
>
> . . . When in such sadness I earnestly elevated my spirit
> into God and locked my whole heart and mind, along with
> all my thoughts and will, therein, ceaselessly pressing in with
> God's Love and Mercy, and not to cease until He blessed
> me . . . , then after some hard storms my spirit broke
> through hell's gates into the inmost birth of the Godhead,
> and there I was embraced with Love as a bridegroom em-
> braces his dear bride. (*Aurora*, xix, 7–11)

A strange break-through—through the gates of hell!

> What kind of spiritual triumph it was I can neither write
> nor speak; it can only be compared with that where life is
> born in the midst of death, and is like the resurrection of the
> dead. (*Aurora*, xix, 12)

"Like the resurrection of the dead"! How could Boehme
know what this was like? In *I Apol. Tilke* he uses other
images:

> I proposed to keep myself . . . dead until God's Spirit got
> a form in me, and I comprehended Him so that through
> Him and in Him I might direct my life . . .

Also I proposed to will nothing but what I knew in His
Light and Will . . .
And what thereupon took place only God and my soul
may know . . .
So I wrestled in God's presence a considerable time for
the knightly crown . . . which later with the breaking of the
gate in the deep center of nature I attained with much joy,
whereupon a remarkable light arose in my soul (Preface,
22–25)

which was, indeed, a sunrise to eternity. His wrestling had
been for a considerable time and was not, as Franckenberg
claimed, instantaneous. Moreover, Boehme broke through
the "gate in the deep center of nature" and so the mystery of
the Godhead was not profaned.

In this light my spirit directly saw through all things, and
knew God in and by all creatures, even in herbs and grass.
. . . In this light my will grew in great desire to describe
the being of God. . . . (*Aurora*, xix, 13)
Now from this light I have my knowledge, as well as my
will and drive; and I will write this knowledge according to
my gifts . . . and let God work His Will; . . . I will attend
and wait what the Lord intends. (*Aurora*, xix, 17)
I shall not hide from you the simple, childlike way I go
in Christ. For of myself I can write nothing, as a child who
knows nothing and understands nothing . . . I never wanted
to know anything about the divine mystery, much less
understood I how I should seek it or find it . . . I sought
only Jesus Christ's heart, to hide myself therein before God's
grim wrath and the devil's violent assaults; . . . I yielded
myself wholly to Him that I might not live to my will but to
His, that He only might guide me, that I might be His child
in His Son Jesus Christ. In such earnest seeking and desiring . . . the gate was opened for me that I saw and knew
more in a quarter of an hour than if I had been many years
in the universities. . . . (*Epist.* xii, 5–7)

Here was no ecstasy, no *nirvana,* no bridal chamber mish-
mash of subject and object, of creator and creature. Here
was no loss of individuality, no melting of the subject into
the formless abyss of being. Here was no rending of the veil
of divine mystery, no merging with the Godhead, no *unio*

mystica in the classical sense! Boehme's mystical experience was gnostic in the sense that from it he gained what was for him new knowledge.

> Therein I first knew what God and man were and what God had to do with men . . .
> Previously I understood little about the high articles of faith . . . much less about nature . . . For the Spirit shot through me like a bolt of lightning . . . I began to write like a school-boy, and so I wrote continuously, but only for myself. (*I Apol. Tilke,* preface, 26–28)

Boehme outlines the knowledge which he had received in this remarkable quarter of an hour and his outline sounds much like the topics of an orderly theological system:

> For I saw and knew the Being of all beings, the ground and the unground (*Ungrund*); the birth of the holy trinity; the source and origin of this world and all creatures in divine Wisdom (Sophia) . . . I saw all three worlds in myself, (1) the divine, angelical, or paradisaical; . . . (2) the dark world . . . ; (3) the external, visible world . . . ; and I saw and knew the whole Being in evil and in good, how one originates in the other . . . so that I not only greatly wondered but also rejoiced. (*Epist.,* xii, 8)
> Moreover, I wrote only my own mind as I understood it in the Deep; and I made no commentary on it as I did not intend that it should be read; I wanted to keep it for myself; had I known that it would be read I would have written more clearly . . . Also my spirit's labor in it and with it was continuous . . . For the Light's spirit moved my soul very much . . . repeating many things very often, ever deeper and clearer, from one step to another—it was the real Jacob's ladder. . . . (*I Apol. Tilke,* preface, 31–37)

Several points are significant in this piecing together of the three extant accounts of Boehme's mystical experience. He sought to resolve the disunities of his experience as he could not accept the medieval cosmology with its sharp separation of heaven and hell and with its transcendence. Moreover, Boehme was asking again the old, old question of religious philosophy, the question of evil. Why does the all-good, omnipotent God appear indifferent to good and evil? Here the young shoemaker's heart, tutored by the pious pastor Moller, became the collision-ground where two Renaissance trends met head on: mystical devotion and nature philosophy.

Secondly, Boehme's mystical experience does not contain the classical element of union with the Godhead in substantial terms. He did not climb a ladder into the Bosom; he did not follow to Dante's Golden Rose there to be lost in contemplation; he was not melted into an abyss of being. What then? Hear his revolutionary words:

> I did not climb up into the Godhead, neither can so mean a man as I am do it; but the Godhead climbed up in me, and revealed such to me out of his Love, which otherwise I would have had to leave it quite alone in my half-dead fleshly birth. (*Aurora*, viii, 7)

This was in full rebellion against the soaring gothic transcendence of medieval thought; this was the mystical heart of Lutheranism, the notion which Staupitz had taught to Martin Luther which was that God's love is in men even before they search for Him. Boehme did use the ladder image, but with him it was merely the repetition of a Scriptural phrase and had no organic relation to his thought:

> Jacob's ladder was shown to me upon which I climbed up . . .

but this ladder was not the old mystical hierarchy of states of being; it was rather the struggling path:

> Therefore if anyone will climb . . . after me, let him be careful that he be not drunk . . . For he must climb through a gruesome deep . . . and . . . hell, and he will have to endure scoffing and mocking . . . In this struggle I had often had to experience it with sad heart; the sun was often eclipsed . . . but it rose again and the more it was eclipsed the brighter and clearer it rose again. (*Aurora*, xiii, 20–22)

Like other mystics Boehme used sensory images to describe this break-through:

> When the Light arises . . . one tastes the other; . . . then the spirits become alive and life's vitality presses through all. In that vitality the one smells the other . . , feels the other. So there is only a heartily loving and friendly seeing, fragrancing, relishing, and loving . . . ; here is love, joy, and delight; here is light and brilliance; here is fragrance; here is pleasant and sweet taste . . . eternally, without end! (*Aurora,* ix, 38ff)

He added:

> But now I have climbed too high and I dare not look back again or else I shall get giddy . . . When I ascend I have no giddiness; but when I look back and want to return, I get dizzy and fear I may fall. (*Aurora,* xiv, 41)

Boehme's moving experience which lighted a new dawn for him was not all joy and exaltation; he never left this world of sin and evil and the consciousness of it was ever present:

> Do you believe that my spirit has sucked this out of the corrupt earth, or out of a felt hat? Truly no . . . for at the time I am describing my spirit . . . did . . . unite with the deepest birth of God. From that I got my knowledge, and from that it is sucked. . . . What I thereafter had to suffer from the Devil . . . who rules my outer man . . . you cannot understand . . . unless you dance in his round. (*Aurora,* xviii, 78ff)

From the passionate character of the latter half of the *Aurora,* Boehme's first book, it is clear that Boehme's initial speculative urge had two sources of confusion. The first was his inability to find answers in the writings of the "high masters" (*Aurora,* x, 27). The fruitless disputes, the endless theological bickering, the bitter confessional controversies of the post-Reformation age, had not resolved man's religious doubt. The second source, related to the first, was Boehme's prophetic discontent with the evil of his time. For Boehme's mysticism was bipolar; to want to seek unity is to

already know both the disunity that exists and the possibility
of its resolution; to seek resolution is to know evil's stubbornness. Boehme's mysticism embraced both joy and misery,
both the mystical elevation and the mystical death. In him
these two poles cannot be separated and his full mystical
experience embraces both. This is clear from the following
lyrical passage in the eighth chapter of the *Aurora*:

O gracious and great Love, how sweet you are! How
friendly you are! How lovely is your relish, who can express
it? . . . Or what do I write—I who stammer like a child
who has just learned to speak! To what shall I liken it? If
I liken it to the world's love it is only a dark vale—and that
large . . . O noble guest! why have you departed from us?
. . . O you wrathful Devil, what have you done? . . . Why
do I complain? you stinking goat! O you cursed stinking
Devil, how you have contaminated us . . . O you lying
Devil! stay a little while and the Spirit will uncover your
shame . . . O woe, you poor blind man, why do you let the
Devil make your body and soul so darksome! . . . O security, the Devil awaits yours; O pride, you are hell's fire; O
beauty, you are a dark valley; O power . . . O ego-centric
will, you are God's grim wrath! O man! Why is the world
become too narrow for you? Would you have it alone? And
if you did have it you would not have enough! . . . O man,
man! Why do you dance with the Devil who is your enemy?
. . . You have but a narrow stage on which you dance;
beneath the stage is hell! . . . O blind man! Is not heaven and
earth yours, and thereto God Himself? . . . O you poor
man, turn around; the Heavenly Father stretches out both
arms and calls to you; come, He wants to fold you in His
Love; you are His child and He loves you! If He hated you
He would be at odds with Himself! . . . O you watchmen of
Israel, why sleep you? Wake up from the sleep of whoredom,
and trim your lamps; the bridegroom comes, your trumpets
sound! O you stiff-necks and drunkards, how you go a-whoring with the greedy Devil! Thus speaks the Lord! Will you
not feed my people whom I have entrusted to you? See, I
have put you on Moses' chair, and trusted you with my
flock; but you mind only after the wool and not to the sheep;
thereby you erect great palaces; but I shall set you on the
pestilential stool and my Shepherd shall tend my sheep
. . . O blessed Love and clear Light! Remain with us for the

evening comes . . . O! why do I write of the world's evil—
I must do it and the world gives me the devil's thanks for it.
O! Amen! (*Aurora*, viii, 96–109)

The reference is obvious. Martin Moller, the good pastor,
had died in 1606, blind and deaf, yet with the welfare of his
flock at heart. As Boehme's experience had "opened" from
time to time he saw the untended sheep and the haughty
rational theology of Moller's successor, Gregory Richter.
This passage, probably written just after 1606, most likely
in 1608, puts Boehme among the prophets and divine am-
bassadors. He was another in the line of farmers' sons who
predicted the victory of God's righteousness over an evil
world. In 1675 Quirinius Kuhlmann, the Silesian *Schwärmer*,
wrote to the then chief pastor in Görlitz: *tres tibi proponam
Dei nuncios nostri seculi, unum Prophetum, alterum Sophum,
tertium Literarum!* [1] The first was Christoph Kotter mentioned above, the second was Boehme, and the third was
Johann Arndt. Thus Boehme found his place in the prophetic
succession; he railed against the world's sin; he fought with
a very personal devil. Apocalyptic urgency is an important
and in some ways exciting aspect of Boehme's growing
mystical experience inasmuch as it emerged from the contemporary situation:

The tribulation and collapse of Babel fast approaches; the
thunderstorm arises in all places; it will rage violently; vain
hope deceives for the tree's destruction is near . . . Babel's
tower has become without foundation; one hopes to keep it
up with props, but a wind from the Lord will collapse it.
Men's hearts and thoughts shall become manifest . . .
Many shall betray themselves . . . Hypocrites and mouth-
Christians shall wail when the false foundation becomes
manifest . . . An eagle [the German emperor] has hatched
out young lions [the Electors] in his nest, bringing them
prey so long that they have grown great, thinking that they
should also bring their prey to him again . . . They take
the eagle in his nest, pluck out his feathers, bite his claws
off . . . so that he cannot fetch prey for them any more
. . . If the rich and powerful knew whereupon their founda-
tions rested they would look to themselves and see to their
end . . . At that time . . . Grace shall flow . . . and the

afflicted and oppressed shall be refreshed. (*Epist.* xli, ps. 1ff.)

Boehme did not work out a dated apocalypse like many of his chiliast contemporaries:

> To me is given to know that the time is now and even now at hand, but the year and day I know not; . . . I leave it to God's counsel, and to those to whom God shall reveal it. (*Letzte Zeit*, I, 59ff.)

Boehme, however, was a prophet in more than a metaphorical sense because he created a philosophy of history more profound than the dated apocalypses of his contemporaries. He saw a new world emerging from a new man, a new level of religious living begetting a new social order, and, so intense had his sunrise to eternity been for him, he gave himself a place in creating this new world. He felt that he was himself a new Luther to a profounder reformation, a reformation of the spirit when Christ's children would not be called shoemaker's blacking (*Epist.* lxiii, 9).

> You shall still hear remarkable things as the time of the reformation is born of which it was told me. (*Ibid.*)

Indeed, this time already was born,

> the time already appears, and soon will come; he who wakes sees it. . . . First there must come a great tribulation before it be fully manifest. The cause is the great contention of the learned. . . . Let no honest man defile himself with such contention. (*Epist.*, xlvi)

This new age was one of certainty, knowledge, truth, righteousness, and peace.

Boehme's apocalyptic was part of his basic mystical experience and he believed, and it appears with sincerity, that his experience of 1600 was a sunrise to eternity, heralding the coming of a new age (*Princ.*, xx, 15). Moreover, he believed, and it appears with sincerity, that God had chosen him to reveal that which had remained hidden to the rest of mankind. He held his revelation to be unique (*Aurora*, xiv,

38) and he said that his life mission was to make the great lily manifest (*Dreyfach* iii, 5). Only his lowly station in the world seemed to bother him:

> Because I here write of . . . divine things . . . the reader doubtless will wonder at the simplicity of the author . . . What was Abel? A shepherd. What were Enoch and Noah? Plain . . . men. What were Abraham, Isaac, and Jacob? Herdsmen. What was David when . . . the Lord called him? A shepherd . . . How came . . . Jesus Christ into this world? Poor, in trouble and misery, and had nowhere to lay his head. What were the Apostles? Poor . . . illiterate fishermen. And what were they who believed their preaching? The poorer and meaner people. . . . What were they who in all ages of the Church . . . have stood by it most loyally and constantly? The poor . . . people who shed their blood . . . But who were they that falsified . . . pure doctrine? . . . Even the learned Doctors . . . popes, cardinals, bishops, professors. . . . Who was it purged out of the German churches the Pope's greediness for money, his idolatry, bribery, deceit, and cheating? A poor depised monk! By what power and might? By the power of God the Father . . . and God the Holy Spirit. (*Aurora*, ix, 1ff.)

Boehme believed himself to be Luther's heir and successor, a prophet possessed of the Spirit, dedicated to the cleansing of a church once again corrupted. Reason and rational theology could not regenerate man. Only an experience born of suffering availed:

> The world . . . supposes that one must see God with the earthly . . . eyes; it knows not that God dwells not in the outer life, but in the inner. It sees nothing strange in God's children, it says: O! he is a fool, he was born foolish, he is melancholy . . . Listen, Master Hans! I well know what melancholy is. I also know what is of God. I know both of these and also you in your blindness. But such knowledge requires no state of melancholy, but a knightly wrestling. (*Menschw.* II, vii, 11)

Boehme knew that rationally discovered creeds could not save man or make him whole. Faith was deeper than reason. Experience of the living Spirit in this world was necessary to overcome its evil. Boehme was not seeking to "go" to heaven any more than he was trying to avoid "going" to hell; he had done with the upward striving of medieval religion; his God had climbed up into him. He believed that the pregnant quarter of an hour had brought the invasion of the Spirit into his heart. This fired his soul.

If all trees were scribes and all branches pens, and if all hills were books and all waters ink, they could not give a sufficient description of the sorrow which Lucifer has brought into this place. (*Aurora* xvi, 26)

Hell was here and now; paradise's lily could grow in the world. Boehme's problem was to regenerate the world.

Conceived in its broadest aspect, Boehme's experience was the sunrise to an eternity within the world, something undreamed of in medieval thought.

NOTE TO CHAPTER TWO

1. Gottfried Arnold, *Kirchen- und Ketzer- Historei*, II, 199ff.

Ich muss die Creaturen fliehen
Und suchen Hertzens Innigkeit,
Soll ich den Geist zu Gotte ziehen
Auf das er bleib in Reineheit.
—ASCRIBED TO TAULER

CHAPTER THREE

BOEHME'S LIFE: 1600–1612

THE YEAR 1600, then, brought Jacob Boehme the sunrise but a long prosaic day of work lay ahead, for man cannot live by "illuminations" alone. He was just twenty-five years of age; he was not yet established as a substantial burgher; he was in reality a young dreamer who thought he had been given special, divinely inspired knowledge.

Outwardly he began to prosper. Obviously a careful and serious workman at his last he soon became established in his trade and a leader in his guild. During this period the tanners and the shoemakers were at loggerheads and Boehme was right in the middle of this controversy. So zealous had he been for success that he had been tanning more hides than he needed himself, selling the surplus to other shoemakers, thus competing with the tanners. On July 24, 1604, he was released from prison on the condition that he would not tan hides for other shoemakers and upon payment of six shillings fine within two weeks.[1] The jealousy of the guilds further appeared in an ambiguous reference in the *Ratsprotokol* for April, 1606, when a Jacob Boehme and Jacob Kissling were imprisoned for calling Max Röhricht a swindler. The trial disclosed that Röhricht had swindled Boehme and Kissling, so he was packed into jail. On May 2 they were all released, bond having been posted by Hans Löwe, Paul Hillebrand, and Hans Seidel.[2] The ambiguity arises from the possibility that the Jacob Boehme mentioned may have been the tanner of that name, although the probability is that it was the shoemaker-theologian as Paul Hillebrand was the man from whom the shoemaker bought his house. Jacob Boehme, the shoemaker, was an active member of his guild.[3]

On July 2, 1607, the theologian's father, whose first wife had died, divided his property among the children of his first marriage, and Boehme was in Old Seidenberg to receive his share of almost two hundred marks. So, in March, 1608, when Boehme's sons took part in the *Gregoriusfeste* they were listed among the *locupletiores* (affluent) and not among either the *pauperes* or the *equites* (nobility).[4]

On July 28, 1608, Boehme sold his house in the Rabengasse next to Paul Hillebrand, mentioned above, to Zacharias Kiesslingen for the sum of three hundred and thirty marks, a profit of thirty marks.[5] Two years passed before he again became a householder; [6] this is why his name does not appear in the list of master-shoemaker property-holders for the period.[7] The fact of the matter is that he had probably already moved into the house he was soon to buy, which was owned by his brother-in-law, Valentin Lange. In 1610 he was made trustee for his unmarried sister-in-law, Rosine, daughter of Hans Kuntzschmann, an act suggesting the death of Boehme's father-in-law [8] and implying Boehme's prosperity. On June 22, 1610, Boehme bought Lange's house in the Neiss gate just outside of the city and on the road to Liegnitz and Hirschberg, one of the busiest highways in eastern Germany. To finance this he borrowed, on November 10, 1610, the sum of fifty marks and contracted for periodic payments.[9] He made them as follows: November 13, 1610, two hundred marks; February 28, 1612, twenty-five marks; February 9, 1613, twenty-five marks; 1614, twenty-five marks; 1616, twenty-five marks; and 1618, twenty-five marks.[10] This sequence seems to suggest the slow settling of Boehme's father-in-law's estate jointly by Lange and Boehme.

Sometime around the year 1610 Franckenberg claims that Boehme experienced his "third illumination." About this Boehme himself is silent and does not hint at anything more than continuing understanding. However, Franckenberg says

according to God's holy counsel . . . about ten years after
. . . he was a third time stirred up and renewed by God.
Whereupon . . . he could not put it out of mind, nor strive
against God. Therefore [he] did . . . write secretly for himself.[11]

In 1612 the strife between the tanners and the shoemakers
again broke out and again Boehme was involved, for Boehme
and Hans Bürger had been sent to Lemberg by the shoemakers to buy leathers. They returned with three hundred
and thirty-two pieces which they had bought at two thalers
apiece. Protesting this invasion of their rights, the tanners
went to court. The *Protokoll* vindicated the shoemakers and
the record in their guild book is in the handwriting of
Jacob Boehme and therefore is the first bit of writing from
his pen. Inasmuch as it is not in his works the German text is
given below in the notes.[12] His authorship, however, has
been questioned [13] but not with convincing argument.

On May 25, 1612, Boehme served as security for Lorentz
Nüssler, a Lauterbach farmer who, as tenant, had allowed
a farm to become vacant and waste.[14]

These few scattered surviving facts present us with a bit
of the outward man—a sometimes boisterous young shoemaker, prosperous, energetic, and immersed in the active
mercantile life of his town. He was no idle dreamer. The
world's turmoil was mirrored in his life. And it was a turbulent age. In 1608 the union of Protestant princes under
Frederick of the Palatinate had taken place, and on July 11,
1609, Emperor Rudolf's *Majestätsbrief* had allowed freedom
of conscience to his Bohemian and Silesian subjects. But
Rudolf's long years of misrule had only intensified religious
hatreds; the Thirty Years' War became inevitable. Imperial
authority was collapsing; the eastern frontier had been saved
only when Rudolf effaced his guardianship, the western
frontier only by the assassin's dagger.[15] Boehme saw his
world composed of

greedy stiff-necks . . . you who . . . seek pride, honor,
praise, power, money, and goods, who sweat and bleed the
poor, oppressed, and distressed, spending their labor on your

vanities, holding yourselves better than simple laymen. . . .
(*Aurora*, xii, 19)

His reference was to the clergy, particularly to Gregory
Richter who had followed Martin Moller as chief pastor.
So in 1612, driven by inner compulsion and by outer pressure, Boehme began to write. On New Year's day he set pen
to paper (perhaps, though, he had already written eight
chapters before 1608) and put down in bold German char-
acters: *Morgen Röthe im Aufgang.* . . . *Die Würtzel oder
Mutter der Philosophie.*[16] A new day was dawning; the old
beaten world was not yet done; a new ground had been revealed to Boehme and he would declare it abroad! The shoemaker's ambition was confident; he knew that the sun had
risen for him; now he was going to reveal the true basis of all
philosophy, astrology,[17] and theology. For he believed that
he wrote not

from the instruction . . . received from men, nor from . . .
books, but I have written out of my own book which was
opened in me . . . the book of the noble . . . image. (*Epist.*
xii, 14)

And the *Aurora*, he says so many times, was not written for
the public but as a memorial to himself and such caution was
prudent in an intolerant age: Giordiano Bruno had been
burned in Rome in 1600; Valentin Weigel refused to allow
his writings to be published; Kepler and Galileo were in difficulties; and Johann Arndt, whose works appeared between
1606 and 1612, paid heavily for his indiscretions.[18] And then
the *Rosenkreutzer* books, however they may have come to be
written, were anonymous and they also advocated thoroughgoing reform. Boehme's *Aurora* suggests that he knew these
last works and in the twelfth chapter he foretells the time
of wonder, with 1604 hinted at as the year when Elias, the
artist, was to have removed man's misery. Paracelsian prophecies also were suggesting the time between 1599 and 1603
as that age of new reformation which was to have come with
"singing, ringing forth, dancing, rejoicing, and jubilating" as
Boehme himself said (xii, 22). And in 1604 that new star
standing in the serpent and crown had appeared and men

searched for its meaning.[19] Boehme, who was no master in courage, knowing the fate of foolish publication,

> intended to keep . . . my writing by me all . . . my life . . . ; but it fell out . . . that I entrusted a certain person with it; by means whereof it was published without my knowledge or consent, and the first book was taken from me. (*Epist.* xii, 12)

This "certain person" was the Schwenkfelder, Carl von Ender von Sercha,[20] who had been associated with Boehme in Martin Moller's conventicle. Of an old family, widely traveled, student at the Görlitz gymnasium between 1586 and 1595, graduate of Frankfurt, von Ender was a man with searching mind and heart.[21]

Now when Carl von Ender discovered that Boehme had written a book, a curious book of promise and prophecy, he had some copies made, unknown to the author, which he circulated. One of these fell into the hands of the churlish successor to Martin Moller, Gregory Richter,[22] chief pastor in Görlitz since 1606. From Boehme's writings Richter appears as a zealous watchdog of orthodoxy, an opponent of enthusiasm in all forms, rational, proud, and eager to persecute. This may be exaggeration. Born on February 1, 1560, probably at Ostritz, son of the monastery smith, he had turned from the anvil to the pulpit where he hammered out stringent Lutheran sermons, becoming orthodoxy's champion in Lusatia.[23] He had helped to protest Görlitz's orthodoxy at court during the crypto-Calvinist troubles.[24] Unpopular as a preacher, his sermons were long and poorly spoken, and not of Martin Moller's spirituality.[25] The Görlitz council reproved him for his reforming zeal and during the plague of 1612, after he had reviled a busy physician for not minding his business and then had himself fled to Sprottau, the council admonished him and ordered him to remain within the parsonage.[26] The burghers had little respect for him and wrote:

> *Quaeritur inclusus cur sit Richterus in aedes?*
> *Me Samaritani calce petavit equus.*[27]

When, then, Richter learned that the shoemaker whose
face he saw near the pillar in Saint Peter's and Saint Paul's
Church every Sunday had written a book, when he knew
that the already suspected Carl von Ender was quietly passing the word around of a new prophet, he was enraged. He
wangled a copy of the book. And his attitude surely was not
helped when he read passages like this:

You teach others the way and you are always seeking it yourselves; you grope in the dark and see it not . . . O you
blind men! Leave off contention and shed no innocent blood;
lay waste no country or city to fill the devil's will; but put on
the helmet of peace, gird yourselves with love to each other,
and practise meekness. Leave off pride and greed, grudge
not one another different forms . . . but live in meekness,
chastity, friendliness, and purity. (*Aurora* xxii, 4ff)

Richter, it seems, was not the man that Moller, his predeces-
sor, had been, and his words did not speak to the condition
of his flock.

But there appears to have been more reason than a *Ketzer-*
buch to turn Richter's wrath, for Cornelius Weisner in his
Wahrhaftige Relation, one of the early biographical materials, records an incident which gives plausibility to Richter's
dislike of Boehme. Richter

did lend to one of Jacob Boehme's nephews, a young baker,
. . . one dollar . . . to buy wheat to make white bread at
Christmas for which he presented him in thankfulness a good
white loaf; soon after the holidays he brought the dollar . . .
to him again; in hope that the preacher would . . . accept
his former present in full satisfaction, as he used it only a
fortnight. The preacher, unsatisfied, pronounced God's anger
. . . against him and so . . . terrified the young baker . . .
that he fell into . . . deep perplexity . . . and despair of his
salvation . . . so that for . . . several days he spoke to no
being . . . but went up and down sighing . . . Till . . . on
the . . . entreaty of his wife, her uncle Jacob Boehme took
the matter in hand . . . till he found what lay upon him
. . . and spoke peace to him . . . and . . . went to the en-

raged preacher and . . . entreated him no longer to be angry with the young man, that he himself would satisfy the en-raged preacher . . . yet thought that the poor man had paid enough . . .

Whereupon the preacher . . . broke forth saying what had that rascal [Boehme] to do with him to . . . molest and disturb him?

But he continued . . . and entreated his favor, promising to make satisfaction . . . Ashamed of his injustice . . . [the minister] would not acknowledge it . . . but showed him the outer door out of which he was to go.

The *Primate* sat on his chair and had his slippers on and when [Boehme] . . . went away, as he was going out of the door, he gave the angry *Primate* a Christian valediction, say-ing, God preserve your worship. The *Primate* was angry . . . , took off his slipper, and threw it . . . at the honest man saying, what have you to do, you wicked rogue, to bid me . . . a good night? . . .

Sunday morning following the preacher . . . vehemently inveyed against [Boehme] . . . and thundered abominably . . . against him by name, . . . threatening the destruction of the whole city. . . .

He admonished the magistrates . . . to be avenged against such tumultuous opposers of the holy office . . . of preach-ing who disturb the preacher . . . and write heretical books. . . .

Upon which the . . . falsely accused man, who sat . . . at the pillar . . . against the pulpit . . . held his peace un-til all the people were gone . . . staying in his seat until the preacher with his chaplain . . . went out of the vestry through the church.

He then followed and . . . in the church-yard spoke to the preacher . . . and asked what harm he had done. . . .

The preacher answered nothing but looked . . . as if he would kill him with his looks and in a rage . . . began to curse . . . , saying, Get thee from me, Satan . . . Do you not see that I am a clergyman? . . .

But the troubled . . . man gave . . . this answer: Yes, reverend Sir, I well see you are a . . . clergyman . . . and [I] esteem you . . . and I come to entreat you as a clergy-man what hurt I have done you.

And turning . . . to the . . . Chaplain entreated him, saying, Reverend . . . Sir, help me in my entreaty to the preacher that he will tell . . . what I have spoken or done against him. . . .

   The preacher was still more enraged. . . . He would have sent . . . a servant . . . for a city bailey to take him away and put him in prison . . . which the chaplain spoke against. . . .

   Monday morning following . . . the magistrates met . . . and sent for [Boehme]; they examined him, perceived no evil in him . . . asked . . . what harm he had done the preacher? He answered he knew not, neither could he know from the preacher himself, and . . . entreated . . . that they . . . would send for the preacher and cause him to say what he had done. . . .

   The Council concluded that it was just that the preacher . . . be . . . entreated to come to . . . the council house . . . to relate those grievances . . .

   Whereupon he was enraged and sent . . . word [asking] what had he to do with the council house . . . he would speak . . . from the pulpit . . . they should banish the vain, wicked heretic from the city . . .

   The Lords consulted and could not find how they should justly help the master, fearing the vehemence of the preacher in his pulpit, and concluded to banish . . . Boehme . . . , in which conclusion some . . . would not consent, but rose and went their way . . . The executioner . . . caused the uncondemned, faithful citizen . . . to be instantly banished out of the gates.

   . . . The patient man . . . answered . . . 'My lords, I will do as you command and depart . . . but may I not go to my house first and take mine along with me . . . ?' But they forbade it . . . , saying they could not alter the sentence . . . Then he said, 'Dear sirs, let it be done, seeing it cannot be otherwise. I am content.' So he was banished and gone away at night . . .

   The following morning, when the council were met, and had reconciled their disagreement they made another conclusion: to hunt the . . . man, and sent up and down . . . and at length found him and brought him solemnly with honor into the city again.[28]

   This account, here stripped of its unnecessary verbiage, may represent the melting together of three different episodes in Boehme's life: 1) the episode of the young baker nephew and Richter; 2) Richter's denunciation of Boehme from the pulpit; 3) Boehme's banishment. There are, fortunately, other sources for the second and third episodes, for July 28, 1613, Burgomaster Scultetus wrote in his *Diarum* that Jacob Boehme, the shoemaker, who lived between the gates behind the hostel, had been brought to the *Rathaus* for examination, that he was questioned about his beliefs, that he was thereupon put in the stocks, and that as soon as Oswald [Krause] had fetched the quarto book from Boehme's house he was released and advised to leave off such things.[29] This was Friday. Sunday, which happened to be the eighth Sunday after Trinity when the Gospel lesson deals with false prophets who come garbed as sheep, Richter preached a sharp sermon against Boehme. Tuesday, July 30, Scultetus records that Boehme was brought to the manse, vigorously questioned about his beliefs, and warned not to continue writing.[30] In *Epist.* xii, 12, Boehme says that in 1613, when he was called before the Görlitz Senate, he wrote an answer to Richter's attacks. This answer has been lost.

This seems to have been the sequence of events. Inasmuch as Boehme was banished in 1624, Weisner's account may be confused, although he may have been banished twice.

In any event Gregory Richter's sharp attack on Boehme was a decisive factor in his development, one which gave him an increasing dissatisfaction with institutional religion. Also his writing brought him trouble; the manuscript of the *Aurora* was confiscated and it circulated only in copies which were not accurate. Boehme said that he

saw this first book no more in three years: I supposed that it was . . . gone until a certain learned man sent me some copies . . . who exhorted me to proceed and manifest my talent, to which the outward reason would by no means agree, because it had suffered so much already . . . ; moreover the spirit was . . . weak and timorous . . . ; my light was for a good while withdrawn from me and it did glow in me as a hidden fire so that I felt nothing but anguish and perplexity within me, and outwardly I found nothing but contempt; and inwardly a fiery instigation. (*Epist.* xii, 13)

NOTES TO CHAPTER THREE

1. *Ratsprotokol,* July 24, 1604. Cf. Jecht, *Böhme,* p. 23.
2. *Ibid.,* April 29, 1606, May 2, 1606. Cf. Jecht, *Böhme,* pp. 23, 24.
3. Jecht, *Böhme,* p. 23.
4. *Ibid.,* p. 27.
5. *Görlitzer Kaufbuch,* 1605ff. Bl. 186a. Cf. Jecht, *Böhme,* p. 10.
6. *Ibid.,* Bl. 45b. Cf. Jecht, *Böhme,* p. 12.
7. *Ibid.,* p. 10.
8. *Ibid.,* p. 24.
9. *Görlitzer Kaufbuch,* 1605ff., Bl. 45b. Cf. Jecht, *Böhme,* p. 12.
10. Neumann, *Geschichte von Görlitz,* p. 367.
11. Franckenberg, *De Vita* . . . , #12.
12. The text is as follows: LAUS DEO! LAUS DEO! LAUS DEO!
   Den 25 August half Gott der Herr, der rechte Augustus, dass
   die Rottgerber mit Schanden ihren hochweisen, übernatürli-
   chen samt ihren Helfershelfern geschmiedeten, unauflöslichen,
   wie sie condeten, Abschied wieder ein antworten mussten und
   den erkaufte Rauleder aus den Häusern in ihr Gerbehaus
   mussten folgen lassen; deren waren 332, so wir, die Schuh-
   macher, zu Lemberg bei einem Kauf- und Handelsmann
   kaufften das Stück pro 2 Thaler und 2 Argent. Wurde getheilet
   und gezahlet. Gott sei ewig Lob! Hans Bürger und Jakob Bem
   kaufften solche Leder zu Lemberg, waren trefflichen Leder,
   also dass wir, Gott Lob, den Schaden und Jammer vergessen
   cunnten, den uns die Gerber gemacht hatten. Wurden geger-
   bet schön und gut hernach getheilet, dafür wir Gott danken!
   Cf. Jecht, *Böhme,* p. 23.
13. Jecht, *Böhme,* pp. 23, 24, 28.
14. B. Scultetus, *Kirchenwesen,* Varia 98, Ratsarchiv 238. Quoted
   by Jecht, *Böhme,* p. 24.
15. *Cambridge Modern History,* III, p. 735.
16. The Ms differs in title from the printed versions. Imperfect
   versions based on Ender's copy have been printed. The text of
   the 1730 edition follows the autograph, and Barker's English
   translation and reprint does not.
17. In Boehme's day astrology meant science generally.
18. Johann Arndt dabbled in astrology. See the fourth book of his
   True Christianity, Mysterium Incarnationis.
19. This star was still being discussed in 1641. Cf. Peuckert, *Die
   Rosenkreutzer,* p. 55ff.
20. Franckenberg, *De Vita* . . . , #3.

21. Heckel, *Geschichte der deutschen Literatur in Schlesien*, p. 164.
22. Richter may have been roughly handled by the Boehmdists. Jecht believes that Richter was a competent, good, and kindly man. Cf. *Böhme*, p. 32ff.
23. Jecht, *Böhme*, p. 61.
24. *Ibid.*, pp. 32–33.
25. Scultetus wrote that Richter had been examined on August 1, 1604, about the quality of his sermons.
26. Jecht, *Böhme*, p. 33.
27. Jechner, *Leben* . . . pp. xlivff.
28. Weisner, *Wahrhaftiger Relation*, #28. Translation modernized from the *Remainder of the Books*, London, 1662. Koyrè holds the episode apocryphal. Cf. *Boehme*, p. 17, note 1.
29. Jecht, *Böhme*, p. 36.
30. Cf. G. Köhler, Görlitzer Wegweiser, 1635, #45. Also Neumann, *Geschichte von Görlitz*, p. 392.

Nur hoffe, wart, und beit,
Es ist noch eine kleine Zeit,
Bis Teufels Reich darnieder leit.
—QUOTED BY BOEHME, *Aurora,* xiv, 107

CHAPTER FOUR

THE *AURORA:* 1612

WHAT SORT of book was it that made such a stir, bringing down on Boehme's head this storm of condemnation? Was it, as Carl von Ender thought, a work of promise and exciting anticipation which the thirty-six-year-old shoemaker had written? Was it really an aurora, a sunrise to eternity?

The *Aurora* is a primitive, profound, chaotic, exasperating, prophetic work of cant and rant as well as of insight and of revelation. It clings to antiquated ideas and yet shows knowledge of Copernican theories and of the circulation of the blood. Brilliant and dull, a hodgepodge of promise and of fulfillment, it shows the Renaissance search for modernity alongside of a valuation of antiquity.

Boehme later called it a work of his "spiritual childhood" (*Epist.* xii, 56), written without full reason by some sort of "magical" consciousness, and the book's structure supports this. It is ungainly, unorganized, incomplete, and revolving around two focal points which rarely meet. It consists of twenty-six chapters, the first eight of which clearly show that they were to have formed a complete work by themselves, and which may have been written before 1612. The Preface was added much later because it mentions the second and third books.

Although the scope and organization of this book may be primitive, the problems which Boehme's mystical intuition proposed were not; they were among the most perplexing of religious philosophy. Koyré suggests that the problem was that of evil and of God's relationship to the world. Boehme formulated this in three questions: 1) that of freedom being manifested in being; 2) that of spirit expressing itself in body; and 3) that of the double necessity of dialectic [1] both in being and in thought. This resulted in a living God of whom nature and man's soul are emanations, in a living world containing the hidden God. Both posit the same problem: how, if God is good, is He the source of all; and if evil is so visibly present in man's soul, how can God also dwell therein.[2]

Boehme also got knowledge from his experience of 1600—the insight that good and evil are in all things. This insight both posited his problems and pointed towards their solution. The *Aurora's* solution was more pantheistic than mystical unless one concedes that mysticism may be a speculative metaphysics which changes outer into inner, historical into eternal, and natural and historical processes into the generation of the gods.[3] Thus conceived, Boehme's pantheizing in the *Aurora* constitutes his first effort at metaphysics, showing his kinship with Renaissance nature-philosophy whose chief idea was the divine unity of the living all.[4] Boehme discloses no cleft between thought and life: evil is not the absence of good. In the *Aurora* it is physical and moral, essentially necessary but existentially irrational. To probe the source, the *Quell*, of nature's dualism he could have become a Manichean; his evil was earth-bound. If he thought of this solution his piety rejected it; the God that he had met in Martin Moller's conventicle could not thus be retained. In the *Aurora* two tendencies collided, creating an empirical dialectic: the one was the piety of resignation and selflessness traditional to German mysticism; the other was Neoplatonic naturalism. The former came to Boehme by way of Moller from Eckhart,[5] Tauler, Suso, Mechthild,[6] the Ebners, Nicolas of Strassburg, the *Theologia Germanica*, Luther, and Schwenkfeld.[7] One form of mysticism was absent—the Dionysian search for the names of God. The other tendency came to Boehme from Platonism, Neo-Platonism, and from Renaissance philosophy by way of the humanists of Silesia. In the *Aurora* the primary problem was the reconciliation of the pantheizing tendencies of the one with the supranaturalistic dualism of the other; Luther's devil, the target of a loaded inkwell, was not at home in a Plotinian world:

The learned have had many disputations, questions, and opinions about grim evil in all this world's creatures, in the sun as well as the stars; moreover there are some very poisonous beasts, serpents, and growths in this world. Therefore rationalists have preemptorily concluded . . . that God has also willed evil because he has made so much evil. (*Aurora*, xvi, 28)

This is Boehme's problem, the old problem of theodicy,—the impetus of his thought in the *Aurora* where he seeks but never finds a solution. Though he believed that he had the true answer, none here was presented. He emphatically denied that God had made evil; was it not the devil who

taught men sorcery and witchcraft . . . Come on, ye jugglers . . . you who go a-wooing and a-whoring after the devil. Come to my school. I will show you how . . . you are carried into hell . . . Poor man did not fall because of a resolved . . . will but through the poisonous infection of the devil. . . . (*Aurora*, xvi, 1, 3; xvii, 38)

The *Aurora* then was not theology for its author sought to know the world, its being and becoming, its divine birth. He wanted to know how in a divinely created world, evil, wrathful nature came to be. Here he was not yet focused on redemption, on the removal of that evil; but he looked, searched, probed, inspected; he was, in short, a metaphysician. However, as the *Aurora* was unfinished, such matters may have been reserved for the end of the book; no solution was even broached and so the fragment is a pansophic book which seeks the wisdom of the all within nature:

What still remains hidden? Christ's true teaching? No; but the philosophy and God's deep ground, the heavenly joy, the revelation of angelic creation, the revelation of the devil's gruesome fall from which evil comes, the creation of this world, the deep ground and mystery of man and all the creatures in this world, the youngest judgment and the transmutation of this world, the mystery of the resurrection of the dead, and eternal life. (*Aurora*, ix, 8)

These Boehme sought to disclose because he believed that a new vision of eternal nature had been given him. Nature was a book containing the "great mystery" (*Epist.* x, 36) and to reveal this hidden God was his aim. To do this the arrogant, self-centered nature was not adequate; the Holy Spirit was wanted (*Aurora* ii, 13) as the same divine Spirit is both in God and within eternal nature which is His "body."

. . . in nature all qualities are in one another as one quality in the way and manner that God is all and how all comes from and proceeds from Him; God is the heart or source of nature; from Him all comes. (*Aurora* i, 6)

Those who propose to search God's being in nature must be enlightened by the Holy Spirit for this Spirit is in God, in nature, and in man (*Aurora* i, 16–18). Though good and evil are in all things, in God there is only good (*Aurora* ii, 63); so evil cannot come from God. It

has in God no substance . . . He is a spirit in whom all powers are (*Aurora*, ii, 69) . . . If God should be angry with Himself then all nature would be afire. (ii, 64)

God was here the coincidence of contraries where contrasts are reconciled—the One. He was unity, an idea, the consequences of which were theodicy and "negative theology." How the harmony and joy of God's inner being became the divided natural world is Boehme's problem.

The *Aurora* was an original work in that it raised questions without bringing answers and in that Boehme did not accept the false identification of evil with nonbeing. For him evil was in positive and powerful struggle with good, a struggle which begat life. Resolution is victory but victory was less satisfying than struggle—*in der Ueberwindung ist Freude!* (*Myst. Mag.*, xvi, 6) And perhaps Boehme's *Aurora* was more struggle than victory, more an effort to overcome the irrationalities of his vision than final delineation of his own matured philosophy.

Boehme was held by an ancient antimony: God and the world should both be united and apart. God, however, can be put so far beyond the world as to be out of it, or so much in it as to be one with it. At first Boehme struggled with deistic transcendence in the earlier years, and this struggle bore him his "illumination." Later he struggled with immanence in *Bedenk. Stief.* and *Irrth. Stief.* He made two solutions: from the world to God during his alchemical period, and from the soul to God during the period of his maturity. Neither of these solutions is present in the *Aurora.*

Boehme saw good and evil struggling in all qualities, a struggle of contraries which was nonexistent in God (*Aurora* ii, 35), angels, or demons. These had but one quality. Man stood between good and evil, able to choose.

Here Boehme's characteristic idea of quality appears: the Holy Spirit "qualifies" the good while Lucifer "qualifies" evil. This struggle assumed special meaning for Boehme for the conflict is endured within nature too, for good and evil stand there in contradiction; he conceived of *Qualität* as *ein quellende Kraft,* a surging vitality.

Here man must consider what the word quality means . . . A quality is the mobility, surging, or drive of a thing. (*Aurora* i, 3)

It is an egressive energy, an inherent libido—to use a modern term—an urge much like Bergson's *élan vital,*[8] a "power of life" (*Aurora* i, 6). In the *Aurora* Boehme adopted the four qualities of Galen and medieval medicine: heat and cold, bitter and sweet. To these he added sour and salt. Heat burns and also illuminates, thus combining fierceness and light in an internal dialectic, operating within nature to warm all reality (*Aurora* i). Light opposes heat's fierce rage, allaying it; it is likewise made of two activities: the power to reduce heat and the power to freeze to immobility. From heat and light come two elements, air and water, the former chiefly from heat and the latter from cold. Between them life is created. The bitter attracts the air's water and makes the earth's vegetables, dissipating evil and producing a joy (*Aurora,* i, 30) wherein the Holy Spirit works; yet, at the same time, if it be too preponderant, it contains a house of death (*Aurora* i). Sweet opposes the bitter, tempers all creatures, makes them pleasant, causes vegetables to be fragrant, tasty, yellow, ruddy, is a source of divine meekness; although when it dominates it breeds disease, plagues, pestilence, corruption, and fermentation (*Aurora* i). Sour opposes both bitter and sweet and it is the flowing vitality in all things in which spirit dwells (*Aurora* i, 38); also, however, when it predominates it begets melancholy, putridness, and sadness. Salt is the bitter's good temper which opposes bitterness and makes things pleasant as a pleasant life-source; but it makes for hardness, producing scabs, sores, pox, and a "mourning house of death."

Boehme, possessing a smattering of medical knowledge, here was seeking adequate psychological terms to describe the inner life; also, he was convinced of the relationship between physical and psychological states. These qualities [9] were really spiritual modes and, writing before modern subjective language had been created, he was searching for terms to describe the substantial as well as spiritual character of reality. This suggests one of the dominant motives of Boehme's thought: the effort to find correspondence between God, nature, and human nature. This "great analogy," as Schleiermacher called it,[10] was conceived substantially:

If you will not believe that in this world all descends . . . from the stars, I will demonstrate it to you, if you are not a blockhead . . . (*Aurora* ii, 52) If not, it will be . . . with you as with the wise heathen, who gazed . . . at creation, and would . . . sift it with their ego-centric reason; and though with their fictions . . . (*Dichten*) they came before God's countenance, yet they were not able to see it, but were stark blind. . . . (*Aurora* ii, 21)

Nature was for him God's body; He was the all in All; reading nature's mystery gave knowledge of God. And man, chief of created beings, was made in God's image and anatomical allegorization revealed all nature: the abdomen signified the deep between the stars and the earth while the whole body signified the entire heaven and earth. Flesh was earth, blood water, breath air, the heart fire. The head, seat of the mind, signifies heaven and contains the "astral principle" as well as the five senses (*Aurora* ii, 19ff). Boehme enjoins the reader to open here the "eyes of the spirit" and see the Creator. His interest in this great analogy was to the minutest detail. Each created form was an analogy to the divine world. As all things existed in fire, air, and water they had a threefold meaning.

Everything in the world has become a similitude of the trinity . . . Thus you find three fountain-heads in man: first the vitality in your whole mind which signifies God the Father; then the light in your whole mind which enlightens the mind and which signifies the Son. And thirdly there goes forth from all your vitalities, and out of your light too, an understanding Spirit. (*Aurora* iii, 36, 41–42)

Boehme saw this ternary in all created things (*Aurora* iii, 101) but man is made of nature's pith while beasts are made of nature's wilder nature. This threefoldness dwells in (*einwohnt*) all nature (*Aurora* xiv, 91) and Boehme believed that natural insight was therefore also divine insight, the vision he himself had attained in his illumination. He felt compelled to communicate this analogy between nature and God:

When one considers all nature and its properties he then sees the Father; when one beholds heaven and the stars then he sees His eternal energy and wisdom . . . All the vitalities in nature come from God the Father; all light, heat, cold, air, water; and all earth's vitalities, bitter, sour, sweet, astringent, hard, soft, and more . . . all begin from the Father. (*Aurora* iii, 8–9)

God does not dwell in a transcendent heaven nor is he shut off from His creation. He is the generator, begetter, creator, the beginning beyond whom and before whom there is nothing. The Son is the source of joy (*Aurora* iii, 23). God is symbolized in nature, but more than symbolized for he is nature and yet He is more than nature.

Now I will show you a similitude. Look at heaven which is a round sphere having neither beginning nor end but is everywhere beginning and end; so also is God in and above the heaven having neither beginning nor end . . . The stars denote the Father's various energies and wisdom . . . Now the whole deep between the stars along with the earth signify the Father . . . The seven planets signify the seven spirits of God . . . The sun goes around in the deep between the stars in a round curve; it is the heart of the stars, giving light and energy to all the stars . . . Even so is God's Son . . . the Father's heart. (*Aurora* iii, 18–21)

In the *Aurora* this kind of symbolism does not yet go beyond the pantheist's identification of God and the world and as the initial urge to Boehme's speculation had been dissatisfaction with deist separation of heaven and earth, so here in the *Aurora* he expresses this in an image which is close to pantheism, an image which links God and the world by symbolic conjunction and union.

This "great analogy" either is tomfoolery or else it has meaning in a metaphysical sense in the same fashion that Thomas Aquinas, opposing Maimonides,[11] taught knowledge of God by analogy. Boehme, however, asserted that God dwelt beyond analogy [12] because he was not the aethereal deep: He is *like* the heavens but He is not the heavens. His Christ was *like* the sun, but He was not the sun. This analogy interpenetrates all reality.

In wood, stone, and herbs are three things and nothing can be born or grow if one of the three be left out. First there is the vitality from which a body comes, be it wood, stone, or herbs; then there is juice in the same which is its heart; thirdly, there is therein an up-surging energy, smell, or taste which is the thing's spirit and by which it increases and grows . . . So you find the similitude of the Trinity in the Divine Being and in all things, look wherever you will. . . . (*Aurora* iii, 47–48)

The trinitarian image therefore inhabits all reality and this is the key to God's power over the world. The Father, moreover, is the organic as well as the psychic vitality of all reality and the pattern of its essential structure. The Son is consciousness, life, rational being. The Spirit is the living essence, life's support. Not only has the world been generated by God, not only has He borne it, but it also expresses His inner nature and all creatures are patterns of His three-fold being. Yet in some passages Boehme seems to suggest that only the Father is God and that a cleft has appeared between Him and the other forms of life. This, however, presages a profounder solution yet to come, his idea of the *Ungrund.*

The order of creation is thus explained in a passage which, like so many in Boehme, is hard to put into English.[13]

From God's vitalities the heavens came; from the heavens came the stars; from the stars the elements, from the elements the earth and the creatures. So everything had its beginning. . . . (*Aurora* ii, 44)

The difficult word is vitality.

So Boehme's general point of view is clear from the *Aurora's* opening chapters: God is in the natural world. Having reacted against barren deism in his basic experience, he was pitched into deeper difficulties; in one sense God was both nature and the cosmos but in another sense he was neither because He was "beyond nature and creature." Yet this transcendent God has manifested his threefold structure within nature which he also inhabits (*einwohnt*), thus becoming both source and synthesis. The world has come from Him, exhibits His inner nature, and returns to Him again. At each step God has expressed himself by intermediaries. These sensible symbols, material or spiritual, are expressions of God, admittedly spatial symbols the final overtones of which are noumenal.[14]

The *Aurora's* first eight chapters form a complete book, even to a final Amen! The ninth chapter begins in a new mood, speaking of the dawn of the day when man no longer may sleep, when the proud shall be humbled and the lowly exalted! A new note has been added—the prophetic—and Boehme's style becomes repetitive, wandering, and centered in two foci: explanation of his nature philosophy and deep-grounded Christian piety. Here the basic "rift" in his consciousness appears, one that separated his metaphysics from his devotion, the tension between reason and passion. He starts, stops, starts again, following no orderly road as in the first eight chapters. He begins one theme only to break into another. Like the psychoanalyst's patient there comes a point where his mind jumps and the flow of his ideas is broken off. All his works from the *Aurora's* eighth chapter to *Sig. Rer.* reveal this schizoid character.[15]

The cause of this rift is clear. It was the harsh treatment he had gotten from Gregory Richter, pastor of the Görlitz church. Boehme's prophetic denunciations, his holy discontent with institutional religion, produced a divided heart: he could not forget his vision nor could he forgo the piety he had learned from Martin Moller. So the *Aurora* was perhaps not meant to be finished, remaining an incomplete, preliminary, provisional statement. No higher synthesis could yet appear: repetitions occur, the story of the three realms being told three times (xii, 17ff, xv, 26ff, xxii, 11ff). One new idea does creep in, one which later becomes important, that of the seven qualities of the divine nature. Here the influence of the Jewish Cabala is apparent [16] and so his connection with Jewish traditions is already evident.[17]

But the *Aurora* remains a hodgepodge reworking of one central theme, the manifestation of God within the world, showing deep insight into nature philosophy on the one hand and breathing living religious spirit on the other, promise of a twice-born man struggling towards solution of one of man's profoundest problems.

NOTES TO CHAPTER FOUR

1. Dialectic is used in meaning E in André Lalande, *Vocabulaire Technique et Critique de la Philosophie*, Paris, 1951, p. 227.
2. Koyré, Boehme, p. 72. I am heavily indebted to Koyré's brilliant analysis of the *Aurora*.
3. Cf. Windelband, *A History of Philosophy*, p. 366. This definition agrees with Schleiermacher in the *Reden:* "It does not arise from being sated and overladen by external influences, but, on every occasion, some secret power ever drives the man

back upon himself, and he finds himself to be the plan and key of the whole. Convinced by a great analogy and a daring faith that it is not necessary to forsake himself, but that the spirit has enough in itself to be conscious of all that could be given from without, by a free resolve, he shuts his eyes forever against all that is not himself." (Oman's translation, London, 1893, pp. 133–134). Here the Peripatetic-Stoic doctrine of analogy between macrocosm and microcosm is the "great analogy." In the Renaissance this doctrine was revived by Weigel and Paracelsus.

4. Windelband, *op. cit.,* p. 367.
5. Eckhart was not yet known as a name although his ideas were in Tauler and others.
6. Cf. A. M. Heiler, *Mystik Deutscher Frauen im Mittelalter,* Berlin 1929.
7. Some of Tauler's prayers were in Moller's *Meditationes sanctorum patrum, Vide: Bornkamm, Luther und Böhme,* p. 77.
8. *Vide:* Jacques Chevalier, *Bergson,* Paris, 1926, pp. 192, 193, 221.
9. Boehme's use of quality bears no relation to the word's usual philosophical use. *Vide:* "Qualité" in Lalande, *Vocabulaire . . .*
10. See note number 3.
11. Cf. R. L. Patterson, *The Conception of God in the Philosophy of Aquinas.* London, 1933, pp. 227ff.
12. This idea of analogy was found in Babylon and India. Cf. H. Olderberg, *Die Weltanschauung der Brahmantexte,* Göttingen, 1919; also, Conger, *Microcosmos und Macrocosmos,* New York, 1923; E. Cassirer, *Das Erkenntnisproblem in der Philosophie und Wissenschaft der neueren Zeit,* Berlin, 1911, pp. 200-244.
13. The difficulty is not with the words but with their meaning. Here the only difficult word is *Kräften,* but what does it really mean? Energy, vitality, power? Is it to be translated in vitalistic terms?
14. See part two for discussion of the symbols.
15. The books become increasingly coherent as he matured and a solution is finally achieved.
16. Koyré, *Boehme,* p. 126.
17. During this period knowledge of the Cabala was not unusual. Reuchlin's works were available for those unable to read the Hebrew, and it was not hard to find someone who had read him. Agrippa von Nettesheim and Paracelsus were also well known. In his later works Boehme even used the word Cabala twice (*Theos. Frag.* iii, 34, vi, 11).

> *But is not solitude, too, a gate?*
> *Is there not at times discovered,*
> *in stillest loneliness, an unsus-*
> *pected perception? Can concern*
> *with oneself not mysteriously be*
> *transformed into concern with*
> *the mystery?*
>
> —MARTIN BUBER, *I and Thou*

CHAPTER FIVE

PERIOD OF SILENCE: 1612–1619

THE YEAR 1612 was, then, the turning point. Boehme had become an author. But other events were taking place, too. In 1611 his mother had died, and on March 12, 1613, he sold his shoemaker's bench to Georg Süssenbachen for four hundred seventy marks,[1] the value of his business having doubled since 1599. In spite of the two recorded borrowings of thirty-six marks, November 19, 1605, and of fifty marks, November 16, 1610, his business seems to have been well-managed.[2] Upon selling his shoemaker's bench he was engaged in the linen and wool business in the interests of which he made yearly journeys to Prague and perhaps to the Leipzig Fair.[3] He is known to have bought woolen gloves from the farmers and sold them at retail.[4] But times were worsening. In 1566 the *Thaler* had been worth sixty-eight crowns; in 1614 it was worth ninety-two; and in 1618, one hundred eighty-six.[5] War inflation and paper currency became prevalent; the rulers sought funds by any means: Emperor Matthias tried to boil gold and was searching his destiny in the stars.[6] This economic instability was mirrored in an incident of October 10, 1616, when Catharina Boehme, with seventeen other women, was prohibited from trading cotton yarn in the Görlitz streets. Fourteen days later Boehme was himself punished for the same offense.[7] He was not forbidden to trade in yarn, but only to peddle it from house to house as the free and open selling of yarn was a privilege of free merchants.[8]

As long as times were good and trade was moving freely Boehme was prosperous; but crop failures, inflation, devaluation of monies, and the miserable plague undermined business. Carl von Ender became Boehme's patron and began to send him provisions.[9] Rudolf von Gersdorf and Augustin Cöppin sent him food.[10] Near the end of 1618 Boehme's father passed away and he shared the inheritance.[11] In 1620, probably in return for permission to copy manuscripts, Boehme received money from Christian Bernhard, but as early as 1613 times of scarcity had arrived (*Epist.* xxxiv, 6) and Boehme could read the signs, for he knew that wars, uproars, calamities, and death were to come. The systematic deterioration of currency by the kippers and wippers, as they were called, almost brought an insurrection among the lower classes.[12]

For Boehme, however, economic considerations were no longer basic. He was established well enough as a substantial burgher with a widening literary fame. Frankenberg relates:

One day there came a stranger to his door, . . . little in stature, cunning in look, and quick in . . . understanding. After an overture of civilities he began by acquainting Jacob Boehme that, whereas he had been informed of his being endued with a singular spirit, such as is not to be met with in common, and it was incumbent . . . to let his neighbors share in the good which had been communicated to himself; he, . . . Jacob Boehme, should do him the favor of bestowing the same singular spirit upon him, . . . making it over to him . . . for a sum of money. Upon which . . . Jacob Boehme . . . gave the man to understand that he . . . esteemed himself . . . unworthy of the supposed extraordinary gifts and arts . . . that he could lay claim to nothing more than a life and conversation grounded upon . . . faith in God and brotherly love to his neighbor . . . that he was as little acquainted as he was fond of any singular . . . spirit. But that, if he would needs be possessed of a spirit, he must take the . . . same course . . . , repent of his sins, fervently imploring the heavenly Spirit of grace . . . in which case He would surely give it to him. Which advice the poor . . . creature was so far from taking, that without much ado . . . he wanted to exhort the . . . familiar spirit out of . . . Boehme till he . . . , chagrined, caught hold of him full in the face . . . Upon which the conjurer, trembling and astonished, begged pardon, which made . . . Boehme remit his zeal. . . .[13]

Boehme's increasing fame began to break in upon his inner life; no longer was he the solitary and lonely man of single vision; his *Aurora* was quietly circulating and his name was being admiringly whispered.

After the confiscation of this first book and the Town Council's ban on further writing he endured a "full sabbath of years" (*Apol. Richt.* 69) in silence. This was indeed that significant period of dryness characteristic of mysticism, that dismal desert before the oasis of splendor which was to follow. He felt that he could not work because the breath of the Most High (*Epist.* xii, 13) had been withdrawn. Moreover

After the persecution I proposed to do nothing further but to keep myself still in God and let the devil roar . . . But it went with me as with a grain sown in the earth which grows unreasonably in all storm and tempest . . . My outward man did not want to write more, for it was quite timorous . . . And even then the Great Mystery appeared: then I understood God's counsel and cast myself upon His Will, wanting neither to think or dream according to reason . . . placing my will in God's will so that my will would be dead. . . . (*Epist.* x, 6ff)

A "fiery instigation" was leading him.

During these years of silence Boehme probably wrote the strange preface to the *Aurora*, perhaps in 1615, possibly later. This was an allegory of history and Boehme gave himself a place in the spirit's descent. The Pope had been a merchant who had been opposed not because he sold holy wares but because his wares were not holy:

Now the merchant, seeing . . . that his false wares were discovered, grew very angry . . . and bent his bow against the holy people . . . and destroyed many, and blasphemed the green twig that was grown out of the tree of life. But then the great Prince Michael . . . came and fought for the holy people, and overcame. (*Aurora, Preface,* 59)

Luther's reformation had succeeded.

The Boehme who had written the *Aurora* was no unlettered peasant and shoemaker who had spun his conceits out of vision-stuff; there was, indeed, somewhat of the Faust in him; and he claims to have read contemporary science. In fact, already in 1612 he knew of the circulation of the blood (*Aurora* ii, 7), and was conversant with Copernican ideas (*Aurora* xxv, 43), but he was searching for other treasures. Moreover, he was a humble man who underplayed his learning.

I can neither say anything of myself, nor boast . . . ; I am a simple man . . . a poor sinner, and have need to pray daily, Lord, forgive our sins. . . . (*Aurora,* preface)

Nevertheless, he was well and perhaps even deeply read in contemporary scientific and theological literature according to his own testimony:

I have read the writings of the high masters . . . but I have found nothing but a half dead spirit. (*Aurora* x, 27)

Further:

I understand the . . . meanings . . . and I have perused their writings also, and taken notice how they describe the course of the sun and stars, neither do I despise it, but . . . hold that . . . good and right . . . I do not have my knowledge from study . . . I have read the order and position of the seven planets . . . and find them to be very right. (*Aurora* xxv, 43ff)

The novelty of their science did not disturb his calm confidence in his mystical experience of 1600 and he was not deterred in searching for the key of all knowledge, a *religious* key:

I do not know how to measure their circles: I take no great care about that. . . .

(He here rejects the mathematical analysis of reality)

However, they will have so much to learn that many will not comprehend the ground . . . all the days of their lives. I have no use for their tables, formulae, schemes, rules . . . I have another teacher . . . total nature. From . . . nature . . . have I learned my philosophy . . . and theology. For . . . in the most part they stand upon the right ground, and I will diligently endeavor to go according to their rules and formulae . . . Their scheme of formulation is my master; from it I have the first elements of my knowledge, and it is not my purpose to controvert or amend . . . but rather to leave them where they are. I will not . . . build upon their ground, but . . . I will dig away the earth from the root, that . . . men may see the whole tree with its root, stock, branches, twigs, and fruits, and . . . that their philosophy and my philosophy are one body, one tree, bearing one and the same fruit. (*Aurora* xxii, 10–15)

So Boehme was already writing in 1612, and this statement must surely be qualified by consideration of his later writings. Examining them, however, we learn that during this sabbath of years he learned more than "first principles" from contemporary science; he learned also to hate arrogant, self-sufficient, impious learning and to distrust the capacity of human reason:

I bring in no complaints against them . . . , condemn them for anything, except for their wickedness and abominations, as pride, covetousness, envy, and wrath, against which the spirit of nature complains . . . and not I. . . . They walk up and down in their drunkenness, seeking the key, when they have it about them and they know it not, . . . like the country man looking for his horse who all the while he was looking for him was riding on the back of that very horse. . . . What could I . . . poor . . . layman, write of their high art if it were not given me by the spirit of nature in whom I live and am? (*Aurora* xii, 16ff)

Boehme was then not a vision-snatching shoemaker illuminated by a quick gleam from a pewter dish—this is indeed the Boehme myth! Already in 1612, in the same work in which he first described his experience, he affirms his understanding of contemporary science. But he rejected its mathematical basis, asserting that insight was more germane. This is an astonishing claim.

In any event, how did Boehme come to such knowledge? And the answer appears plain: he received from his Silesian neighbors, as Silesia and especially Görlitz itself became, after 1580, a center of "alchemy," especially among physicians whose affinities were Schwenkfeldian.[14] In 1589 Elias Schadeus had brought together the Silesian Schwenkfelders and the Paracelsians.[15] The following were leaders: Balthasar Flöter and Francis Kretschmeyer in Sagan; Johann Huser and Paul Linck in Glogau; Marcius Ambrosius in Neisse.[16] Görlitz was the center of a larger group: Christopher Manlius, Johann Rothe, Balthasar Walter, Tobias Kober, Michael Kurtz, and the burgomaster Scultetus.[17] Alchemists in a metaphysical sense only, these men were philosophers whose "first principles" were from Renaissance Neoplatonism as proclaimed by Reuchlin and Paracelsus.[18]

The man who mediated Paracelsus to Boehme was his friend and physician, Tobias Kober of Görlitz. Of an old family, Kober had attended the Görlitz gymnasium and then the university in Basel.[19] Later he wrote *Observationes Castrenses*.[20] The intimacy of the letters Boehme wrote to Kober from Dresden in 1624 show the close personal friendship which existed between them; indeed, while Boehme was in Dresden, Kober cared for his family, and when Boehme died Kober was executor of his will and took care of Boehme's widow and the children.[21]

Another *sonderbare alchemist und adeptus* was Johann Rothe, Boehme's close friend, a student of Tauler, medieval mysticism, and Johann Arndt.[22] Michael Kurtz, *medicinae canditatus et practicus*, and Dr. Kober's assistant, composed a eulogy on Boehme.[23] These physicians were within the immediate circle of Boehme's friends. Burgomaster Scultetus was a Paracelsian who, with Johann Huser of Glogau, edited an edition of Paracelsus; and Huser's son Johann was the addressee of Boehme's *Epist.* xlvii.

So in close association with Boehme were these people who were well-acquainted with contemporary scholarship.

And in this galaxy, one star shines brightly: Balthasar Walther.[24] He had been in Görlitz as early as 1587 and several entries in burgomaster Scultetus' *Diarium* prove Walther's close association with the Görlitz Paracelsians.[25] Between 1592 and 1599 he had traveled into Poland, Wallachia, Greece, Syria, and Egypt, and upon his return publishing an account of his journey which he dedicated to Scultetus and to Sebastian Hoffmann, the Schwenkfeldian lord of nearby Hennersdorf.[26] Walther became acquainted with Boehme in 1617, spending three months in Boehme's house the following year,[27] having been introduced to Boehme probably by Carl von Ender, Hoffmann's nephew.[28] In 1620 he became director of the chemical laboratory in Dresden and personal physician to the Prince of Anhalt.[29] In 1622 he was in Lüneburg where he got to know the north German "lovers of wisdom." [30] In 1624, in association with Morsius, he published a book in Lübeck along with other works.[31] He was Boehme's most learned intimate friend, entirely typical of the times, dabbling in the occult arts and somewhat of a theologian.

What did Walther teach Boehme during these three months? In the 1652 edition of some of Boehme's works which is said to have been edited by Gregory Richter's son Gregory there is a reference to the subjects discussed. It is there said that Boehme's philosophical globe, a part of *Seel. Frag.*, came from these conversations and that Walther had gotten it from Reuchlin.[32] And surely in Reuchlin's *De Arta Cabalistica* there is such a globe. So Boehme learned the Cabala from Walther, for the *Aurora* shows little if any allusion to Jewish mysticism; moreover, Boehme knew merely the contents of the Cabala, the name came later. And Walther gave Boehme the androgynous Adam Cadmon of the Cabala and the *En-sof* or *Ungrund*,[33] neither of which ideas is in the *Aurora*. Walther may also have brought occult materials to Boehme, for in *Gnad.* xi, 21, Boehme mentions the *Fourth Book of Ezra*, a popular Cabalist work.[34]

C. G. Jung's *Psychologie und Alchemie* [35] brings significant psychological insight to bear on the meaning of Boehme's interest in alchemy and Hermetic philosophy. When the Church, he says, by formalism of rite and dogma, separated itself from the roots of doctrine in the unconscious, alchemy sought to bridge the gap to nature again, to the unconscious. The old planetary gods became fate-components of the *spiritus mettalorum*.[36] Hermetic philosophy and alchemy led consciousness back to knowledge of the *Heimarmene*,[37] that is, back to temporal natural forces, giving place for the projection of psychical archetypes which do not appear in more rational Christian processes. This is why alchemy has stood on the border line of heresy; this is why Gregory Richter was enraged when he suspected Boehme of writing alchemical books. Dr. Jung concludes that alchemy represents the projection of the unconsciousness and that the naive *opus* in the laboratories, which Boehme disclaimed, was not the alchemists' goal and that, as Boehme wrote, goldmakers are deceiving themselves. So, *aurum nostrum non est aurum vulgi*, and the serious business was psychical, the process of individuation and the uncovering of Christ within nature.[38] Alchemical symbols stirred both the consciousness and the unconscious, and the usual method of explaining the obscure by the obscure accentuated just those processes which churchly tradition sought to eradicate. The deep-buried traditions of the heresies, especially Gnosticism, re-emerged in alchemy, establishing a fateful dialectic between alchemy and dogma—a conflict evident in Boehme's works between 1619 and 1623.

Alchemy's significance for Boehme lies in Dr. Jung's assertion that for seventeen hundred years it had existed as a dialectical undercurrent to dominant rational theology. There was alternation between the even numbers of dogma and the odd numbers of alchemy.[39] Rational dogma made the Father-Son important; in the unconsciousness this is symbolized by the mother-daughter myth; in Boehme's later works this "male" Trinity stands "opposite" the Virgin Sophia, and that Sophia plays so important a role in Boehme's mature system shows that the unconscious is not only complementary but is consciousness' helper and aid.[40] That the Son-type calls forth as fulfillment image from the chthonic unconscious not a daughter but a son is significant for an idea of God within human nature, an idea made suggestive by the image of the Holy Spirit within the *Beata Virgo*. And the *filius philosophorum* is a manifested androgynous man with masculine names and feminine unconsciousness. The answer from the female-mother world shows that the cleft can be bridged as the unconscious has a kernel of each. The essence of consciousness is distinction, conditioned being. For self-knowableness the *Ungrund's* chaos must be broken and the opposites separated. In manifested being the opposites seek one another, then tending back again to rest.

Dr. Jung's explanation solves the problem cleanly for it tells us why, when Gregory Richter, proponent of rational (square) doctrine, persecuted him for writing a book of natural philosophy, Boehme turned with interest to the alchemical symbolism being urged upon him by his friends. His alchemy then became but the projection of his own inner conflicts and of the outer difficulties emerging from his church life. In 1613 when Boehme had promised the Council that he would refrain from writing, similar silence had been asked of Richter. But the Pastor continued his attacks on Boehme, making Boehme out a fool (*Epist.* liv, 6) and circulating the *Aurora* in strange places where it was sometimes viewed with "other eyes" than Richter's (7); thus it circulated from *einer Stadt zur andern* among the learned, physicians, and nobility who transcribed it, wrote Boehme, pestered him at his house, and begged him to continue "his talents" as he had no right, they said, to hide them in continuing silence (*Epist.* liv, 8). Generously Boehme answered these requests, not meaning to write for general circulation (*Epist.* liv, 9). When he wrote again he was no longer fully Martin Moller's spiritual son; the Richter persecution had driven him deep within himself, and so at his friends' requests, his "external man" became eager again.

When this was done, then the internal man was armed, and got a faithful guide, and to him I wholly yielded my reason, and did not study nor invent anything, neither did I give reason leave to dictate what I should write, save only that which the Spirit did show me in a great mystery. (*Epist.* x, 8)

So during the sabbath of silence Boehme was brought to alchemy both by outer pressure and inner need. He came to

Paracelsus who had been neither interested in the tomfoolery of the laboratories nor allured by gold-cooking quackery,[41] thus becoming an enemy of the endless prescriptions, the daubing and greasing of the apothecary shops. The *Aurora* already betrayed some alchemical knowledge but he denied empirical knowledge:

> Do not take me for an alchemist . . . I write only in . . . the spirit. . . . Though I could here show . . . in how many days and hours these things might be prepared, for gold cannot be made in one day, but a whole month is needed for it . . . I know not how to manage the fire. . . . (*Aurora* xxii, 104)

This "sabbath," however, brought Boehme face to face with a study which dealt with *living* things. For the alchemist's problem was not simple: if God is hidden within living substance then when matter burns does God burn? When a tree grows does the hidden God also grow? Look at burning wood! What is happening? The alchemist said that burning wood was sulphur-like, smoke was mercury-like, and ashes salt-like. These three *Grundsubstanzen* were in all things and to transmute baser into higher these elements have to be known essentially.[42] Alchemy also held that the lower was image of the higher: thus sulphur, mercury, and salt corresponded to God's trinitarian life as well as to man.[43] The process of transmuting lead into the tincture was like the process of changing an impious heart into a pious one.[44] The word "process" came to have soteriological significance. And when the alchemical process or hope of transmutation is understood then God's birth and man's spiritual rebirth become clearer.[45]

The alchemist needed to prepare himself spiritually for the work. To make other things into one he first had to make himself one.[46] Unity was the condition *sine qua non*, for after the *projectio* came *cogitatio*, the identity of the alchemist with his work.[47] Boehme made the seven stages of the alchemical work the later basis of his theogony, cosmology, and regeneration, altering however their psychological implications by saying that regeneration of man was like the process of resolving the contradiction in the elements.[48] He understood that the philosopher's stone which produced natural change was also the corner stone which the builders had rejected.[49] Already in the *Aurora* the seven alchemical steps [50] were different than Boehme's seven stages of creation.[51] Thus the inner decay of alchemy began, not with the Enlightenment, but with Jacob Boehme.[52]

Boehme had already said in the *Aurora* that "their scheme of formulation" was his master and from them he had had the first elements of his knowledge. (xxii, 11ff) What were these first elements? In an important passage of his *Liber de nymphus* . . . Paracelsus had presented Boehme with an important key to nature. Parcelsus had written:

There is more than that which is comprehended by the light of nature . . . It is grounded in the light of man which is above nature. For nature produces a light by which she may be known in her own character; but in humanity there is also a light beyond the light which by nature is within man—a light by which man experiences, learns, and understands supernatural things. Those who search in the light of nature speak about the natural light; those who search in the light of humanity seek beyond nature. For man is more than nature; he *is* nature; but he is also spirit; he is an angel, having all three properties.[53]

Alchemy's field was the light of nature, but the other realm was not natural, although it did have the same goal. For the light of Grace sought union by the mystical process. Paracelsian Neoplatonism allowed older Germanic elements to enter the mystical stream,[54] like that of Hermes Trismegisthos [55] and that of pseudo Albertus Magnus [56]—elements directed towards union with the God hidden in nature.[57] So Paracelsus' teachings were confirmed in Boehme's folk soul.

Finally, nearly a century before, Paracelsus too had seen that in all things there was good and evil.[58] Neither Paracelsus nor Schwenkfeld nor Weigel, who also had seen this duality, saw what Boehme saw—that the goal of this duality was resolution in man and in nature. Between Paracelsus and Boehme there stood the towering figure of Martin Luther with his doctrine of original sin. And Boehme was heir of both, and his natural man had to be born again;[59] for the difference between Paracelsus and Boehme was simply Luther.

It has been proven that Boehme read an anonymous little work, *De Secretis Creationis,* part three of Huser's Paracelsus edition. Dr. Peuckert had found parallel passages between this work and Boehme's *Sig. Rer.*[60]: in this work the three alchemical substances were associated with the medieval mystical methodology of purgation, illumination, and union,[61] a suggestive idea.

These, then, are the things that Boehme learned in the sabbath of silent years after the *Aurora's* confiscation. But his inner spirit grew active too and he hints at further "illuminations":

I was not able to comprehend that light till the breath of the Most High did help me again, and awakened a new light in me, and then I obtained a better style of writing, also a deeper and more grounded knowledge; I could bring everything better into outward expression . . . I have written out of my own book which was opened in me. . . . (*Epist.* xii, 13ff)

This illumination probably took place in 1619 and it produced a strong inner drive to say what his vision gave him.

It behooves the Doctor . . . to study the whole process . . . then he may find the universal, provided he be born again of God; but the selfish pleasure, worldly glory, covetousness, and pride lie in the way. Dear Doctor . . . the coals are too black, you defile your white hands therewith. (*Sig. Rer.* x, 10ff)

Boehme had come again to inward certainty, even when it was opposed to institutional religion, and achievement of intellectual courage which was remarkable for his time. The theologians

wrangle and contend about the church, yet none will take care of the poor, forsaken mother of Christ. They are mad . . . they are wolves and lions . . . foxes and hares. . . . They continually contend, wrangle, grin, and bite one an-

other for the letter. . . . Let these wolves, bears, and lions
go. . . . Take John, the Disciple, . . who teaches love and
humility. (*Sig. Rer.* xi, 61ff)

Historical faith was sterile and believers were welcome in the
churches. Preachers only tickle consciousness and do not lead
to living religion (*Gelassen.* ii, 51); the churches are full of
books about the new birth composed by research but are
empty of those who have been reborn (*Princ.* v, 12). The
churches cannot live by meanings.

Boehme's prophetic spirit in the *Aurora* now was turned
against institutional religion as well as against formal theology. His seven-year silence brought him courageous as-
surance that the gifts he had were enough. So why should he
remain silent?

Seeing I know experimentally in power . . . that it is a . . .
gift of God . . . I must write what I know and see. Therefore I will obey God rather than man, lest my office . . . be
taken from me again. (*Epist.* iii, 8)

These gifts, though dormant, were not quite dead

and gone, albeit they were hid . . ; yet now they often appear and show themselves more deep and wonderful. (*Epist.*
iii, 17)

Nowhere did Boehme describe his illumination of 1619
though he hinted at it several times. The nearest he comes
to full description is in the tenth chapter of *Princ.*

I followed the words of Christ when He said, 'You must
be born anew . . .' which at first stopped my heart, and I
supposed such . . . could not be done in this world. And
then my soul was in anguish to the birth, and would have
tasted the Pearl; and gave itself up more vigorously to the
birth until finally it obtained a jewel. According to which I
will write, for a memorial to myself, and for a light to them
that seek . . . When I found the Pearl, then I looked Moses
in the face. (x, 142)

His timidity vanished. Requested by noble and learned
friends to continue writing, driven by an inner urge to share

his knowledge, he was finally led to produce during the next five years some twenty books and eighty or more letters, writings that belong to the most profound which man has produced.

NOTES TO CHAPTER FIVE

1. *Görlitzer Kaufbuch*, 1605ff. Bl. 383. *Vide:* Jecht, Böhme, p. 25.
2. Jecht, *Böhme*, p. 25.
3. See the 1715 edition of Boehme's works, Appendix, pp. 62ff.
4. *Ibid.*
5. Peuckert, *Die Rosenkreutzer*, p. 108.
6. *Ibid.*, p. 6.
7. Ratsprotokoll, 22 October, 1616, *vide*, Jecht, *Böhme*, p. 24.
8. G. Aubin, *Die Leinwandsachen in Zittau, Bautzen u. Görlitz*, n.p., 1915, p. 596.
9. *Epist.* v, 2; vi, 1. At the end of 1618 and in May, 1620, Boehme received wheat from Ender.
10. *Epist.* xxxii, 2; xxxiii, 6; xxxvii; lxv; lxvi, 10.
11. *Schöpenbuch, Alt Seidenberg*, Bd. I. Cf. Jecht, *Böhme*, p. 1.
12. *Cambridge Modern History*, IV, p. 7.
13. Franckenberg, *De Vita . . .* , #22.
14. Hans Heckel, *Geschichte der deutschen Literatur in Schlesien*, p. 164.
15. Peuckert, *Die Rosenkreutzer*, p. 225.
16. Peuckert, *Pansophia*, pp. 524–525, also, Peuckert, *Böhme*, pp. 50ff.
17. Heckel, *op. cit.*, p. 164.
18. Hahnemann, founder of homeopathy, was a Boehme student.
19. Jecht, *Böhme*, pp. 57–58.
20. Peuckert, *Böhme*, p. 60.
21. Jecht, *Böhme*, pp. 57–58.
22. *Ibid.*, p. 58.
23. *Ibid.*, p. 59.
24. Three entries in Scultetus *Diarum* mention Walther as from Liegnitz; Franckenberg says that he came from Grossglogau. The *Diarum* is probably correct.
25. Jecht, *Böhme*, p. 63.
26. *Balthazari Walthari vera Descriptio Rerum ab Dno. Jon Michaele Mold. Transalp. S. Walachiae Duce et Platina Gestarum.*

27. Koyré, *Boehme*, p. 48, note 1.
28. *Mehrere Merckwürdigkeiten*, #48.
29. Peuckert, *Böhme*, p. 100.
30. *Ibid.*
31. *Ibid.*, p. 63.
32. This Richter reference is from *Mehrere Merckwürdigkeiten*, 1715 edition, *Vide:* Peuckert, *Böhme*, p. 101.
33. Peuckert, *Böhme*, p. 101, quoting from Don Georg Morhof, *Polyhistor*, 1732, III, v, #6–11, 111, p. 55. Peuckert lists the passages which Boehme wrote which recall the Cabala. *Vide: Böhme*, p. 177.
34. Walther was the praeceptor of the children of Lord Schweidnitz, Balthasar Tilke. This is how Tilke came to read Boehme.
35. Zurich, 1944.
36. Jung, *op. cit.*, p. 57.
37. The doctrine of individual and cosmic faith was significant for Gnosticism, especially *Pistis Sophia*. *Vide:* Leisegang, *Die Gnosis*, pp. 363, 367.
38. Jung, *op. cit.*, p. 39.
39. *Ibid.*, p. 42.
40. *Ibid.*, p. 43.
41. *Vide:* Franz Hartman, *Paracelsus*, London, 1887.
42. Paracelsus wrote: "All things (man included) are composed of three substances . . . These three . . . are . . . sulphur, mercury, and salt, and they are acted upon by a fourth principle which is life. These . . . are not seen with the physical eye . . . [but] are held together in forms by the power of *life*. If you take these three invisible substances and add . . . the power of life, you will have three invisible substances in visible form . . ." Cf. Hartmann, *op. cit.*, p. 165.
43. The poet Angelus Silesius wrote in *Cherubinischer Wandersmann*, I, 251:
    Dass Gott dreieinig ist, zeigt mir ein jedes Kraut;
    Da Schwefel, Salz, Merkur in einem wird geschaut.
44. Cf. Angelus Silesius, *op. cit.*, I, 104:
    So bald durch Gottes Feuer ich mag geschmeltzet sein,
    So drückt mir Gott alsbald sein eigen Wesen ein.
45. Cf. Angelus Silesius, *op. cit.*, I, 246:
    Der Heilige Geist der schmeltzt, der Vater der verzehrt,
    Der Sohn ist die Tinktur, die Gold macht und verklärt.
46. Quoted by Jung, *Psychologie und Alchemie*, p. 349, from Dorsius, *Theatr. Chem.*, 1602, I, p. 472.
47. Jung, *op. cit.*, p. 366.

48. Peuckert, *Böhme*, p. 56.
49. Cf. Angelus Silesius, *Cherubinischer Wandersmann*, I, 280:
    Dein Stein, Chymist, ist nichts; der Eckstein, den ich mein,
    Ist meine Goldtinktur und aller Weisen Stein.
50. The stages were: distillatio, solutio, putrefacto, nigredo, albedo, rubedo, projectio. *Vide:* Peuckert, *Böhme*, pp. 166ff; Peuckert, *Rosenkreutzer*, pp. 81ff, 85ff, 112, 117ff, 155ff.
51. Cf. *Myst. Mag.* ilviii. *Vide:* Brinton, *The Mystic Will.*
52. *Vide:* Jung, *The Integration of the Personality*, New York, 1939, pp. 205ff.
53. Quoted by Peuckert, *Pansophia*, p. 209. Colberg in *Platonisch-hermetisch Christenthum*, I, 314, says that Erasmus Francisci in *Gegenstrahl der Morgenröthe*, found more than thirty passages where Boehme directly quoted Paracelsus.
54. Peuckert, *Pansophia*, p. 227.
55. Gunholf, *Paracelsus*, Berlin, 1927, pp. 69–70.
56. *Vide:* Albertus' widely read folk books on "sympathetic" medicine.
57. Cf. Walterhausen, *Paracelsus am Eingang der deutschen Bildungs-Geschichte*, Leipzig, 1936, p. 1.
58. Cf. Peuckert, *Böhme*, p. 54.
59. *Ibid.*, p. 55.
60. *Ibid.*, p. 56.
61. *Ibid.*, p. 164.

*Here Christ, the Serpent-bruiser,
stands in Man,
Storming the Devil's hellish,
self-built Plan;
And hence the Strife within the
human Soul,—
Satan's to kill, and Christ's to
make it whole;
As by Experience, in so great Degree,
God in His Goodness causes you
to see.*

—JOHN BYROM: *A Poetical Version of a Letter from Jacob
Behmen*

CHAPTER SIX

ALCHEMICAL SEARCH:
JANUARY, 1619–MARCH, 1620

H AVING THUS spent seven years obeying the Görlitz Council's order not to write, Boehme again took pen to expound what he believed were his God-given intuitions. But
when in January, 1619, he resumed his writing he was no
longer the naive young shoemaker who had dreamed of unlocking the secrets of all reality. He had now met the intellectual forces of his age. And, stretched by these contacts,
he nevertheless remained convinced of the importance of his
inner convictions:

I have no controversy with God's children because of the
diversity of gifts. I can reconcile them all in myself . . . I
only bring them to the center . . . There I have the proof
and touchstone of all things . . . If you will . . . follow
me, then you shall find it so by experience, and later perhaps
bitter experience what I have written. (*Epist.* xii, 38)

His new purpose was evangelical: to communicate to and if possible to reproduce his experience in other people. It was not to dogmatize. Even though his theology was gained as *gnosis* in mystical experience, what Boehme sought to share was not the knowledge but the experience which had produced it.

What good does knowledge . . . if I live not . . . according to the same. The knowing and . . . will . . . and performance . . . must be within me . . . Not only to contend . . . about knowledge . . . , but you must become a new man . . . Then what need I then contend . . . about that which I myself am—which I have essentially within me, and of which no man can deprive me? (*Epist.*, xii, 62ff)

By refusing to make his experience a new law Boehme's purpose thus gained a new focus after 1619.

I have . . . a fair garden of roses; which I do not want my brothers to partake of, but I desire . . . that the golden roses might . . . bloom in them . . . When I go to the center . . . I find the whole ground . . . for I find . . . understanding both of good and evil, of God's Love and anger . . . These I set . . . in Christ's humanity . . . I write not as one dumb and blind, without knowledge; I have myself found it by experience. I have been as deep in your opinion as yourself . . . I wish . . . that you might have the insight into my seeing and that you might see out of my seeing. (*Epist.* xliii, *passim.*)

Before 1619 his sources had been Moller, Paracelsus, Luther, and Christian mysticism. Now these became peripheral. Eclectic, synthesizing, he learned only what suited him, retracing in each book the old ground. His theme, like Bach's in the *B Minor Mass*, was repeated, growing, never the same.

Boehme was himself aware of his growth. In 1621, writing to Caspar Linder, he grouped his writings: 1) the *Aurora;* 2) *Princ., Dreyfach, Seel. Frag.;* 3) *Menschw., Sig. Rer., Theos. Punkt.* (*Epist.* xii, 66–70) This classification was made before the apologetic works and before those of 1621 and following.

The earliest surviving *Epist.* sets the tone for Boehme's alchemical search. Writing in answer to a query from Christian Bernhard, a stranger, Boehme did not admit authorship of other works beyond the *Aurora;* he did, however, suggest that Bernhard might find out what they were by asking Dr. Balthasar Walther. Boehme then suggested that the noble stone was an acquisition of great joy and once possessed it was more valuable than silver. (*Epist.* xxvi, 1–4)

It is more beautiful than the sun, more costly than the heavens, and he who finds it is richer than any prince . . . He has the entire art and understanding of the earth. (*Epist.* xxvi, 3)

While not admitting authorship, Boehme asserts that his writings will show Bernhard

many beautiful and noble things, which . . . have remained hidden . . , around which the learned have searched and danced, thinking that they had discovered the noble stone. (*Epist.* xxvi, 4)

Because a wonderful time was coming when the sun would shine at midnight (*Princ.*, Pref, 21) he felt that the time was short. So, with uncharacteristic courage, he screwed up his determination and wrote: *Beschreibung der Drey Principien Göttliches Wesens.*[1] It was a book of twenty-seven chapters and in manuscript it came to a hundred sheets. He finished it in October, 1619. He says that it is

a key and alphabet for all those who desire to understand my writings. It treats of creation, of the Deity's eternal birth, of repentance, of the justification of man, of his Paradisaical life; also the Fall, and then the new birth, and of Christ's Testaments, and man's total salvation. Very profitable to be read, for it is an eye to know the wonders of the mystery of God. (*Epist.*, xii, 67)

But nothing about the world's generation!

This book's essential problem was the same as the *Aurora's:* justification of God.[2] The *Aurora's* simple solution was forsaken and Boehme now was convinced of the world's necessity because Christ's Incarnation had been willed eternally, thus making the world eternally necessary.

The *Aurora's* three realms of angels became the dialectical idea of the three principles (*Aurora* xii, 37ff). Where Paracelsus, Schwenkfeld, and Weigel had seen good and evil, Boehme understood that good and evil between them generated substantial being, a body.[3] Like the trinity, these principles were then in all things—in God, the world, and man. These principles are not the Trinity's persons, Plotinus' three modes, nor Hegel's logical stages. They are rather psychological types: wrath, love, and movement—or in the language of science, plus, minus, and creative power. Life, like the power in an electric appliance, is produced only when the opposites agitate each other.

For Boehme principle was a birth, a mode of divine activity, a life-source, a mode of divine revelation. Each principle bore and ruled a world: wrath gave hell, love gave paradise, and life the sensible world. The first, symbolized by sulphur, was an ardent life-source like libidinous pride; the second, symbolized by salt, was meek, self-yielding love. The first was fire, the second light. These two are necessary to each other and between them they set up a dialectical tension. The wrath[4] is demonic but not wholly evil; self-will is evil as long as it remains untinctured by self-giving, for as Boehme says, and in this instance his German is quoted to show his newly found style,

So wir nun von Gott wollen reden, was Er und wo Er sey, so müssen wir ja sagen, dass Gott selber das Wesen aller Wesen sey: Denn von Ihme ist alles erboren, geschaffen, und herkommen, und nimt alles Ding seinen ersten Anfang aus Gott . . . Dass aber nun ein Unterschied sey, dass das Böse nicht Gott heisse und sey, das wird in dem ersten *Principio* verstanden: dass da ist der ernstliche Quell der Grimmigkeit, nach welcher sich Gott einen zornigen, grimmigen, eiferigen Gott nennet. Denn in der Grimmigkeit stehet des Lebens und aller Beweglichkeit Urkund: so aber derselbe . . . mit dem Lichte Gottes wird angezündet, so ist nicht mehr Grimmigkeit; sondern die ernstliche Grimmigkeit wird in Freude verwandelt. (*Princ.* i, 1–2)[5]

God is the source of being, not of evil. Potentially this will-to-be is good or evil, depending on how the second principle "tinctures" it. When no tincturing by love takes place eternal stillness results. Life is then the result of the interplay of forces.

Boehme's ideas on the generation of being in *Princ.* have advanced far beyond those of the *Aurora.* A new range of ideas also appears—redemption, a theme lacking in the first work. The chastened Boehme who wrote *Princ.* was no longer the chesty pantheist of the *Aurora;* he tackled those disruptive ideas which upset the earlier smooth-flowing pantheism. *Princ.* alternates around two poles: emanation of all from God and man's need of the new birth. There is as yet no connection between them and they are merely analogic.

In *Princ.* the way of redemption is from the world to God; however, this doctrine was not yet fully spun. Boehme here conceived of it as regeneration and for this Christ's work was symbolic: He had brought new life out of the darksome earth (*Princ.* viii, 9) and Boehme interpreted Logos substantially (viii, 9); this was here vaguely expressed. His chief problem was to tell how Jesus got a body without *Grimmigkeit* in it. This drove him, as it has driven the Roman Church, into Mariology; this, however, only pushes the Incarnation back to Mary's lap. In *Princ.* Boehme still held that Mary bore the new man's heavenly image and that Christ got His perfection from her, receiving from her the "pure element" which He incorporated in a body free from wrath. (*Princ.* xxii, 48) In this body He brought the pure element also to death, separating the natural soul from this world, from death, and from hell, thus opening a gate for us all (*Princ.* xxii, 49). This "pure" flesh is appropriated in the Holy Supper by the believer who thus gets a "pure" body. Before this, man must walk the road from Jerusalem to Jericho. In a beautiful passage, Boehme said:

When I was at Jericho, there my beloved Companion opened my eyes for me, that I saw and beheld a great generation of men and multitudes of peoples and nations were together, one part were like beasts, and one part like men,

and there was strife between them. And beneath there was
the abyss of hell, and the beasts saw that not, but the men
were afraid and were gone; to which the Devil would not
consent, because his garden had no gates; but they broke
open his garden so he had to watch at the door so that they
would not run away from him; but the beasts . . . did eat
of his food, and drank his drink, and he did nothing to them,
because he fattened them for the slaughter. . . . Do you
suppose that this is not true? . . . Then come with me to
Jerusalem, we will go together along the way to Jericho, and
see it well enough. (*Princ.* xxiv, 10–11)

But in *Princ.* this lonesome road to Jericho, however much
trodden, escapes clear definition and there is as yet no understanding of how "grim nature" is to be renewed.

In November, 1619, immediately upon finishing *Princ.*,
Boehme plunged into another work, designed perhaps as a
sequel, entitled: *Vom Dreyfachen Leben des Menschen nach
dem Geheimniss der Dreyen Principia Göttliche Offenbarung*.[6] Writing to Carl von Ender on November 29, 1619,
Boehme said that soon he would be able to send something
which clearly "opened" what man is, what man must be,
and what he must do to attain the highest good (*Epist.* v, 9).
Sixty sheets in length, it was probably completed by August,
1620 (*Epist.* x, 11). Boehme said that it showed

the whole ground of the three principles. It serves everyone
. . . He may sound the depth and resolve all questions. . . .
(*Epist.* xii, 68)

The problem of *Dreyfach* is like that of *Princ.* and the
Aurora; however, Boehme now no longer asks why is evil? If
God is good then how did an evil world come to be? A good
God cannot be responsible either for a fall which He has not
willed nor for sin which He has not decreed. So Boehme
came to freedom, fall, and restitution; his focus now was
narrowed to creation. Two ideas here were in conflict: God's
goodness and the worth of His creation. Boehme's solution
in *Dreyfach* tried to safeguard freedom while maintaining
creation's worth and man's freedom.[7]

Why was the world created? Because God wanted to manifest Himself.[8] The God who is the will-to-be is also the will-to-be-manifested, an *ens manifestativum sui* (*Aurora* xiv, 9–10). By creating a world He expressed Himself in nature and creature. As the eternal no-thing, beyond nature and creature, He cannot be conscious of Himself, as no being can be conscious of nothing. To be conscious He needs something to be conscious of; this is His *Gegenwurf* or *Wiederwille;* in *Dreyfach* this is the created world. Although this will not be Boehme's final position it is nevertheless a step from the *Aurora's* frank pantheism: God no longer brims over in self-manifested creativity; here the world is the counter-image of God's self-consciousness, the dialectical precondition of self-knowledge. To be conscious of self God first must create the image which He may contemplate.

Boehme's mystical *gnosis* that good and evil were in all things was here enlarged so that these tendencies to self-projection and to self-knowledge govern all life-forms. Opposed to the creative urge is a self-negating denial; the one is anxious, defiant, self-assertive; the other is calm, silent, free.

Each principle has a mother from which it springs. To change the principle must return to the mother and be "born again." The source of the selfish desiring will is the *centrum naturae* (*Dreyfach* iii, 56; vi, 44; viii, 5, 61); however, this is not ultimate for behind this is the inmost center's *centrum.*

The image of this change is borrowed from alchemical transmutation—fire, and this image dominates the works of Boehme's alchemical period; indeed, the use of this image determines the nature of this period. In alchemy fire was the agent of change. In Boehme's mind fire was the purgative which brought the new birth. In a remarkable simile Boehme described this idea of mystical union:

Behold a bright flaming piece of iron which of itself is dark and black, and the fire so penetrates through the iron that it gives light. Now, the iron does not cease to be; it is iron still; and the source of the iron retains its own property; it [the fire] does not take the iron into it but it penetrates through the iron; and it is iron then as well as before, free in itself; and so also is the source of the fire; in such a manner is the soul set in the Deity; the Deity penetrates through the soul, and dwells in the soul, yet the soul does not comprehend the Deity, but the Deity comprehends the soul. (*Dreyfach* vi, 84ff)

He continues:

> if the flaming iron be cast . . . into the water then the property of the fire and the . . . heat which proceeds from it are all quenched together. (*Dreyfach*, vi, 87)

This image, which appears also in other writers,[9] reveals the relationship between Boehme's mystical regeneration and transmutation.[10]

Boehme's fire, however, like that of Pythagoras, was not merely the peripatetic element or even the mysterious event on the hearth in Balthasar Walther's laboratory. His fire was spiritual calcination, a power capable of making hard metals pliable, changing them; it was an "ardent source" which begot being and conscious life—the burning, self-consuming life-heart (*Dreyfach* viii, 18). Fire was life, the passionate *libido* at the center of conscious, willing reality. Holy Fire was the source of regeneration and of the new life's center in God (*Dreyfach* ix, 71–72).

Alchemy's goal was not laboratory work; ever since Hermetic philosophy [11] an eclectic Platonism had continued in Neopythagorean and Neoplatonic guise those Gnostic speculations which had been basically mystical,[12] the central axiom of which was expressed by Maria Prophetissa: the One becomes two, the two three, and out of the third the One becomes a fourth.[13] Here creation also becomes the process by which consciousness is achieved; here too is what Schelling called "theogony."

Balthasar Walther, who had been Boehme's guest for several months, was responsible for the form of Boehme's next work, *Seel. Frag.*,[14] or forty questions concerning the soul. The English translator of 1665 wrote in his introduction,

> Boehme wrote [answers to] these questions . . . chiefly for the benefit of all such as love the knowledge of mysteries.

This friend . . . was Dr. Balthasar Walther, who, travelling for learning and hidden wisdom, and on his return home, happened to hear of this author in the city of Görlitz; and when he had obtained acquaintance with him, he rejoiced that at last he had found at home, in a cottage, that which he had travelled for so far, and not received satisfaction; then he went to several universities in Germany, and did there collect such questions of the soul as were thought and accounted impossible to be resolved . . . , which he made this catalogue of, and sent to the author, from which he received these answers to his desire.[15]

Boehme probably had Walther's questions on January 18, 1619 (*Epist.* i, 47); the manuscript was done August 3, 1620,[16] consisting of twenty-eight sheets. (*Epist.* xii, 69) The supplement, entitled *Das Umgewandte Auge,* an appendix to the first question's answer, was probably written in 1622. Naively Boehme says that this work

treats of all things which are necesssary for man to know. (*Epist.* xii, 69)

Seel. Frag., being answers to set questions, lacks structural unity, but it marks a significant step ahead. Two important ideas appear: *Ungrund*[17] and Wisdom. Both poles of Boehme's mystical theology—God as *Nichts* and God as *Alles*—are more evident. *Ungrund* is his word for the absolute devoid of determination and as Schopenhauer suggested it probably came to Boehme from his environment, perhaps from Walther who had spent some time in the East and was probably familiar with the Hindu Brahman.[18] The idea of the divine all—Wisdom—is also an Eastern idea.

When Boehme achieved his ideas of the Unconditioned and of Sophia, as Wisdom became known, his thought achieved a new center because his problem had found a new focus: how can God exist in determination? This embraces the question of God's self-manifestation in two clearly distinguishable creative acts. *Seel. Frag.* posits but it does not solve this problem: his next work, *Menschw.,* which is a logical sequel, attempts solution (*Menschw.* I, 1, 15).

This change appears in Boehme's use of the fire image. In

Seel. Frag. fire dominates his thought, appearing as sufficient manifestation of the essence of all essences (*Seel. Frag.* i, 11). It is life's first principle, the soul's first root. God, who called Himself a consuming fire, becomes reality's burning center; *Seel. Frag.* uses fire, however, more than metaphorically for here is broached a metaphysics of light (*Lichtmetaphysik*) for when Boehme wrote fire he had luminosity in mind too, the *Feur-blitz*.[19] Fire is both light and heat

the light-life has its source and drive, and the fire-life its source and drive, each in itself; but the fire-life is the light-life's cause, and the light-life rules the fire-life. (*Seel. Frag.* i, 62)

He thinks of this in psychological terms:

. . . look at glowing fire . . . First there is matter from which it burns . . . Fire has a wrathful, harsh, strong, bitter, desiring source, a devouring and consuming . . . which has all essences of life in it and is the vitality . . . That makes a . . . seeking for freedom, and in the fire it attains freedom . . . thereby we know that one spirit separates into two principles, two spirits . . . Now fire in itself is first a seeking to draw into itself (Die Sucht, in sich zu ziehen). (*Seel. Frag.* i, 63–66)

Fire bifurcates into concupiscent passion and freedom (*Seel. Frag.* i, 72).

Boehme here transforms the alchemical image of fire[20] into an interesting analogy of the vital urge at the center of conscious being. His fire, however, is not artificial like the fire of Heracleitus[21]; it was "depth psychology," a pantheistic image because the same divine fire which kindled life sustains it too. From fire came freedom; out of life's central passion came fulfilled stillness. He pictured this idea graphically in the Philosophic Globe which he borrowed from Reuchlin, a fanciful picture of the world-soul's generation which he based on his theory of the "natural language," an idea adapted from the Cabala.[22]

The ideas of *Ungrund* and Sophia, along with the change in the fire image, brought Boehme new confusion,[23] and his philosophy was still more confused by the new tension between God as the no-thing and as the All. He was not to resolve this easily.

Transformation of the fire image also transformed alchemy. Fire was no longer the tool or an element; it was life, an *élan vital*, a drive, an energetic source.

Man's place in this fire-flaming world is not yet clear to Boehme. He was writing about the soul's flaming center because he wanted to change men—even the old fire-consuming Adamic man.[24] His vision of regeneration did not yet embrace the way to Christ, for it still arose from reality's burning heart.

Sometime before the middle of August, 1620, and probably as early as May,[25] Boehme completed *Of the Incarnation of Jesus Christ* (*Menschw.*), the most lucid of his alchemical works and showing his growing mastery of the German language. Of it he said:

> The fifth book has three parts: the first is concerning the Incarnation of Jesus Christ; the second part is very deep and profound, treating of Christ's passion, suffering, and death, and how we must enter into Christ's death, and both die and rise again in and with Him, and why Christ was to die, wholly brought forth, enlarged, and confirmed out of the center through the three principles, very deep. The third part is the Tree of Christian Faith, also demonstrated through the three principles, very profitable to be read. (*Epist.* xii, 70)

He no longer believed that God had to manifest Himself; incarnation was voluntary. Here he achieved new focus:

> If we would write of the Incarnation . . . we must reflect upon the cause, and consider what moved God to become man, seeing He was not in need of this for the realization of His being. (*Menschw.* I, i, 5)

Evil is no longer his central problem; now it was Christ in the world. God was both fire and light; Christ united both in equivalence.

> For there have been from eternity only two principles, one

in itself, the fiery world, and the other similarly in itself,
the light-flaming world; although they were not separated,
the light dwelling in the fire, without being laid hold of by
it. We are thus to understand two kinds of spirits united
into one another. (*Menschw.* I, i, 7–8)

The adjustment here implied brought Boehme further clari-
fication of his doctrine of principles. In *Princ.* he had identified them with the alchemical *Grundsubstanzen*. His changing fire image projected these into Christ.

[the] nothing has in the nature of fire and light advanced
into a ground, and yet issues from nothing but the spirit of
the source which gives birth to itself in itself in two properties, and likewise separates into two principles. . . . For the
Father's *proprium* stands in fire and light. He is Himself the
Being of all beings. He is the unground and ground, and in
the eternal birth divides into three properties, or into three
persons, or into three principles, although in eternity there
are but two in being, and a third is the mirror of the first two,
from which this world has been created a palpable existence
in a beginning and an end. (*Menschw.* I, xi, 11ff)

Boehme could not yet forget his fire image; His God was
light only (*Menschw.* I, iii, 3) whose light-majesty could not
be laid hold of by consuming fire. Light became freedom

because we were gone from the freedom of the angelic world
into the dark source, with fire as its abyss, there was no necessity for us unless the power and Word of the light . . .
became a man and brought us out of the darkness through
the torment of fire, through death in fire, again into the freedom of the divine life. . . . (*Menschw.* I, iii, 5–7)

Into darkness beyond the fire-world was the Devil cast because, despising the light, he remained consuming fire; other
angels became light, receiving love (*Menschw.* I, iii, 10–11).
This light was Christ and in the Incarnation He took on the
dark consuming anguish of the fire to change man:

And let this be plain . . . : if you would find the *lapis*

philosophorum set yourselves to attain the new birth in Christ. (*Menschw.* I, iv, 10)

This tolls the doom of speculative alchemy, transforming it into Christian mysticism. Hear these words and then consider whether Boehme was a gold-cook:

Man was created to be lord of the tincture, and it was subject to him; but he became its servant . . . He seeks only for gold and finds earth . . . As the tincture of the earth is shut up in the wrath, till the judgment of God, so also is the spirit of man shut up in the wrath, unless he go out and be born in God . . . Man . . . had power to disclose the tincture and bring forth the noble pearl . . . if he had remained in innocency. (*Menschw.* I, iv, 10–11)

Boehme's alchemy, if such it was, here led to religious regeneration.

In *Menschw.* Boehme continued to play with the fire image, ringing the changes on it, conceiving of the religious change in similar fashion. This is the period when he had worked through alchemical imagery, found it lacking, and was nearing the later solutions of Christ-mysticism. For the early Boehme, then, alchemy afforded analogy of regeneration:

Lying in view is a rough stone, and in some we find the best gold . . . This stone is inert, and knows not that it contains . . . noble gold. This holds also of us: we are an earthly sulphur, but have a heavenly sulphur in the earthly, where each is its own possession . . . The rough stone is not the gold, but only the receptacle of it. . . . So it is also with man: the earthly man is indicated by the rough stone, and the Word that became man is indicated by the sun, which makes the corrupt man pregnant. . . . The new man is not mere spirit; he lives in flesh and blood; just as the gold in the stone is not merely spirit. . . . So is it also with the old earthly man; when he receives the Word of Life . . . he receives it in . . . his flesh and blood, in the . . . center that is shut up in death, and there the rough earth covered his gold . . . so that the heavenly nature had to remain in death. . . . In the same center the Word of life, which in Mary became man, moved itself; there the essence that was shut up in death obtained a living tincture. (*Menschw.* I, xiv, 4–7 *passim*)

In various alchemical images Boehme here speculated about problems which were widely discussed during the sixteenth and seventeenth centuries—the problems of *communicatio idiomatum, communio naturarum,* and *propositiones perso-nales.*[26] All these have to do with the relation of Christ's two natures; how were they joined? how were they united in one being?

So, during this period which can be called the alchemi-cal, fire was for Boehme the root of life (*Menschw.* II, i, 5) and Christ is the flame of love in the light-world (II, iii, 14) who begets a soul purified by fire (I, xiv, 3). Even this new life is conceived of in terms of fire:

Dear children, let us discourse together deeply . . . Our true life . . . is a choked fire; in some even as the fire shut up in a stone; we must kindle it by right and earnest turning to God . . . so that [we] . . . may become capable of the divine fire. . . . Historical faith is tinder which glimmers as a small spark; it must be enkindled. (*Menschw.* II, viii, 1)

So the man who wrote *Menschw.* was basically religious, one who thought of the religious transformation in unusual terms; surely he was not an alchemist who seriously sought the tincture of transformation.

Following *Menschw.* Boehme wrote *The Six Theosophical Points* (*Theos. Punkt*) which were a lucid step forward in his fast-maturing thought. This was late in 1620.[27] Of it he said,

The sixth book . . . is the six points, treating . . . how the three principles do mutually beget, bring forth, and bear each other . . . it is a key to all. (*Epist.* xii, 71)

Truly it is a philosophical work of strength which deals with the idea of the *Ungrund* and like all works of this period also with the fire image. For

all sense . . . must have fire. Nothing springs from the earth
without fire's essence. (*Theos. Punkt,* iii, 13)

Here he treats the problem with more objectivity and he is
beginning to understand that knowledge is not enough:

> It is not merely a question of taking comfort (in know-
> ing) but of keeping down the impostor lest he become mas-
> ter in the house. (*Theos. Punkt,* vi, 22)

His mystical salvation by knowledge was starting to break
down and a new interest was emerging:

> There must be doing . . . a striving against the Devil's
> will. . . . Man must here be at war with himself, if he wishes
> to become a heavenly citizen. He must not be a lazy sleeper.
> . . . Fighting must be his watchword, and not with tongue
> and sword, but with mind and spirit, and not give over.
> . . . (*Theos. Punkt,* vi, 22ff)

Boehme has traveled a long and roundabout way from nature philosophy to the struggle for penitence, or, in Kierkegaard's phrase, to the place where he again became subjective,[28] thus achieving that inwardness which has been the
continuing treasured heritage of German mysticism.

Sometime during 1620 [29] Boehme wrote *The Six Mystical
Points (Myst. Punkt),* another short, clear discussion of six
ideas. Of it he wrote in the preface:

> The precious knowledge is not found unless the soul has
> once conquered . . , so that it obtains the knight's garland
> . . . Then a wonderful knowledge arises, but with no perfec-
> tion.

Here he was beginning to probe the relationship between
faith and knowledge.

On May 8, 1620,[30] Boehme wrote nine short texts, *Of The
Earthly and Heavenly Mystery (Ird. u. himl. Myst.),* short,
succinct, clear recapitulations of his main ideas. The third
text records a major change, and here Boehme supplants
the central fire image with will; his voluntarism finally

emerges from his alchemical search. Originally fire had been the central ἀρχή of being; now however

We recognize . . . the eternal will-spirit as God . . . there is nothing prior . . . [it] is an eternal knowing of the unground. (iii, 3)

Along with these works of the alchemical period Boehme also wrote eight letters to friends who were beginning to form a Boehme "circle."

NOTES TO CHAPTER SIX

1. The autograph ms is lost. The printed text comes from the corrected copy of Michael von Ender which Prunius found in Görlitz with Hans Rothe. The Appendix was written later, either on December 27, 1623, or in February, 1624. The first English version of 1648 varies from the standard German version.
2. Koyré, *Boehme*, p. 179.
3. Underhill, *Mysticism*, London, 1930, pp. 144–145.
4. The demonic is described in Book Twenty of Goethe's *Dichtung und Wahrheit*.
5. Translation: Seeing we are not to speak of God, what He is, and where He is, we must say, that God Himself is the essence of all essences; for all is generated, or born, created, and proceeded from Him, and all things take their beginning out of God . . . But there is yet this difference: that evil neither is, nor is called God; this is understood in the first principle, where it is the earnest fountain of the wrathfulness, according to which God calls Himself an angry, wrathful, jealous God. For the original of life, and of all mobility, consists in the wrathfulness; yet if the same . . . be kindled with the light in God, it is then no more tartness, but the severe wrathfulness is changed into great joy.—Comparison will show how the English words do not convey the spirit of Boehme's words.
6. The autograph ms is lost. Six early copies, each with a slightly different title, survive. Michael von Ender's was the basis of the printed text.
7. Koyré, *Boehme*, pp. 240–241.
8. This is good scholasticism: *deus non destruit, sed perficet eam!*

9. Fire's cleansing power is an Eastern idea. St. Macarius the Egyptian wrote: "As iron, or lead, or gold, or silver, being cast into the fire, are melted from the hardness which belongs to them by nature, and are changed into softness, and so long as they are in the fire, their natural hardness continues to melt and be altered on account of the vigorous heat of the fire, in like manner also the soul which, having renounced the world, is possessed by the desire for God alone, in great searching and pains and conflict of soul, maintains an increasing watch for Him in hope and faith, and having received the Celestial fire in the Godhead and of the Love of the Spirit, it is then, in truth, freed from all the love of the world and is set at liberty from all evil affections and casts all things out of itself and is changed from its own natural habit and hardness of sin and sets aside all other things for the sake of the heavenly Bridegroom alone, whom it receives, as rest in this fervent and ineffable Love." (Margaret Smith, *Studies in Mysticism in the Near and Middle East*, London, 1931, p. 64) Here the fire image is only metaphor, but in the following from John of Lycopolis it is more: "As when iron is placed in the fire, and the fire passes into it and becomes one substance with it, the iron partakes of the fire, and assumes its likeness and colour, and no longer appears as it formerly did, but takes on the aspect of fire, because it has become absorbed in it, and so they have become one, so when the Love of Christ comes into the soul, it becomes one substance with Him and He with it. That which was old has become new, and that which was dead is now alive." (Smith, *op. cit.*, p. 192.) *Vide:* Bernard of Clairvaux' use of this image in T. L. Connolly, *Saint Bernard on the Love of God,* New York, 1937, p. 45.

10. Cf. Underhill, *Mysticism,* p. 143. ". . . the proper art of the Spiritual alchemist . . . was the production of the spiritual and only valid tincture or philosopher's stone, the mystic seed of transcendental life which should invade, tinge, and wholly transmute the imperfect self into spiritual gold."

11. *Vide:* E. Zeller, *Philosophie der Griechen,* Leipzig, 1903, III, ii, pp. 242–254; E. Reitzenstein, *Poimandres,* Leipzig, 1904; J. M. Creed, "The Hermetic Writings," in *The Journal of Theological Studies,* Oxford, 1914, xv, pp. 513–538.

12. Willoughby, *Pagan Regeneration,* Chicago, 1929, p. 223.

13. C. G. Jung, *Psychologie und Alchemie,* p. 41.

14. Also known as *Psychologia Vera.*

15. In Barker's 1911 London reprint, p. xxi.

16. Cf. W. Buddecke, *Verzeichniss*, p. xx.
17. "We have already explained what we assume in the first respect: that there must be a being *before* all basis and before all existence, that is, before any duality at all; how can we designate it except as 'primal ground,' or rather, as the 'groundless.' " Schelling, *Of Human Freedom*, tr. Gutmann, Chicago, 1936, p. 87. *Werke*, vii, p. 406ff.
18. *Ueber die Vierfache Wurtzel des Satzes vom zureichen Grunde*, Ch. ii, #8, in Werke, *Inselverlag*, III, p. 31.
19. Koyré, *Boehme*, p. 284.
20. "God made the body of the All of fire and earth—joining them by the natural property of proportion," Plato, *Timaeus*, 310.
21. "This ordered universe, which is the same for all, was not created by any one of the gods or of mankind, but it was ever and is and shall be ever-living fire, kindled in measure and quenched in measure." Fragment 22. *Vide:* Freeman, *Ancilla to the Pre-Socratic Philosophers*, Oxford, 1948, p. 26.
22. *Vide:* C. Dornsieff, *Das Alphabet in Mystik u. Magie*, Leipzig, 1925, *passim.*
23. It is significant that the world soul arises in the book where Boehme tries to expound the human soul.
24. *Seel. Frag.* presents the strange distinction between the Son of God and the heart of God. The latter is reality's divine center but not its Redeemer! Cf. Koyré, *Boehme*, p. 300.
25. Buddecke, *Verzeichniss*, p. xxi.
26. Luthardt, *Kompendium der Dogmatik*, Leipzig, 1937, pp. 253ff.
27. Buddecke, *op. cit.*, p. xx.
28. Cf. Kierkegaard's *Concluding Unscientific Postscript*, tr. Swenson, Princeton, 1941, pp. 115ff.
29. Buddecke, *op cit.*, pp. xx.
30. *Ibid.*

Still live in me this loving strife
Of living Death and dying Life,
For while Thou sweetly slayest
me
Dead to my selfe, I live in Thee
—RICHARD CRAWSHAW

CHAPTER SEVEN

RELIGIOUS APOLOGETICS:
AUGUST, 1620–JUNE, 1622

AFTER A BURST of creativity, stemming from his sunrise to
eternity, had thus produced an astonishing group of
works which sought to interpret Christian regeneration in
the imagery of alchemy, Boehme's spirit, pushed from within
by mystical drive, grew weary. Having driven his initial insight to its speculative limits he again met life and found
existential demands again decisive. The conclusions to which
his thought was tending became clear and he recoiled from
distortion in a series of apologetic works which were written
at a more leisurely pace, without the pressing intensity of the
earlier works of the alchemical period.

First, his insistence on urgency in religious decision tended
towards chiliasm and, as the region in and about Görlitz was
full of precise apocalypses, Boehme's two letters to Paul
Kaym sought to reject this millenarianism. Secondly, his pantheistic tendencies were challenged by Crypto-Calvinist predestinarianism and his two apologies against Balthasar Tilke
protected him in this direction. Thirdly, his emanationism
tended towards the deification of the world and of man and
Boehme had to dissociate himself from the messianism of
Stiefel and Meth. So Boehme's spirit rejected the three dis-
tortions: chiliasm, predestinarianism, and Methism.

But Boehme was no housebound prophet. Business took

him abroad. Traveling over eastern Germany and Bohemia, the theater of the Thirty Years' War, Boehme probed the spirit of those exciting times. Beginning November 1, 1619, he spent a week in Prague just when the new king, Frederick of the Palatinate, was there:

> I was present at the coming of the new king. . . . He came in at the fort upon Retskin of Shlan, and was received of all the three orders with great solemnity. . . . I exhort you well . . . whether the time of the great expedition be not at hand upon the mountains of Israel in Babel . . . especially with respect to the *Siebenbürger* (Bethlem Gabor) who should get help from the Turk, and very easily come to the river Rhine, where the great slaughter of the children of God then will come to pass.[1] We know for certain the ruin of Babel to be nigh. (*Epist.* iv, 38ff)

For war had come! Before going to Prague Boehme had known that Upper Lusatia had become more closely bound to Bohemia, Silesia, and Lower Lusatia.[2] After the Union of 1619 Upper Lusatia had become an ally. With the death of doddering old Emperor Matthias, March 20, 1619, the boom was lowered and the hordes came on.[3] The Royal Brief accorded in 1609 by Rudolf II to Hussites and other Protestants in Bohemia, Moravia, and Silesia, securing religious freedom, was withdrawn. The Emperor's regents suppressed popular liberties. An election of August 22, 1619, found Upper Lusatia outvoted by the other provinces.[4] Bohemia, Moravia, and Silesia declared themselves independent from the successor, Ferdinand II, and attached themselves to the Palatine Elector, Frederick V, champion of the Protestants. Revolt was general. Villagers sided against burghers, evangelicals against Romans, Lutherans against Calvinists. The divisions were not just between prince and prince, creed and creed, but it was between neighbor and neighbor and the whole world seemed to be divided into a Yes and No. Boehme shared in this revolt: he disobeyed the Görlitz Council's order not to write.

The war came to Boehme's doorstep. On March 10, 1620, Ferdinand came from Breslau to Görlitz with an entourage of 329 people and over 400 horsemen.[5] On April 25 the citizens were put under arms,[6] the mild Boehme among them. Soldiers were recruited and mercenaries enlisted.[7] When in August a detachment of British and Scottish troops passed through the city they brought along the fever [8] and for six weeks Boehme was ill with what he called *der bösen Soldaten zugefügten Kranckheit.*[9] The Congress of Lesser Nobility met in Görlitz on September 4 and when the Saxon Elector took Bautzen, Görlitz pledged him allegiance.[10] Ferdinand maneuvered Saxony, a Protestant prince, over to the Catholic side, thus enabling Saxon soldiers to be quartered in and around Görlitz.[11] In September General von Jägerdorf made Görlitz his headquarters and trenches were dug.[12] The burghers were commanded to win God's Grace by "earnest prayers, faithful attendance at services, and repentant living." [13] Houses and bridges were destroyed, soldiers went about plundering, Calvinist services were allowed.[14] Meanwhile Frederick had been defeated in Bohemia and had fled to Britain. The Saxon Elector occupied Löbau and Bautzen.[15] The Silesians begged for mercy and, as the Elector passed through Görlitz on his way to Silesia, passing right by Boehme's house, the citizens asked for mercy and love. Boehme subscribed his ninth letter, written during these days: The Lord's name is a mighty fortress; the righteous flee to it and are lifted up.

Boehme's mind, long concerned with its own thoughts, now was drawn out into the external course of events. In a letter to Christian Bernhard, November 11, 1620, he asked for news about the war's progress in Sagan and Lower Lusatia. He told Bernhard that on Martinmas the Elector and his entourage had entered Görlitz, that houses were full, and that the festival of allegiance—the reason for Ferdinand's visit—had been shortened by skirmishing near Lübe in Bohemia where the Elector had been camping. The previous summer there had been skirmishing around Görlitz; half the land was ravished and plundered. Boehme felt that the countryside was done for. The encampments near Rackenwitz were so close to one another that skirmishing was almost continuous, spreading even as far as Raudnitz. Nearly all areas both in Leutenmeritz and Sals, as well as parts of Schlau, had been burned out. Boehme reported that the battle of Prague had had enormous casualties. (*Epist.* lxvii, 1–4)

No wonder chiliastic dreams arose! Boehme himself felt that God's ruin was at hand, that the time of "the great expedition" could not be long delayed. But he could not go along with those who dated the end. On July 20, 1620, Paul Kaym, tax collector at nearby Liegnitz, had written Boehme asking for his ideas about the "end of time" and sending along two tracts. Boehme answered Kaym in two letters dated August 14 and November 18, the eighth and eleventh *Epistles.*[16]

Kaym was no ordinary chiliast, frightened into believing that the world was soon going to end; Gottfried Arnold called him a learned man,[17] author of some important works including *Biblische Rechnung, wie lange die Welt gestanden und noch zu stehen habe* which probably was read by Boehme and may even have been one of the tracts which Kaym sent him. Kaym also wrote commentaries on the Song of Songs and Revelation,[18] and he displayed his ecumenical ideas in his *Bekänntniss eines unpartheyischen Christen wegen des seligmachenden Glaubens unter allen religionen und völckern auf Erden,* which was an early plea for the union of Christendom appearing in 1646 and sought to reunite Orthodox and Roman Churches too.[19] Kaym argued that the Logos which illuminates all men was also present among the Jews and the heathen as "natural law";[20] he also asserted that inward illumination was the only basis for spiritual growth. Gottfried Arnold says that Kaym's writings were Quaker in tone,[21] for he spoke of internal absolution, inward baptism, inner union, stressing inwardness at the expense of the external church.[22] These anti-ecclesiastical ideas brought Kaym into conflict with one "P.C.," a pastor who accused him of being a follower of Weigel.

Kaym seems to have had greater spiritual maturity than one gathers from Boehme's epistles, although Boehme was friendly, making a sympathetic effort to explain his eschatological views. Boehme suggested that

the manifestation of the thousand years sabbath is not of much importance or concern to the world, seeing we have not sufficient ground of the same, it should of right rest in the divine omnipotence. (63)

Boehme confessed to have found earnest purpose and diligent labor in Kaym's book, even though he could not agree to the dating of the end. Boehme denied that the world's state was unusual, as evil was, but insisted that it was coming to fruit so that man could recognize it. He repudiated the popular *Fourth Book of Esdras* and denied knowledge of computed dates,[23]

but whether they shall be a thousand solar years, or how it may be referred . . . , I leave to God. (36)
Concerning the end . . . (viz. that Babel should be wholly destroyed about the year 1630, according to your computation, and . . . many more be of the same mind), the same likewise is not . . . manifest to me. To me indeed is known that the time is night and even now at hand, but the year and the day I know not. (73–75)

Boehme's second letter to Kaym,[24] a reply to a second query from him, is a short and at times brilliant exposition of the still more excellent way of Christian love.

When we attain the new man in Christ then we are . . . already in the Sabbath. . . . For we are with Christ in God, we are together with Him planted into His Death, we are buried in Him, and arise with the new man out of the grave . . . and live eternally in our own essence. . . . We are with and in Christ in God, and God in us. Where should we then keep the sabbath? (ii, 48)

Here Boehme inwardizes the thousand years of peace, rejecting outward ages. His final answer is that apocalypse is spiritual,

it requires a high illuminated mind and understanding which has power to enter into the mystery of God. (ii, 57)

Here Boehme recognizes a divine knowledge which is the highest form of knowing. (58)
Towards the end of 1621 Boehme wrote the *First Apology Against Balthasar Tilke*.[25] Tilke, a Silesian nobleman, had written a refutation of Boehme's *Aurora* on April 13, 1619.[26]

Sometime during 1620 Boehme got hold of this and, at the request of Abraham von Sommerfeld, proceeded to answer it. Tilke, a strict Crypto-Calvinist, contended that nature was the hidden God's manifestation as were also other acts and that Boehme was a false prophet because he argued that Christ was natural (*I Apol. Tilk.*, 108, 126) and that he was seeking to

make Christ . . . pure humanity, natural; and thereby prepare an entrance . . . for His seduction from God. (220)

Tilke, in good Calvinist tradition, argued that by nature man is a child of wrath and that natural man perceives no spiritual things. (221)

Is Christ a man in the wild nature? Then He was by nature vain or corruptible as other men. And how then has He revealed the mystery of God? . . . Could He pay our debts, and offer an acceptable sacrifice . . . and reconcile us to the Father? (221ff)

Tilke here raised orthodox Calvinist objections to Boehme's nature philosophy, especially at its most vulnerable point, soteriology.

At Luther's death Protestantism had been torn apart by deep-rooted party and doctrinal antagonisms.[27] The enmity of the Schmalkaldic War had been expanded into tension with Frederick of the Palatinate.[28] Part of these difficulties arose from Melanchthon's affinities to Calvinism. Three points of controversy had appeared: synergism, the necessity of good works, and the Lord's Supper. Gottfried Arnold lists [29] these marks of the Crypto-Calvinists: they denied that the sacramental elements were blood and body, they suspected the union of Christ's two natures was impossible, and they disputed the *communicatio idiomatum.*[30]

During the latter half of the sixteenth century Crypto-Calvinist troubles increased, especially in eastern Germany where Lutheranism dominated. In Eilenberg some yokels had waylaid Pastor Kempf and almost killed him.[31] In Zwickau Pastor Held was driven from his pulpit. In Freiburg so many broadsides were being published each day against Pastor

Riedel that the authorities intervened.[32] In Wittenberg the students called Pastor Pierum *Bier-Urben*. In 1591 matters came to a head when Friedrich Wilhelm became Saxon Prince Elector, for he ordered all secret Calvinists purged and appointed a Committee of Visitation [33] to examine pastors in the various creedal tests,[34] on the Lord's Supper, Christology, Baptism, and Election.[35] Uproars continued; two Dresden court preachers, Salmuth and Steinbach, were attacked [36]; indeed, not only Saxony but all Silesia was aroused.

Tilke forced Boehme to clarify his views on Christ, one of the controversial points. Boehme did this, discussing Christ's human nature (226ff), the incarnation (229ff), election (360ff), and the divine within nature. Boehme knew the significance of the controversy. He was dealing with

Criers at Babel, the Grace Electioners, the cripple electioners at Babel (613). . . . He [Tilke] need not contend with me; I have written for myself, and not for the Grace-Electioners; much less for the new Babel. . . . It is now high time to prepare for the gossip's gift.[37] (67)

In controversy like this Boehme could take care of himself in robust seventeenth-century fashion; and he did not spare personal attack, for the "libeller"

is a false . . . judge . . . an advocate of God's anger (563) . . . but hearken libeller, why should I talk long with you about it; you are wholly blind as to my writings; you bring everywhere other meanings thereinto (417). . . . He thinks he has caught a mouse and sees not that he himself sticks in the trap. (110)

After spirited defence Boehme wrote "instructions in time of temptation for a continuing sad heart and soul"—texts of comfort for the afflicted. This was his next tract, *On the Four Complexions* (*Complex.*), written in March, 1621.[38] In the Preface to the English version, translator Sparrow says that *Complex.* was compiled by Boehme who had been asked to write a work for one who was afflicted and tempted by Satan.

It is a curious and dated work wherein Boehme accepts the four peripatetic elements (earth, air, fire, water) as bases of the four humors (melancholic, sanguine, phlegmatic, choleric)—a formal scheme useless in a modern sense. The essential idea is that as the basic elemental character is changed the humor, or complexion which is dependent upon it, also changes. On April 18 [39] of this same year Boehme completed *Considerations on Esaiah Stiefel's Book* (*Bedenk. Stief.*) which owed its origin to Boehme's friends. On February 24, 1614, the Saxon Elector had signed a mandate directed against Ezechiel Meth and Esaias Stiefel,[40] fanatics who believed themselves to be new Christs. Boehme's friends wanted him to dissociate himself from such harebrained fanaticism and *Bedenk. Stief.* is his refutation of Stiefel's work, *Unterschiedliche Erklärung . . .* which had appeared in 1610,[41] written because an unknown nobleman correspondent wanted Boehme's opinion about the book. The references to "dear brethren" and to "dear Sirs and Brethren" suggest that the work was intended for a group.

You have sent . . . a little book for me, together with your other friends, to peruse; and you desire me to discover to you my knowledge thereupon. (11)

Boehme says that Stiefel, whom he did not know, might have been an honest, virtuous, newborn man (18) but he seemed to want philosophical understanding of the three principles which brought him gross error. Stiefel had claimed to have been transported to Paradise. To this Boehme replied,

If the author . . . has put on Paradise, then he is taken up . . . I can say no such thing of myself at present, yet I have with earnestness sought the Pearl and have . . . also attained a jewel; also it is given to me to know the first man in Paradise, how he was before the Fall and how after the Fall, and have also seen the paradisaical property, but not in the outward man. (57)

Stiefel's perfectionism was abhorrent to Boehme:

also the author mentions: he is thus through Christ transmuted into death; he can sin no more; and for that cause leaves the outward name . . . that needs very much clearer description. . . . For the holiest men or greatest saints have acknowledged themselves sinners, (61) . . . The author says: it is not possible for the regenerate to sin, whereby it may be understood that he does not . . . understand the mystery of the soul. (66)

Boehme here recoiled against arrogation of righteousness because he understood evil's reality:

> If we put on Christ . . . we are rightly called Christians. . . . The new man lives in Christ; but we should not say [as Stiefel did]: I am Christ. (75)
> When the author says . . . : I the living Word of God in this my holy flesh and bones say this or do this; then is God's dear name . . . abused. . . . He is not in flesh and bones the Lord; but in the life of Christ, a fruitful humble little sprout. (84ff)

Boehme agreed with Stiefel that the time was clearly born (104) when the beginning shall find the end and the middle be manifest and revealed. Boehme's epilogue was kind and mild, remarkable in an age of bitter polemic and revelatory of his spirit:

> This . . . I was not to hide from you . . . for my conscience requires it of me in the Lord, not with intent to suppress or reject the author's book . . . ; but in love towards him. I would give him my gifts and understanding . . . as one member to another. . . .
> For I know the author's spirit very well, and I would fain speak with him, seeing he has suffered much for the sake of Christ's name . . . and has willingly brought his life into Christ's foot-steps; therefore I acknowledge him as a right true Christian.
> But he should not be ashamed of this: to learn better to know himself, and to learn more of the spirit of Christ.
> I say nothing of my self but that I first am become an ABC scholar . . .
> I do not ascribe to myself any perfect knowledge yet; for what is any way perfect, that is not from my understanding, but manifested or revealed in the Spirit of Christ in my brethren . . . I myself am nothing.

Therefore I exhort you to understand this . . . Christianly. . . . For I am not a master of your spirit and knowledge but your helper in the Lord; that the author's course might not be in vain; and the name of Christ in His members may not be reproached, as Babel has done. (158–163)

Boehme here protected himself against the charge, so often leveled against the mystics, that they arrogate spiritual perfection to themselves.

On July 3, 1621, Boehme completed the *Second Apology to Balthasar Tilke* (*II. Apol. Tilke*) which he sent to Johann Daniel Koschowitz,[42] Striegau physician, to whom the Preface is addressed. This work resulted from a discussion between Tilke and Boehme at a meeting in the castle of von Tschesch, later one of the editors of Boehme's works under the pen name of H. Prunius. Balthasar Walther had gathered a group, including Carl von Ender and Christian Bernhard, which met secretly at various neighboring landed estates. One such meeting took place in the summer of 1621 at von Tschesch's castle.[43] A letter dated July 3, 1621, has this to say about the discussion with Tilke:

In our late meeting I was ill disposed to . . . disputation, for wine and sumptuous fare hide the Pearl's ground, especially because I am not accustomed thereunto, and do at home fare very meanly and soberly, and Mr. [Tilke] was not sufficiently answered; but I offer to answer him, and all others that mean Christianly, let them but give me their questions in writing . . . I will give them a fundamental . . . expositive answer, and not defend myself with . . . any sectarian name . . . not a Flaccinian, as Tilke supposes . . . I teach no self-ability without Christ to attain the Adoption as D. Staritius thinks, only I am not satisfied with his opinion, much less with Mr. . . . Tilke's, which wholly clashes with Scripture; for I am dead to all opinions in me . . . what have I as a lay, illiterate, unexercised man . . . to do with you who are bred in the high schools. . . . (*Epist.* xv, 7–8)

Boehme now was meeting intellectuals; but this meeting was not merely a gathering for philosophy and theology. Here there was some sort of secret order, a brotherhood, as the context of this letter shows:

> Concerning our secret discourse [44]. . . . you must be patient
> to go on in that known process a good while; and in the be-
> ginning no other will be admitted; it may well, in the sev-
> enth year, be accomplished in this process; for it must be
> opened through all the six properties of the spiritual ground;
> albeit it is already opened through the sun, yet the key is
> scarce come into the first or second degree. . . . (Epist. xv,
> 10)

Next Boehme outlines a seven-stage process which clearly is
some guarded teaching. He concludes that the long dramatized teaching is well known to him for

> I have lately seen it . . . Therein much is revealed to me
> . . ˉ. If I come to you I may entrust you with something
> which I have lately seen and received; yet I shall go as far as
> I dare . . . I come to Breslau about Shrovetide; and so may
> visit you in my return. Mr. Doctor, become seeing, read . . .
> with inward deliberation . . . Be faithful in the mysteries
> . . . ; what you cannot understand parabolically, there ques-
> tions are requisite; somewhat more shall be revealed to you,
> yet, in order to do that, I am prohibited by the Prince of the
> Heavens. (Epist., xv, 17ff)

This is not the confused language of a muddle-headed alchemist; rather, here is man concealing knowledge from the
unworthy and the uninitiated. Boehme, then, was in a secret
society where philosophical and theological problems were
discussed. Dr. Peuckert, erudite in these matters, is convinced that a secret circle grew up around Boehme.[45] It is
known that Schwenkfeld's teachings were preserved in secret
associations of Silesian nobles and physicians. Carl von Ender
was a member of such a group in 1618 [46]; von Sommerfeld
had been denounced as a Schwenkfeldian, as had also von
Schweinichen and von Tschesch; and finally von Franckenberg belonged.[47] (Franckenberg was Sommerfeld's nephew.)
Peuckert believes that these men studied Saint Paul, the Theologia Germanica, Tauler, á Kempis, Weigel, Johann Arndt,
and the Schwenkfelders.[48] Inasmuch as Schwenkfeld's followers were not allowed to meet in public, mystical groups
had to meet secretly.

What kind of meeting took place at von Tschesch's in the summer of 1621? What philosophy was dramatized in secret ritual? Why did Boehme return from a dispute with Tilke to write an apology? Boehme wrote a letter to Koschowitz as preface to the book telling exactly what the subject was: predestination.

> I have . . . presented it before him and other readers . . . to consider . . . ; since I see that not only my opposer but also others . . . are thus perplexed . . . about the predestination of God. (7)

Boehme also felt that Tilke

> lamentably goes astray concerning Christ's humanity, and concerning . . . Mary; which opinion is quite contrary to our Christian faith. (5)

Boehme had little respect for Tilke who dragged "Scripture by the hair of the head" (14) and exchanged words with words; nor did Tilke understand the light of nature. Boehme here achieved the same respect for Scripture as had energized Luther and Calvin—the "ground and corner stone of faith." Such faith, however, was not

> an historical conceit but a right life; the spirit of God must be generated in the Center . . . and spring up in the mystery of the mind; and therein rule and shine; it must be man's will and deed, yes, it must be his inward life and understanding, and man must be resigned to it. (16)

Boehme next recounted the philosophy on which his views rested, showing, although not as clearly as in his later works, the ontological basis of freedom. He spoke of the generating Virgin, but in the tract his perplexity appeared and he resorted to proof-texts to show man's moral freedom.

The second part of *II Apol. Tilke* dealt with the Incarnation, another point in the Crypto-Calvinist controversy.[49] The Calvinists said that the

> children of God must be generated out of the woman's seed,

as the dew of the morning redness, and reject Adam and
Eve's seed, and make a strange seed. (230)

Here again the union of Christ's two natures (*communicatio
idomatum*) was again central and Boehme was strictly orthodox. Mary was Eve's daughter. He concluded the tract with
a plea for the end of theological wrangling:

What now are the Christians so-called better than Turks and
heathens if they live Turkishly, and more than Turkishly or
heathenishly? Where is the Christian and Evangelical Truth?
(319)

About the same time that he was writing his second
Apology to Tilke he also wrote his *Reply to Stiefel's Exposition* (*Irrth. Stief.*). It was completed either on the sixth or
twenty-sixth of April.[50] The origin of this book is clear from
its preface:

There has lately come into my hands a treatise, sent from
good friends, concerning some points. . . . Thereupon I
have been entreated . . . to give my . . . understanding and
explanation upon these points. Seeing, therefore I observe
that some . . . opinions . . . run contrary to the Holy
Scriptures and true understanding . . . therefore I would
take the labor and express it in a more rectified language.
(1–3)

Stiefel was seeking to explain Genesis i, 27, I Timothy iii, 16,
Isaiah liv, 5, and I Corinthians ix, 2. Stiefel, whose confused mind did not escape Boehme, sought to prove these
points: 1) that when God created man in His image He
made man visible in Christ who was the first-begotten image;
2) that God manifested Himself in Adam and Christ was the
second Adam; 3) that God was related to Christ in various
ways; and 4) that Christ's androgynous nature transcended
asexuality.

All this Stiefel expressed with dull confusion and Boehme
was performing an onerous duty to which he had no mind,
for he confessed that Stiefel's writing is altogether contradictory and runs counter to itself (426). Nothing new is
added to Boehme's thought by this tract.

During this period, then, Boehme moved out to challenge contradictory ideas in the world around him. No longer the visionary shoemaker set only on the exposition of his own vision, now he was the dynamic center of a group of men whose interest in intellectual discussion was strong. Thus meeting the turbulent, seething welter of ideas in the world outside, Boehme was forced to adjust his own thought, thus disciplining his growing, maturing mind.

NOTES TO CHAPTER SEVEN

1. This slaughter took place, but not quite as Boehme had anticipated.
2. H. Knothe, "Der Anteil der Oberlausitz an den Anfängen des 30 jährigen Krieges" in *Neues Lausitzisches Magazin*, lvi, 1890, pp. 19ff.
3. Arnold, *Weingartens Zeittaflen und Ueberblicke zur Kirchengeschichte*, Leipzig, 1906, p. 190.
4. Knothe, *op. cit.*, p. 23.
5. *Epist.* lxvii, 2.
6. Knothe, *op. cit.*, p. 44.
7. *Ibid.*
8. *Ibid.*, p. 47.
9. *Epist.* xvii, 1.
10. Knothe, *op. cit.*, p. 66.
11. *Ibid.*, p. 48.
12. *Ibid.*
13. *Ibid.*
14. Phrases and cadences of the Palatinate liturgy, basis of Calvinist worship, were evident in Boehme's work for this period.
15. Knothe, *op. cit.*, p. 68.
16. Buddecke, *Verzeichnis*, p. 3.
17. G. Arnold, *Kirchen- und Ketzer Historei*, II, pp. 21–23.
18. *Ibid.*, II, pp. 1095–1096.
19. Arnold asserts that Kaym wrote the popular devotional tract, *Helleuchtender Hertzenspiel* (*Op. cit.*, II, pp. 21–22), a work based on Tauler.
20. Ritschl, *Geschichte des Pietismus*, II, p. 304.
21. *Op. cit.*, II, p. 236.
22. *Ibid.*, II, p. 236.

23. Peuckert holds that Boehme's chiliast works are lost. *Böhme*, p. 82.
24. Buddecke, *Verzeichnis*, p. xx.
25. The autograph ms has been rediscovered.
26. The first work on Boehme was by this Silesian nobleman. No copy has been found.
27. Heussi, *Kompendium der Kirchengeschichte*, Tübingen, 1933, pp. 316ff.
28. *Vide:* J. G. Walch, *Historische und Theologische Einleitung in die Religions-Streitigkeiten*, Jena, 1734.
29. *Op. cit.*, I, 865a.
30. *Vide:* Luthardt, *Kompendium der Dogmatik*, Leipzig, 1937, pp. 253–259. Also, J. A. Dorner, *Entwicklungsgeschichte der Lehre von der Person Christi*, Berlin, 1853, pp. 613ff.
31. Arnold, *op. cit.*, I, 865a.
32. *Ibid.*, I, 965b.
33. Selneccer, Mirus, Mylius, Hunnius, Horbart.
34. Arnold, *op. cit.*, I, 866b.
35. *Ibid.*, I, 866b.
36. *Ibid.*, I, 868a.
37. The "gossip's gift" was doubt about parenthood.
38. Buddecke, *Verzeichnis*, p. xx.
39. *Ibid.*, p. xx.
40. *Ausführlicher Bericht*, #39.
41. Herzog-Hauck, PRE3, "Stiefel."
42. Buddecke, *Verzeichnis*, p. xx.
43. Peuckert suggests the date as 1623 (*Böhme*, p. 98). This presumes incorrect dating of five letters and of *II Apol. Tilke*. If this meeting was at Christmas it must have been either in 1621 or 1623 for Boehme was at Seifersdorf in 1622 (*Epist.* xv). The probability is that it was a summer meeting.
44. This discussion must have been heated and personal (*Epist.*, xviii, 1).
45. Peuckert, *Die Rosenkreutzer*, pp. 254ff.
46. *Ibid.*, p. 258. Peuckert believes that the Conventicle around Moller had been a secret one too.
47. *Ibid.*, pp. 258–263.
48. *Ibid.*, p. 261.
49. Sparrow in the preface to the 1661 English edition.
50. Buddecke, *Verzeichnis*, p. xx.

Dein Stein Chymist, ist nichts;
der Eckstein, den ich mein,
Ist meiner Gold-Tinktur, und aller Weisen Stein.
—ANGELUS SILESIUS

CHAPTER EIGHT

THE FUTILITY OF ALCHEMY: 1622

BOEHME came to grips with alchemy. In February, 1622, while busy with his apologetic writings, he began what should have become his greatest work, that is if his alchemical presuppositions had endured.[1] *The Signature of All Things* (*Sig. Rer.*), however, became instead the book which marks the failure of his alchemical quest. Though alchemical works continued to appear in European literature, Boehme's *Sig. Rer.* marks the end of serious Faustian search for the philosopher's stone and perhaps even the end of alchemy itself. Boehme says that *Sig. Rer.* is

a very deep book . . . of the signification of the . . . forms and shapes of creation. . . . It shows what the beginning, ruin, and cure of everything is. . . . (*Epist.* xii, 73)

Sparrow, early English translator, said that it

sets forth . . . the birth, sympathy, and antipathy of all beings; how all beings originally rise out of one eternal mystery, and how the same mystery begets itself from eternity to eternity; and likewise how all things, which take their original out of this Eternal Mystery, may be changed into evil, and again out of evil into good.

Sig. Rer. is a deep, powerful, profound book, conceived in wide terms, yet missing greatness because of the falsity of its presuppositions. While likening regeneration to alchemical transmutation, Boehme adopted the old idea of the sympathetic signature. Sympathy was the influence that one thing was thought to be able to exercise on another. This was accomplished through the core, or what may perhaps be termed the idea, of the thing. Thus, bloodstones cured hemorrhages, yellow flowers cured jaundice, because their signatures were sympathetic. Boehme elevates this medical idea into an epistemological process; transmutation proceeds from the knowing of a thing's signature.

Whatever is spoken, written, or taught of God, without the knowledge of the signature is dumb and void of understanding; for it proceeds only from an historical conjecture, from the mouth of another, wherein the spirit without knowledge is dumb; but if the spirit opens to him the signature, then he understands the speech of another; and further, he understands how the spirit has manifested and revealed itself. . . . For though I see one to speak, teach, preach, and write of God, . . yet this is not sufficient for me to understand him; but if his . . . spirit enter into my own similitude . . . then I may understand him . . . be it either spoken or written, if he has the hammer that can strike my bell. (i, 1–2)

Sympathy, an affinity between similar things, is here a principle of knowing as well as of therapeutic. To change, to heal, and to know one must exert sympathetic power on the signature, which is perhaps but a popular version of the Platonic form, as it is

no spirit, but the receptacle, container, or cabinet of the spirit, wherein it lies; for the signature stands in the essence and is as a lute that lies still; and it is indeed a dumb thing that is neither heard nor understood; but if it be played upon [by sympathy] then its form is understood, in what form and tune it stands, and according to what note it is set. Thus likewise the signature of nature in its form is a dumb essence; it is a prepared instrument of music, upon which the will's spirit plays. . . . (1, 5)

In the human mind this signature must remain passive until the "wise master" comes to strike his instrument.[2] Each person's instrument was tuned at his conception (6) and his knowledge comes from how it then was tuned. All things, including men, are known by their signatures, and by external manifestations in sound, form, voice, and speech a thing's hidden spirit is expressed. The signature is the expressed form of an individuated being's inner essence.

Boehme's world of signatures was the "language of nature." Here he comes close to Plato's theory of language in the *Cratylus*. But with Plato names never were immediate intimations of things; for him language was imitation of imitations, copies of copies.[3] But for Boehme language conveyed inward essence by suggesting the signatures.[4]

Boehme's signature is an epistemological and an ontological key at the same time: a man's face shows his inward self, and by it the self can be known. As a principle of knowledge it is neither inductive nor deductive but productive, the necessary basis of created being. The doctrine of signatures is antagonistic to reason: the scientist who describes, measures, classifies things is interested in repeatable similarities and separating distinctions. Boehme sought to understand nature from within without mathematics or logic because he held that meaning rested on the concordance of inner κερκίς and external form. His symbol was the blooming lily. Evil, disease, and pain were a contradiction between inner will and outer form. When once this conflict is understood cure becomes possible; thus the old principle that "like cures like" here attains a religious meaning, for then there comes

the satisfaction of the will, viz., its highest joy; for each thing desires a will of its likeness, and by the contrary will it is discomfited; but if it obtains a will of its likeness it rejoices in the assimulate, and therein falls into rest, and the eternity is turned into joy. (ii, 3)

Here at the close of the alchemical period Boehme saw evil as disharmony between signature and outer form.

Alchemy attached significance to qualities. If a metal looked like gold it was gold—all that glittered was gold! The external quality was meaningful. Metals as well as heavenly bodies were given spiritual qualities. Gold was the sun's earthly image, silver the moon's. Copper signified Venus, iron Mars, tin Jupiter, and lead Saturn. To this heavenly hierarchy of elements there was added the idea that the lower always seeks to become transmuted into higher.

In this early period Boehme's thought was dominated by the notion that Christian regeneration takes place like the supposed alchemical transmutation:

> You must eat of God's Bread if you will transmute your body out of the earthly property into the heavenly. Christ said, 'He that eateth not the flesh of the Son of Man hath no part in Him'; and He says further, 'He that shall drink of the water that I shall give, it shall spring up in him to a fountain of eternal life.' Here lies the pearl of the new birth. It is not enough to play the sophister; the grain of wheat brings forth no fruit unless it falls into the earth; whatever will bring forth fruit must enter into its mother from whence it first came to be. (x, 49ff)

Boehme's alchemical language, however, described merely the archetypes of the psyche. It was projection.[5] Reason, formulated in dogma, found difficulty in combining spiritual and psychical; alchemy made this junction. The laboratory "artist" worked with physical stuff, yet gold-making was not the goal. Nor was it bluff. The secrecy came from the fact that the "work," done in substances, was symbolical projections of inner states. Projection, therefore, is not studied; it happens. What Boehme says in his speculative alchemy was the inner needs; what the alchemist experienced was his inner self.

Spiritual "preparation" was needed. "You will never make One out of other things if you do not become one yourself," said Dorneus.[6] After *projectio*, the casting of the tincture on the lead, came *cogitatio*. Boehme used the word *imagination* to describe this process by which the soul's lost image is restored (*I Apol. Tilke*, 82), for Adam fell through imagination and so through it we are again restored (*Letzte Zeit* II, 7, 8). Imagination was the voice of the "other," the Unconscious, and its development is basic.[7] In a remarkably apt phrase Boehme writes that imagination is the projection (*Aushauchen*). (*Test.* I, i, 6)

Boehme said that he wrote only "in the spirit of contemplation" (*Sig. Rer.* xiv, 1), and the fifteenth chapter of *Sig. Rer.* finally brings junction between alchemical symbolism and Christian thought. The significance of this final integration is that the threatened schizoid separation of Boehme's experience, which was also the focus of his age and time, was avoided. He no longer felt that his own inner struggles were foreign to the language of Christianity. Burdened by a powerful Yes and No, alchemy served to project his schizoid psyche, but it could not, and did not, bring regeneration.

All during his alchemical period, up to this fateful fifteenth chapter of *Sig. Rer.*, Boehme had been playing with alchemical images: fire, transmutation, process, work, and all the quackery of Faust's laboratory. Now it changed. He read his Bible, the Gospel of John, and with Nicodemus asked the old, old question:

'How can one being old enter his mother's womb, and be born again?' . . . 'Except ye be converted, and become as children, you cannot see the Kingdom of Heaven.' (x, 51)

Here is Boehme's newly found answer:

Hear, O man! understand what you are to do: behold yourself in yourself, what you are, whether or no you stand in the resignation of your mother (out of which you were generated and created in the beginning), whether you are inclined with the same will; if not, then know that you are a rebellious, stubborn, disobedient child, and have made yourself your own enemy. . . . For your will is entered into selfhood; and all that does vex, plague, and annoy you, is only your own selfhood; you make yourself your own enemy, and bring yourself into self-destructive death. (xv, 8ff)

Here the old Christian way of German mysticism—regeneration, resignation, repentance, disinterestedness—is put into the alchemist's imagination, and it becomes the key to all transmutation. All this is foreshadowed in a beautiful use of a beloved Christian metaphor:

Christ said, "Seek and you shall find; knock and it shall be opened to you": You know that Christ signifies in a parable

concerning the wounded traveler, that he fell among murderers, who beat him and wounded him, and pulled off his
clothes, and went away, and left him half dead, till the
Samaritan came, and took pity on him, and poured oil into
his wounds, and brought him to an inn: This is a manifest
and lively representation of the corruption of man in Paradise, and also of the corruption of the earth in the curse of
God, when Paradise departed from it. Now, would you be a
magus? Then you must become a Samaritan, otherwise you
cannot heal the wounded and decayed; for the body you
must heal is half dead, and sorely wounded; also its right
garment is torn off, so that it is very hard for you to know
the man whom you will heal, unless you have the eyes and
will of the Samaritan. (vii, 39, 40)

By thus discovering again the inwardness of Tauler and the
German mystics, Boehme finally achieved his place as a
mystic of stature and depth. He had learned that the "artist"
must be first transformed before he can change wrath into
love and evil into good (viii, 53; xi, 86). This he can learn
only from Christ's "process":

Both have wholly one process. Christ overcame the wrath
of death in the human property, and changed the Father's
anger into love in the human property; the philosophers likewise had even such a will. He wills to turn the wrathful
earth to heaven. (xi, 6)

And the more Boehme pondered this process the greater his
discontent became. Knowing was not being changed. There
must be earnest striving too.

A true Christian is a continual champion, and walks wholly
in the will and desire in Christ's person. . . . He desires to
die to the iniquity of death and wrath, and gives himself up
to obedience, and to arise and live in Christ's obedience in
God. Therefore . . . take heed of putting on Christ's purple
mantle without a resigned will; the poor sinner without
sorrow for his sins, and conversion of the will, does only take
it in scorn to Christ; keep you from that doctrine which
teaches selful abilities and works of justification. (xv, 35)

Here Boehme entered upon his mature synthesis. He was

now no longer the naive natural philosopher. Before *Sig. Rer.* he had sought knowledge symbolized by the philosopher's white stone. Now, however, he sought the rejected corner stone as keystone to his mystical theological arch. But the development of his mind needed one more step, the deepening of his own inward struggle, before he could find his way to Jesus Christ.

NOTES TO CHAPTER EIGHT

1. Buddecke, *Verzeichnis,* p. xx.
2. Cf. Plato's theory of the technician who discovers the instrument naturally fitted for each purpose. *Cratylus* 389c.
3. Cf. *Thaetetus* 206D. *Vide:* Demos, *The Philosophy of Plato,* New York, 1930, p. 263; Taylor, *Plato, the Man and His Work,* New York, 1936. Taylor does not believe that Plato's language theory was seriously intended. But the κερκίς imposed on a piece of wood by the carpenter is not far different from Boehme's passive receptacle or even from the κλίνη of the *Republic,* X.
4. Boehme, though, is not too far from the ideas of Pseudo-Dionysius.
5. Jung, *Psychologie u. Alchemie,* p. 333.
6. Quoted by Jung, *op. cit.,* p. 349, from Dorneus, *Theatr. Chem.,* 1602, I, p. 472.
7. Underhill, *Mysticism,* pp. 144, 146.

I know what is expedient for me; now I am beginning to be a disciple. May nothing of things seen or unseen envy me my attaining Jesus Christ. Let there come on me fire, and cross, and struggle with wild beasts, cutting, and tearing asunder, racking of bones, mangling of limbs, crushing of my whole body, cruel tortures of the Devil, may I but attain to Jesus Christ.
—ST. IGNATIUS TO THE ROMANS, V, 3

CHAPTER NINE

THE WAY TO CHRIST: JUNE TO DECEMBER, 1622

JACOB BOEHME came from his alchemical search to the search for Jesus Christ, thus confirming the ancient subjectivity of German mysticism in his own experience. He had been looking for the Logos incarnate within natural reality but he came to the knowledge that nature's wrath could not be changed into harmony without first changing himself. This momentous experience, which has been confirmed over and over again in the inner life of Teutonic mystics, was the watershed dividing the pansophist of the first period from the Christian of the last. At the end of *Sig. Rer.* he had written:

The election is set upon him who departs from sin; he is elected who dies to sin in Christ's death, and rises to Christ's resurrection, who receives God in Christ . . . in the will and new birth . . ; knowledge apprehends it not, only the earnest desire and breaking of the sinful will. . . . (xvi, 43)

Here his age's second impulse asserted itself and conquered his gnostic search for the philosopher's stone.

This second mood had, of course, not been absent from his earlier writings. It had been a second theme. The *Aurora* had shown knowledge of older mystical traditions and he had already learned the best of this tradition in his association with Martin Moller. Sometime around 1620, however, he came into serious contact with Schwenkfeld, Franck, Tauler, Weigel.[1] Thus he combined the two streams from which Protestant mysticism derives: the first is that which stems from Paracelsus and the hermetical-alchemical tradition and which dominated Boehme's first years of productivity; and the second is that which comes from Tauler, the *Theologia Germanica*, Luther, and the Spiritual Reformers.[2] Boehme is their full union.

But Boehme also hints of new "illuminations," unrecorded by Franckenberg. He said:

> For the time is born of which it was told me three years since by a vision, namely of reformation. (*Epist.* lviii, 13)

Having written this in 1624, the passage hints of a vision sometime around 1621.

Boehme, however, was born, bred, and buried a Lutheran. This was the most significant fact about him.[3] He may have strained its strict orthodoxy; he may even have strayed in a few details; but even throughout his alchemical period he did not wander far from the *Smaller Catechism* of Luther. And even his rebellion against self-appointed guardians of orthodoxy was shared by Luther.

As a child of the reformer, Boehme was a Bible-reading Protestant. He knew the great, good book. The booming cadences of Luther's version echo themselves in Boehme's clear German. Hear now the rhythm of the Lutheran psalms:

> Freuet euch ihr Himmel mit uns, und die Erde jauchtze, denn des Herrn Lob gehet über alle Berge und Hügel: Er thut uns auf die Thüre zu Mutter, dass wir eingehen; lasset uns freuen und fröhlich seyn, denn wir waren blind gebohren, und sind nun sehend worden. Thut auf die Thoren des Herrn ihr Knechte Gottes, dass die Jungfrauen mit ihrem

Spiel einhergehen; denn es ist ein Reihen, da wir und sollen mit den Jungfrauen . . . fröhlich seyn, saget der Geist des Herrn. (*Dreyfach* xii, 10)

This strongly rhythmed language was from a mind filled with the cadences of Luther's mighty Bible.

The Saxon reformer—and, it will be recalled, the Lutheran jubilee had been celebrated in 1617—gave Boehme the insight that God approaches man in love and wrath. The *Smaller Catechism*, basis of study in schools like the one in Seidenberg which Boehme had attended, repeatedly admonishes, *wir sollen Gott lieben und fürchten.* Lutheran phrases occur in Boehme's writings: in *Busse* and *Gebet* Boehme repeats the familiar Lutheran prayer formula: *Ich armer unwürdiger, sündiger Mensch;* [4] in *Busse* baptism is called a *Bund* (11); in *Apol. Richt.* 57 and *Aurora* xiv, 133, he quotes Lutheran hymns. Indeed, the Lutheran hymnal like the one used in worship in the Görlitz church was a thesaurus of Lutheran faith and, as with German churches generally,[5] was used as a book of devotion.

Now Luther's hymns explained his views on atonement, ideas which had significant bearing on Boehme's mystical conversion. Neither Luther nor Boehme accepted Anselm's Latin view but insisted that Christ fought death and overcame.

Boehme recorded his estimate of Luther in the *Aurora's* Preface. The great merchant Pope had sold divine knowledge, saying,

I have power in heaven and earth. Come to me and buy for money the fruit of life. Whereupon all nations flocked to him, and did buy and eat, even until they fainted. All the kings of the south, the west, and towards the north, did eat of the fruits, and lived under a great impotence . . . and there was a miserable time. . . . But in the evening God in His mercy took pity on man's misery and blindness. . . .

People flocked to eat; but true religion was being revealed in a new twig [John Huss] growing from the great tree's root. Men heard and were

mightily rejoiced, and did eat of the tree of life with great
joy and refreshing, and so got new strength from the tree of
life, and sang a new song concerning the true real tree of
life. . . .

The Pope again seduced man, tempting him with false wares,
hawking about the fruit of life . . .

But then the great prince Michael [Luther] . . . came and
fought for the holy people, and overcame. . . . But the
Prince of darkness, perceiving that his merchant had a fall,
and that his deceit was discovered, raised a tempest from
the north . . . and the merchant of the south made assault
upon him.

But the reform's glory soon faded too

when the . . . holy tree was revealed to all nations, so that
they saw how it moved even them and spread its fragrancy
over all peoples, and that any one that pleased might eat of
it, then the people grew weary of eating its fruit. . . . They
forgot to eat of the fruit of the sweet tree, by reason of the
controversy about the root of the tree.

Boehme thought that he was living in a time of controversy
about the root of the tree, a search for definitive creeds
which circumscribed the nature of the tree's life and which
neglected the tree's fruit.

For Boehme, Luther was Prince Michael who had fought
the southern merchant and brought good fruit again to all
people. However, having seen good fruit, people again became blind and the post-Reformation controversies spoiled
the fruit.

Luther's influence on Boehme's mature thought was large
for Boehme came from nature mysticism to Lutheranism; the
opposition of love and wrath, of law and Gospel, the problem
of justification, man the lord of creation, freedom of the will,
and interpretation of stories of creation [6]—these were Lutheran. Moreover, Boehme's idea of divine omnipotence, his
dualism, his clear voluntarism were also Lutheran, and on
the main points of his Christology Boehme followed the
Saxon reformer. [7]

The tracts of 1622, gathered together under the title of *The Way to Christ*, united the better elements of Paracelsian nature philosophy with traditional German mysticism, thus creating a new area which covered the fields least cultivated by the reformers: the doctrine of God, of Trinity, of creation, of man's relation to God, and of knowledge and revelation.[8] Classical mysticism, true to its Dionysian and Neoplatonic affinities, had aimed at self-annihilation in God. Medieval mysticism had become somewhat more subjective, seeking forgetting of sin and individuality in the next life. The Reformation, proclaiming pardon now, anticipated Protestant mysticism by emphasizing nature within the divine order, thus discussing nature's relationship to the soul.[9]

Boehme's search to define his soul's relationship to the natural world was furthered by his contact with both Schwenkfeld and Weigel. Boehme mentions Schwenkfeld twice only to say that he "stumbled" at some points. In a note on the cover of a Schwenkfeld manuscript there is this note:

C.S. was born Ao. 1490, came to Lutheranism in 1519, and came to a true knowledge of Jesus Christ in 1527.[10]

In the Wolffenbüttel catalogue of Boehme's writings there is a parallel reference:

J.B. was born Ao. 1575, reborn Ao. 1600, and newly enlightened 1610.[11]

Schwenkfeld and Boehme both had been grasped by gracious visitation: the nobleman had been "baptized by the Holy Spirit"; the shoemaker had seen more than the universities could teach. The experiences were not alike: Schwenkfeld's spirit was theological, Boehme's philosophical.[12] Dr. Peuckert has found many parallel passages between Schwenkfeld and Boehme, some so similar that Boehme must have copied them.[13] The shoemaker took the title of one of Schwenkfeld's tracts: the nobleman had written *Von dem dreyerley Leben des Menschen*; Boehme wrote, *Von dem Dreyfachen Leben des Menschen*. Both men were dualists in the same sense.[14] In *Test.* II, iii, 11, Boehme used the same

Biblical references for the Lord's Supper as Schwenkfeld; also, Boehme's doctrine of regeneration was a copy of Schwenkfeld's. Sometimes, however, Boehme's words seem to be in direct contradiction of Schwenkfeld (*Dreyfach*, 12, 39a). Boehme also changed Schwenkfeld's repudiation of Tauler's idea of resignation, accepting medieval disinterestedness. Boehme knew Schwenkfeld less than he knew Paracelsus.

The *Aurora* betrays no knowledge of Schwenkfeld but *Dreyfach* was different, for the book's theme was the new birth although not in the exact Schwenkfeldian sense; Boehme called it *ewige Geburt*.[15] In the works that followed, especially those in *The Way to Christ*, there was a growing stress upon the eternal birth until in *Test.* we come to a fully Schwenkfeldian work.

Who brought Boehme to Schwenkfeld? Carl von Ender, Boehme's patron. Erasmus Francisci, in his *Gegenstrahl der Morgenröthe*, suggests this to be so.[16] Others were Abraham von Sommerfeld, Abraham von Franckenberg, Hans Sigmund von Schweinichen,[17] David von Schweidnitz, and Hans Dietrich von Tschesch, all loosely known as Schwenkfelders, for ever since Valentin Krautwald's death the Schwenkfeldian church had embraced more than the reformer's strict followers,[18] and the denomination's official history suggests that the churches had secret congregations of Schwenkfeld's adherents.[19] After Boehme's death Boehmists continued to exist among Schwenkfelders, although most leaders went to Amsterdam;[20] upon migration to Pennsylvania in the eighteenth century the church still had a Boehmist party,[21] showing his continuing influence upon them.[22]

Boehme also may have come to Schwenkfeld's writings through Valentin Weigel for he said that Weigel wrote about the eternal birth as well as Schwenkfeld (*Epist.* xii, 59ff). Valentin Weigel, meek pastor at Zschopau, continued German mystical impulses and united Paracelsian and Schwenkfeldian traditions. After his death in 1588 his writings circulated in manuscript and beginning in 1609 they were being printed.[23] Although banned they continued to appear just during Boehme's period of silence.

Weigel, having seen good and evil in all things, likewise

asserted that their opposition could be removed by a new birth. This, good German mysticism, revived Eckhart, Tauler, and the German Theology. Weigel, however, was basically a Neoplatonist, as his *Dialogus de Christianismo* suggests.[24] From Weigel Boehme received Tauler's deep spirit, as Prunius says.[25] Weigel's pantheism gave Boehme [26] words like *Ichheit, Gelassenheit,* and *eigene* which he also shared with Tauler.[27] New problems were added to the traditional ones of German mysticism: Christology and the *communicatio idiomatum*,[28] the Lord's Supper, and freedom.

Schwenkfeld had two kinds of ubiquity: natural ubiquity, *presentia potentia,* pantheistic in implication; and ubiquity of faith, resulting from participation in the Eternal Word.[29] This doctrine realized Luther's two divine modes, the hidden God and the revealed God, becoming the hook where the Paracelsian "light of nature" was jointly hung with the "light of Grace." In Schwenkfeld's doctrine of ubiquity, then, Boehme found place for the theogonic ideas of his doctrine of God, and Neoplatonism, working in the area of God's relationship to creatures, needed Schwenkfeld's doctrine of the Lord's Supper for logical integration. This joining was Boehme's rôle.

In Schwenkfeld's and Weigel's writings Boehme thus found confirmation of his own insight and the clue to his inward apprehension of Christ. As with Osiander this indwelling Christ—*iustitia essentialis*—implied substantial regeneration through acquiring Christ's mystical body, an idea which opposed the reformer's *iustitia forensis.* These doctrines were what alchemist Boehme had been searching for and when he found them he gave them their finest expression.

There are veiled intimations that new visions were appearing but nowhere did Boehme describe them. (*Busse* i, 11)

On June 1, 1622,[30] Boehme began to write *Of True Repentance* (*Busse* I). Writing to Christian Bernhard on June 21, 1622, Boehme said

By exhortation and request I have written a fine tract, *Of Penitence and True Repentance,* along with a Prayer Formulary . . . which on request I send to Herr Rudolf von Gersdorf zu Weicha. . . . As this tract will lead you to the *Praxis*, you will experience its good since it was born through the fire of an anguishable twig, and it was and still is my own process through which I have attained the Pearl of divine knowledge. (*Epist.* xiv, 3, 4)

This process was not transmutation of elements but the conflict of penitence and the psychological steps by which this might be obtained.

On June 24, 1622,[31] Boehme completed *Of Regeneration, or Of the New Birth,* (*Wiedergeburt*). Here he did not profess to write psychologically but wrote

for a service to the simple children of Christ and at the request of good friends, a short summary of regeneration . . . for the hearts that hunger and thirst after God's fountain. . . . For scorners I have not written. (*Preface* 1, 3)

In his own words, here is his newly achieved inwardness:

For the righteousness of a Christian is in Christ; [in His Righteousness] he cannot sin. For Saint Paul says: For our conversation is in heaven, from whence we look for our Saviour Jesus Christ. (*Phil.* 3:20) If our conversation is in heaven, then heaven must be in us. Christ lives in heaven, and if we are His Temple, then that same Heaven must be within us. But sin nevertheless attacks our being, by which the Devil has access to us, then hell also must be within us, because the Devil lives in hell. (i, 7–8)

Boehme here saw the world's Yes and No within his own being, and resolution of his conflict was the beginning of the way to Christ.

Of True Resignation (*Gelassen.*) was written in 1622, whether before or after *Wiedergeburt* is not clear.[32] Weigel also had written a tract entitled *Von der Gelassenheit* which contained little of Boehme's depth and his solid distrust of reason. Boehme here showed the same "learned ignorance" as found in Nicolas of Cusa, an attack upon the elevated human will, selfhood's rational life (i, 2), by which man conceives great and wonderful things (14).

From out of this sort of reason false Babel in the Christian

Church on earth arose, wherein men rule and teach by rational conclusions and have enthroned as a fair virgin that child which is intoxicated with selfhood and ego-centric passions. (16)

Resignation supplants transmutation as the way out of man's misery:

> The creaturely will . . . must . . . descend into itself, becoming like an unworthy child which is not worthy of so high a Grace. It must not arrogate to itself any knowledge nor understanding, nor should it, in creaturely selfhood, request or desire any knowledge from God. But, simply, and plainly, it must resign itself to the Grace and Love of God in Christ Jesus, becoming dead to its desires, yielding itself freely to the life of God so that He may do what and how He wishes with His own instrument. (i, 23)

Here was Boehme's way, that of absurd ignorance, allowing the Devil no prideful place where he might take hold. Here was no fire and flame and tincture and substantial transmutation! Here was German mysticism's traditional inwardness.

During the time that Boehme was writing these tracts he achieved a good, plastic German style. His writing was no longer barbaric and, buoyed by confidence in his literary abilities, he wrote his next tract, *Of the Supersensual Life* (*Uebersinn. Leb.*), as a dialogue between a master and a disciple. It was completed late in 1622.[33] It traces the course of the conflict in the soul, for its theme is the psychology rather than the mechanics of penitence: "How will it happen that I shall love that which despises me?" (25) "How can man hate and love himself at the same time?" (24) "Why must love and suffering, friends and foe, live together?" "Would it not be better if Love were alone?"

Near the end of 1622 Boehme began *Of Divine Contemplation* (*Beschau.*) but he never finished it.[34] It was the rejected beginning of a new philosophical work, a new synthesis. Its central problem was stated in its first paragraph:

> Reason says: I hear many say of God that there is a God who has made all things, who also sustains and supports them; but I have not yet seen anyone, nor heard tell of any-

one, who has seen this God, or could tell me where or how He is. For when they look at the world's essence, and consider that it goes as well with the pious as with the impious, that all things are mortal and fragile, also that the pious can find no redeemer to free them from the anguish and perversity of evil . . ; then they think that all happens capriciously, that there is no God who accepts the sorrowing since He rejects those who hope in Him and allows them to stew in their miseries; and no one has ever been heard to return from corruption and claim that he has been with God. (1)

Thus did Boehme begin again to try to solve his ever-changing yet inwardly consistent problem. *Beschau.* was broken off at the end of the fourth chapter as he was coming to clarity of style and expression.

On February 9, 1623, in the middle of important other matters, Boehme wrote *On Penitence* (*Busse* ii)[35] which usually appears as the second book of *Busse* i.

Considered together these tracts of the latter half of 1622 present a new Boehme, one who was no longer the pansophist of the *Aurora* but a man who was now seeking the marriage of the Lamb (*Busse* ii, 1). He has forsaken alchemical imagery and symbolism, although a few words, phrases, and conceptions continue to appear; now he has worked through to the traditional inwardness of the German mystics.

This change was accomplished sometime during the year 1622. The bizarre and occult speculations with their outmoded ideas, however significant for his development, were rejected because they had brought him to a *cul de sac.* Two facts support this: the scope and kind of the books he wrote after his mystical conversion, and the change in the nature of his central imagery. But even more important was the change from *gnosis*, or saving knowledge, to regeneration. Now he knew that reason was a false way to a false God; only by overcoming Yes and No within his soul was evil to be overcome.

What led Boehme to this conflict of penitence? The writings for the period are silent. The Boehme of *The Way to Christ* was still seeking knowledge, but only in a superficial sense; now "knowledge" was metaphor:

Therefore it is necessary for God's children to know what they are to do with themselves if they want to learn God's way. As they destroy and cast off even their thoughts and desire nothing and want to learn nothing, they will then experience true resignation. They will discover that God's Spirit leads, teaches, and instructs the human spirit, and that the human egotistical will towards ego-centric passion must be completely broken and resigned to the Lord. All speculation about the mysteries of God is a very dangerous thing by which the will-spirit may be captured soon enough.

—And all this from a man who had sought to probe the whole of philosophy!

I do not say that man should not investigate and learn from the natural arts and sciences. No, this is useful for him. But ego-centric reason should not be the energizing of it. Man is to rule his life, not through the external light of reason—this is all very good—but he should sink himself down into the deepest humility before God and employ the Spirit and Will of God at the beginning of his investigations so that the light of reason can see through God's light. (*Gelassen.* i, 33ff)

The most striking change was Boehme's doctrine of sin. In the *Aurora* sin had been dark, mysterious, formless vitality capable of being subjugated by knowledge. Now sin was a separated will that wanted to be like God. He said:

God hardens no one. On the contrary, the ego-centric will, which persists within the sinful flesh, hardens the mind, for it brings the vanity of this world into the mind by which the mind remains closed. God, in so far as He is and is called God, can will no evil; for in God there is only one single will, and that is eternal Love—a desire for similar things, as for vital energy, beauty, and virtue. God desires nothing but what is like His own desire; His Desire appropriates nothing except that which it itself is. (*Gelassen.* ii, 25ff) [36]

Life's end was not knowing, but unknowing. A pure branch was to grow—Aaron's rod shall bloom again. Boehme pictured the total restitution of substantial existence in eschatological symbols which command respect from imaginative minds: this is the blossoming of the noble lily-twig, the finding of the pearl, the joyous love-play of God. The old imagery of Solomon's Song pictured union not of God and the soul but of Sophia and man. For the transcendent Abyss of undifferentiated Being remains inviolate! New birth was substantial; the earth too was renewed with man's renewal. This was the celebrated restitution-of-all-things doctrine which contrasts so sharply with Eastern *Nirvana* and reincarnation. The true wedding of the lamb was the "passing from history to substance" (*Wiedergeburt*, 97).

For his growth in spirit a second major experience is needed. Boehme hints at it, but nowhere does he describe it. Perhaps, in his pilgrimage, the transcendent had become passingly familiar.

The year 1622 was, then, the second watershed, dividing the pansophist from the Christian.

NOTES TO CHAPTER NINE

1. He mentions the following books: *Der Wasserstein der Weisen* (*Epist.* xviii, 14), the third part of the pseudo-Weigelian work, *Gnothi Seauton* (*Epist.* ix, 14), the *Fourth Book of Ezra* (*Letzte Zeit* i, 27). He also mentions Luther, Calvin, Schwenkfeld (*Aurora* xx, 51ff), Hans Weyrauch, Weigel (*Epist.*, xii, 51ff), and Paracelsus (*Letzte Zeit*, i, 6, 8, 9).

2. *Vide:* R. M. Jones, *Spiritual Reformers in the Sixteenth and Seventeenth Centuries*, New York, 1928. Cf. also, C. G. Jung, *Paracelsica*, Zürich, 1942.

3. Erich Seeberg returned from Boehme to a renewed interest in Luther. "Mein Weg zu Luther setzte bei Jakob Böhme ein; ich spürte unmystischen Züge in seinen Denken und fand den Grund dafür in seinen Beeinflüssen durch Luther." *Luthers Theologie, Motive u. Grundformen, I. Gottesanschauung,* Göttingen, 1929, p. 5.

4. *Vide:* Taufe, I, 4, iv, 15.

5. Anabaptist hymnals for this period are of much interest.

6. Bornkamm, *Luther u. Böhme*, p. 103.

7. *Vide:* Erich Seeberg, *Christus Wirklichkeit und Urbild*, Stuttgart, 1937, *passim*.

8. Dorner, *History of Protestant Theology*, Edinburgh, 1871, p. 178.

9. *Ibid.*, II, p. 179.
10. Peuckert, *Böhme*, p. 69.
11. *Ibid.*
12. *Ibid.*
13. *Ibid.*, pp. 171–173. The parallels are with these Schwenkfeld works: *Caspar Schwenkfelds Schriften, Der Erste Theil der Christlichen Orthodoxischen Bücher und Schriften,* n.p., 1564; *Epistolar I,* 1566; *Epistolar, Ander Theil,* 1570; *Das 2. Buch des andern Theils des Epistola,* 1570.
14. Schwenkfeld taught that God's plan did not rest with one person but on Adam and Christ, created one and begotten one.
15. *Vide* especially the last part of Ch. xiv. Cf. also *Dreyfach,* iii, 49; *Menschw.*, I, 8, xii, 17; *Princ.* iv, xxii, 23; *Epist.*, xxviii, 6; *Gnad.*, viii, 97ff.; *Myst. Mag.* v, 19; *Irrth. Stief.*, 66.
16. Quoted by Peuckert, *Böhme*, p. 73.
17. Peuckert, *Rosenkreutzer*, pp. 244, 245. Cf. *Das Geschlecht derer von Schweinichen,* Breslau, 1906, I, p. 42.
18. Peuckert, *Rosenkreutzer*, pp. 244, 245.
19. *Erläuterung für Caspar Schwenkfeld,* Sumneytaun, Penna., 1834. The Enders (now Anders), Johns, and Schweidnitz's are still Schwenkfelders in Pennsylvania.
20. Gichtel, *Theoscopia Practica,* Amsterdam, 1722.
21. H. W. Kriebel, *The Schwenkfelders in Pennsylvania,* Lancaster, Pa., 1904, p. 57.
22. Schwenkfeld also thought of redemption in medical images. *Vide: Von der Himmlischen Arzeney,* Allentown, Pa., 1820.
23. Peuckert, *Böhme,* p. 78. *Vide:* Opel, *Valentin Weigel,* Leipzig, 1864; A. Israel, *M. Valentin Weigels Leben und Schriften,* Zschopau, 1688.
24. Peuckert, *Pansophia, passim.*
25. *Einleitung in den Edlen Lilien Zweig,* Amsterdam, p. 44.
26. Bornkamm, *Luther u. Böhme,* p. 170. (*I Apol. Tilke,* p. 174.)
27. Boehme did not accept Tauler's self-negating mysticism.
28. Weigel stressed Christ's double identity.
29. Bornkamm, *op. cit.*, p. 169.
30. Buddecke, *Verzeichnis,* p. xx.
31. *Ibid.*
32. *Ibid.*
33. *Ibid.*
34. *Ibid.*
35. *Ibid.*
36. This is an old German mystical idea. *Vide: Theologia Germanica,* ii.

All men are led to heaven by
their own loves; but these must
first be sacrificed.

—COVENTRY PATMORE

CHAPTER TEN

THEOLOGICAL
RECONSTRUCTION: 1623

AFTER Boehme's interest had thus centered in the problems of the soul he became a kerygmatic apostle of regeneration and redemption in Christ. In an Epistle to Christian Bernhard, October 13, 1623, he recounted the results of his unordained ministry.

God has opened his door of Grace to me more and more, and not only to me, but many others, who get these writings to read, whose hearts God has touched so that they entered into repentance and conversion, and come to the divine vision within themselves. . . . Indeed, several days ago, such a stirring up of two persons . . . was presented . . . ; in whom I saw the new birth take place with great power . . . I never saw the like since my childhood, except that which God worked in my own person . . . One of whom despised himself with regard to his earthly world-affairs, and disesteemed his former mode of living; and did sink down into resignation and repentance . . . considering himself . . . dead and wholly unworthy . . . Thereupon the divine Sun shone upon him. And for three hours he spoke nothing else . . . than: 'God-Dung, God-Dung, God-Dung,' . . . Whereupon he, together with another man in like condition, came to me. After I had seen that awakening in him, they greatly rejoiced with me in that through my tract *Of Repentance* they were drawn to it. As indeed in a short while many more also were seen in like condition. . . . (*Epist.* xlv, 1–6)

Boehme's new evangelical role brought Pharisees to God's Light in converted "renovation of the Spirit of Christ," those who teach

that all disputation is dung, and an unprofitable frivolous thing . . . [and who are directed] to the Life of Christ. (*Ibid.*, 10)

So Boehme got a new focus for his theology which necessitated that he recast it. This produced three major works, the writings which contain his nature thought: *On the Election of Grace* (*Gnad.*), the answer to the theological problem of election; *On the Great Mystery* (*Myst. Mag.*), the answer to the cosmological problem; and *On Christ's Testaments* (*Test.*), the answer to the Christological problem, a work not of the stature of the other two.

Gnad. was completed February 8, 1623.[1] It was written at the request of learned, well-placed gentlemen (*Epist.* xxiii, 3) among whom was Balthasar Tilke (*Epist.* xl, 2, 4), now one of Boehme's most ardent admirers. Boehme himself thought it to be his greatest work (*Clavis*, 147) and many would agree with him, as Franz von Baader did. Writing to Friedrich Krause, Boehme said:

I have written a pretty large book concerning Election . . . I hope that the same shall put an end to many contentions and controversies, especially of some points between Lutherans and Calvinists, and other controversial sects. . . . (*Epist.*, xxxix, 5)

In another letter to Krause he wrote:

Upon the advice of yourself . . . and Tilke I have considered those sayings of Scripture which . . . Tilke set down in his letter . . . wherein I was exhorted to expound the same in Christian Love, according to my gift and understanding but especially the ninth and eleventh chapters of . . . Romans. . . . (*Epist.* xl, 2ff)

This ground was more fully explained in a letter to Abraham von Franckenberg:

The work is so deeply grounded that not only the ground of the question concerning God's will may be understood; but likewise the hidden God may be known in his manifestation in all visible things, with a clear explanation how the ground of the mystery has brought itself through the expression . . , through the Word of God . . , into a severation . . . and how the original of good and evil is to be understood . . . and then a clear explanation of the phrases of Scripture. . . . Yet not in a logical way as 'tis treated of in the schools. . . . (*Epist.*, xli, 5ff)

Indeed, Boehme's treatment of this great theme was antirational and a far cry from the way it is treated in the schools and in Jonathan Edwards' *Careful and Strict Enquiry into the . . . Freedom of the Will,* and he emphasized to a remarkable degree the nonrational element in freedom. *Gnad.* was mainly directed against false reason and Boehme's writing often took the form: "reason says . . . answer." Sometimes he simply addressed himself to reason:

Hearken, you blind Babylon. . . . What is the election and the Grace with which you comfort yourself, and spread the mantle of Grace over yourself, over your whoredom and vices? . . . Where does it stand in Scriptures that a harlot can become a virgin by royal warrant . . . Can that indeed be? (x, 28–29)

The key to Boehme's solution of the problem of freedom is the simple proposition: no externally imputed Grace avails. This rejects any legalistic view of Christ's work. Grace is an uncovering, unveiling, and unmasking of the God hidden within man by the revealing power of Christ, for

it is not the individual born of man and woman from the corrupted nature that attains to the Grace of filiation, so that he can comfort himself and say, 'Christ has done it! He has freed me from sin! I need only believe that it is done!' No! The Devil knows this. . . . Now, what is the will which they must do to attain this filiation? . . . For Christ's will is the will of God, and they who would do this will must be new born from Christ's flesh and blood, from the Word which became man. . . . (x, 29–31)

The unveiling of the divine spark in man, the fanning into flame of the fire of divinity until the creature becomes new— this is freedom. All men were created with this divine spark; there was no election at creation! The rekindling of freedom's fire is an inward experience.

Not by comfortings from an adopted external shine or luster, but an essential way, as self-subsisting children of Christ, in whom the inspoken covenant of Grace is fulfilled substantially, in whom the soul eats of Christ's flesh and blood, has life, and that not from without, but in itself, in whom Christ continually says . . . Take, eat my flesh and drink my blood, so abidest Thou in me and I in Thee. *John vi*, 36 (x, 32)

This rich mystical indwelling, a precious Protestant form of sacramentalism, became possible only when the Mass had been rejected as a "cursed idolatry," as the Heidelberg Catechism called it, and in the tradition of Calvin (whose mystical doctrine of the Supper is frequently misunderstood), along with Schwenkfeld and Osiander. Historical faith must be followed by regeneration, and Boehme was aware that this was but partly achieved in this life and he awaited the resurrection at the end of time.[2]

. . . it is not a question of external knowledge, as that I know I have in Christ a gracious God who has cancelled sin . . ; but rather . . ; 1) that such take place likewise in me; namely that Christ . . . rise up also in me, and rule over sin in me; 2) that He kill sin, viz. nature in its evil will, in me; 3) that a new will proceeding from nature in Christ's Spirit, Life, and Will arise in me, which has God for its object. . . . This will fulfills the law . . . gives itself up in obedience to the law and fulfills it with the divine love-will. (x, 34)

The "freedom" of regenerate man unfolds itself from within out of the primal freedom which was in him at creation. The end comes to the beginning again.

The renewed Boehme who had known victory was now readjusting the focus of his interest. The devotional piety of his earlier years, molded by Martin Moller, and which had been overclouded by his alchemical speculation, now reasserted itself in a deeper form which was enriched by nature mysticism. Indeed, Boehme's mature works reconciled medieval piety with Renaissance nature-mysticism, creating a philosophical theology of depth and devotion. The God who created man became the God who redeemed man.

Faith is not an outward thing, that any should say: 'With this is the Election of Grace, for Christ has taught and acknowledged; he has chosen us before other peoples, that we may hear His voice. And though we are wicked, yet he has forgiven us our sins, in His Purpose . . . We need only appropriate this and comfort ourselves therewith; it is imputed to us from without and bestowed on us as a Grace.' No! No! This is of no effect. Christ Himself is the imputed Grace, the gift along with the merit. He who has Christ in him, and in whose inward ground Christ Himself is, and is crucified and dead with Christ, lives in His Resurrection. . . . It is not a question merely of knowing and taking comfort, for Christ dwells not in the body of iniquity. (*Gnad.* x, 35–38)

This final heart of Boehme's theology portrays his resolution of the disunities of his experience. Here is the completion of the inward process of regeneration:

If Christ is to arise in you, then must the will of death . . . die in you. For Christ has broken death . . . and become Lord over death and hell. When he makes his entry in a man, there must death and hell in the inward ground of the soul break and give way. He destroys the Devil's kingdom in the soul . . , makes the soul into God's child . . . gives it His will . . , slays the will of the corrupt nature. (*Gnad.* x, 38ff)

This was the final end of Boehme's groping. Now he had his "Pearl"; God was still distant, and the God-man dualism remained; but now he knew where to look for the ever-lingering Love.

O God! the time of Thy Visitation has come, but who recognized Thy Arm before the great vanity of Anti-Christ. . . Destroy him, Lord, and break down his power that . . . Jesus may be revealed to all languages and peoples . . . Hallelujah! From the east and north the Lord roars with His

Power and Might; who shall prevent it? Hallelujah! His Eye of Love sees into all lands, and His Truth remains eternally. Hallelujah! We are delivered from the yoke of the oppressor, no one shall build it up any more; for the Lord has shut it up in His wonders. Hallelujah! (*Gnad.* x, 49)

Towards the end of 1622, even before *Gnad.* was finished, Boehme had begun the second great work of his maturity, *The Great Mystery* (*Myst. Mag.*), which he finished on September 11, 1623,[3] but already as early as February, 1623, forty-eight signatures had been completed (*Epist.* xxiii, 6). Completed, it contains seventy-eight chapters.

Its theme is breath-taking. Boehme had nothing to do with allegorical, tropological, and analogical meanings. His doctrine of the three principles gave him, he believed, his key to unlock creation's story in Genesis. Boehme's book is a *tour de force* because each character, incident, figure, or event in Genesis became part of his scheme of three principles. Each fact had three meanings in each of Boehme's three worlds. Yet this is not all! Here is allegory on a grand scale. Here nature philosophy became also a philosophy of history; the order of creation became also the order of salvation. The whole scheme is so astounding that, as Schopenhauer remarked, one can withhold neither admiration nor tears.

The central insight supporting this work was not original with Boehme but came, however indirectly, from the Calabrian Abbot, Joachim of Flora,[4] who had divided history into three ages: of the Old Testament, of the New Testament, and of the Spirit. Boehme's scheme was not chronological but dialectical. Reality was threefold, and Genesis, the record of creation, had therefore a threefold meaning. In the preface Boehme wrote:

And we will enlarge this exposition through all the Chapters . . . and signify how the Old Testament is a figure of the New; what is to be understood by the deeds of the holy patriarchs; wherefore the Spirit of God did give them to be set down in Moses, and at what the figures in these written histories do look and aim; and how the Spirit of God in His children . . . did allude with them . . . concerning the Kingdom of Christ. . . . And how the whole time of this world is portrayed and modelized, as in a watch-work; how afterwards it shall go in time; and what the inward spiritual world, and also the outward material world is; also what the inward spiritual man of the essence of this world is; how time and eternity are in one another, and how a man may understand this. (12, 13)

Each figure of Genesis had meaning for each of these three principles, and from the account time and history could be deduced. Nature-philosophy was also Bible history and a Protestant like Boehme saw all of reality within the ideas of the Bible. One has to understand, he says, that God's vitality is

hidden to visible elements, and yet dwells through and in the elements; and works through the sensible life and essence, as the mind in the body. For visible sensible things are an essence of the invisible; from the invisible and comprehensible the visible and comprehensible proceeded. (Preface 4)

So from the Biblical account of creation Boehme proceeded to deduce the inner spiritual world.

Genesis, then, comprehends Boehme's system. The seven days of creation are prototypes of God's seven spirits and of the seven natural principles. His philosophical-theology here is reoriented to the Biblical structure and it is hard to see how the writer of the chaotic *Aurora* achieved the self-discipline to write also on the great mystery. His style has become mature.[5]

A few alchemical terms survive, but on the whole he has forged a new and adequate vocabulary.

Myst. Mag. is bold and thorough. Here he explains how God operates within nature and history. Here is a philosophy of history far more profound than Augustine's parallelism because it is Biblically grounded and does not make God transcendent. The book's third part, sometimes printed with the title *Iosephus Redivivus*, describes the prototype of the New Being in the figure of Joseph who was the "cleerest figure of the new man regenerated out of the earthly Adam," as the 1654 London edition calls him. Joseph was the prototype of the true Christian.

Boehme's method is clear from the following sample passage wherein he seeks to explain several Scriptural passages:

He will wash away his garment in wine, and his mantle in the blood of the grape. That is, Christ will wash our humanity, viz. the garment of the soul, in the wine of His Love, and with the Love wash away from the defiled Adamical flesh the earthly dross and spawn of the Serpent that Adam had received with his desire and lust, from which the earthly man became a beast; and leave the spawn of the serpent to the earth, and in the end burn it up with the fire of God.
And His mantle in the Blood of the Grape. The mantle is the cover which covers the washed garment, and is even the precious purple mantle of Christ, viz. the scorn, affliction, torment, and suffering; when he thereby washed our sins in His Blood, that is, the right blood of the grape, wherein He washed His mantle, which now he casts over our garment and covers it, viz. over our humanity; that God's anger and the Devil may not touch it. (*Myst. Mag.* lxxvi, 59, 60)

Scriptural figures point forward towards Christ's work and the restoration of man by reunion of opposites within history. For Boehme the reunion of opposites remained for the end of time. Individual men could not be saved alone, apart from the race. When Adam fell the race fell; so, when the new man comes, the race will rise again. His mystical idea of restitution was a social idea because no one could be renewed unless nature itself was restored to her original purity. A universal fall means a universal redemption. This presages the true unsectarian–*unpartheyisch*–religion when Babel and Fabel will disappear, when good and evil will be supplanted by a harmony in which the conflicting wills have become one.[6] History stands under dialectical tension; eternity is beyond desire.

Boehme traced the line of the covenant with skill and originality and Joseph prefigures the new Adam to come.

As the next book, *Of Christ's Testaments* (*Test.*), now stands it contains a preface, two versions of a tract on Baptism, one on the Supper. Boehme partially re-wrote the one on Baptism "for the simple-minded," which follows as Book Two in most editions. The first composition was November and December, 1623,[7] and the revision was begun on April 1, 1624.[8]

Boehme's sacramentarian views form a central point in his thought, expressing the idea of the indwelling Christ. Just as the medieval Mass rested on Anselm's legal atonement, so Boehme's views rest on the Protestant view that Christ conquered death and brought new life to man as it was expressed by Luther, by Schwenkfelder, and by Osiander (however they may have differed in detail). Boehme's *Test.* is really a thoroughgoing Schwenkfeldian work, confirming that trend in his thought which began with his nature-philosophy and moved towards the more specifically religious inwardness of traditional German mysticism. Though Boehme employed words like *Bund,* his idea of substantial indwelling and his conception of substance mark his views as his own. Then he also used the old fire image again, an image which Luther shared.[9] Baptism was by fire as well as by water.

For when the Logos and life-force of the Holy Fire became man, revealing itself in Christ, the holy Logos in the Holy Fire spoke through this assumed humanity into its fellow-members of the Covenant. (I, ii, 29)

Through the fire-sacrifice Israel was redeemed, and the new birth was conceived as sacrifice through fire (I, ii, 12). Fire baptism was baptism of the primitive human libido; water baptism was renewal of the image, the prototype of which was circumcision. The Supper was communion first with Christ's vitality and secondly with fellow believers. But man should not cling to the medium, for

faith, when it hungers for God's Love and Grace, always eats and drinks Christ's flesh and blood, through the medium of the hallowed food, or without the medium of the food. (ii, iii, 42)

Now, after vicissitude and devious search, Boehme gained stature as a front-ranking philosophical theologian. He had met the stressing viewpoints of his time and, contrary to his own claims to ignorance which were born of his humility, he was a moderately learned man. He did not spring up unheralded and unsung, an untutored peasant's son who stood in the direct beam of divine illumination. He won his way through struggle to victory.

NOTES TO CHAPTER TEN

1. Buddecke, *Verzeichnis*, p. xx.
2. This point needs emphasis. Union was anticipated, not experienced, forming the irreducible core of his thought.
3. Buddecke, *Verzeichnis*, p. xx.
4. D. 1202. Joachim wrote a harmony and other works. *Vide:* Peuckert, *Rosenkreutzer*, pp. 41ff.
5. Example of this maturity of style is the first paragraph: Wenn wir wollen die neue Wiedergeburt verstehen: was sie ist, und wie es geschehe; so müssen wir erstlich wissen, was der Mensch ist, und wie er Gottes Bilde ist, und wie die Göttliche Inwohne sey; Auch was der geoffenbarte Gott sey, dessen der Mensch ein Bilde ist (i, 1).
6. Erich Seeberg, *Gottfried Arnold, Die Wissenschaft und Mystik seiner Zeit,* Meerane, 1922.
7. The date of this tract depends upon the correct date of *Epist.* xliv, which is given as May 7, 1623, but which was more logically dated May 7, 1624. Here he mentions a printed version of *Test.* Where? We here accept Buddecke's order, *op. cit.*, pp. xxii ff.
8. Buddecke, *Verzeichnis*, pp. xx, xxi.
9. "Why could Christ not confine His Body within the substance of bread, just as in the accidents? Fire and iron are two substances; yet they are so mingled in red-hot iron that any part is at once iron and fire. What prevents the glorious body of Christ from being in every part of the substance of bread?" Luther, *The Babylonish Captivity. Vide:* also Plato, *Timaeus,* 52D.

La agonía es, pues, lucha. Y el
Cristo vino a traernos agonía, lu-
cha y no paz.
    —UNAMUNO: *La Agonía del*
    Christianismo

CHAPTER ELEVEN

BOEHME'S LIFE: 1619–1624

THE Boehme who had written the *Aurora* had been an obscure young shoemaker, but the Boehme who emerged from enforced silence to continue one of the most creative periods in modern philosophical theology was a sensation. For a book-writing "illuminated" shoemaker was as much of a curiosity as the bears, camels, and five-legged calves at the Leipzig Fair.

Boehme's fellow burghers mistrusted the strange, high-browed little man who lugged fat books to his shop, who had intercourse with nobility and learned people, who made mysterious journeys to visit the landed gentry, and who entertained visitors from far-off places in his house for lengthy periods. Unlike the Nürnbergers of the previous century, who had held shoemaker *Meistersinger* Hans Sachs in esteem, the Görlitz citizens suspected their cobbler neighbor whose fame then was spreading over all Silesia. Tension between landed gentry and the middle classes was rising; Boehme, the merchant, was a *protegé* of the nobility; his class resented it and rejected him. But a band of disciples in aristocratic, medical, and official classes arose who hung on his every word, who copied out his books even before they were finished, who paid him for the right to transcribe, and who wined and dined him in their manors.

Balthasar Walther had won the first Boehme converts, among them Christian Bernhard, as early as 1618 (*Epist.* xxvi, 3). Along with Carl von Ender, Bernhard proved to be a devoted friend. In 1619 he had further intercourse with "high persons" who urged him

> to write what I saw in an effectual manner, and knew in spirit. (*Epist.* i, 2)

The "good and known" Doctor Walther already had given the forty questions to answer, but Boehme wrote

> I am much busied with worldly affairs and employments, else a part might have been finished. (*Epist.* i, 17)

Boehme now was a prosperous man although there is no suggestion about the kind of business he pursued after selling his shoemaker's bench; most likely he was a linen merchant and draper.

Business, however, no longer was primary; he was an author—an "illuminated" man. He had a large correspondence with noblemen, officials, and physicians. Among the nobility were Carl von Ender and Michael von Ender, Abraham von Sommerfeld auf Falchenheim und Wartha, Rudolf von Gersdorf, Abraham von Franckenberg. Among the officials were the tax collector at Sagan, Christian Bernhard, the Electoral Superintendent at Lissa, Augustin Cöppin, the tax collector at Beuthen, Casper Linder, the mintmaster at Glogau, Johann Jakob Huser, and the Imperial Tax collector at Liegnitz, Paul Kaym. The physicians were Balthasar Walther, Christian Steinberg, Friedrich Krause of Goldberg, Gottfried Freudenhamer von Freudenheim of Gross-Glogau, Johann Daniel Koschowitz of Striega, and Tobias Kober of Görlitz. Other correspondents whose professions are not known were Johann Butowski, Martin Moser, and Valentin Thirnes. Balthasar Nitsch was a cloth-maker. Moreover, Boehme had close friends among some of his neighbors in Görlitz, mostly the professional people with whom he was in close rapport.

Boehme, although flattered by the attentions of the learned, seems to have kept his head. But when they asked him to continue his writing he dared not refuse. Although his literary activity was secret, his fame was spreading. He admitted that he knew that "haughty" people were reading his works and he cautioned against careless exposure. (*Epist.* ii, 11) In

October, 1619, writing to Carl von Ender, he said that he had gotten his writings back from Zieger. Late in September or early in October he spent several days journeying "to another country where . . . my outward man was not at home"; he also mentions his impending journey to Prague (*Epist.* iii, 3). On November 14th he wrote to Christian Bernhard,

I have been so busied with travelling . . . and other affairs, that I could not pleasure you therein . . . for I have yet so much to do by reason of my brother's daughter (who [the brother] is lately dead) that I must run every week into the country. . . . So do worldly affairs hinder God's Kingdom. Yet I know at present no other remedy or means to maintain the earthly body, with wife and children. (*Epist.*, iv, 28–31)

He went on to say that the transcribing of his writings should not be done by anyone; not everyone could keep peace. Near the end of November he spent a longish time at Carl von Ender's; he finished *Princ.* there (*Epist.* ii, 11). This work was also sent to a Mr. Fabian (*Epist.* v, 14). Boehme and his friends were circulating the manuscripts and printed works:

As for the other two books, viz. the New Testament and the third part of *Gnothi Seauton* [a pseudo-Weigel work], have a little patience, for they are not yet in my hands, till the Leipzig Fair, but I am confident, then they shall be sent you. (*Epist.* ix, 4)

The most interesting of Boehme's *Epistles* was addressed to Abraham von Sommerfeld und Falckenstein auf Wartha, scion of a well-known house, answering an inquiry about the *Aurora*. Boehme wrote in fawning, flattering style, admitting authorship of the work, describing his experiences, saying that he was going to send some later writings including a copy of *Seel. Frag.* Apparently Boehme had sufficient copies to lend them out.

Not only books but food as well was shared during these trying times when the Thirty Years' War was beginning. On November 10, 1619, Boehme asked Christian Bernhard to send a letter through Michael Specht to Balthasar Walther and to have three sacks filled with wheat at Mr. Weigel's, and then returned. He asked for war news, saying that the Saxon Margrave had come to Görlitz after a skirmish at Lübe, and that other skirmishes had resulted in damage which Boehme had seen on his visit to Prague (*Epist.* lxvii). Boehme's relationship to these friends is not fully known; but their effect upon his spirit is clear. That Boehme was impressed by the coterie of important people who hung on every word that he wrote, is evident from a letter to his patron, Carl von Ender, wherein he acknowledged the urgent pleas to continue writing as coming from God (*Epist.* xi, 2). Writing to Abraham von Franckenberg he said,

Seeing, Sir, that you together with your brother, Mr. H. S., and likewise the deep learned doctors, J. S., and J. D. K., are very much respected friends; and in the life-tree of Christ my eternal fellow-members . . . I . . . do rejoice with them . . . I have taken order that they should get a copy of this treatise . . . and communicate it to each other for the transcribing. . . . (*Epist.* xl, 11)

Franckenberg was a serious student of German mysticism; Boehme, whom he learned to know in 1623, introduced him to it and he went on to read Tauler, Kempis, the *Theologia Germanica*, Schwenkfeld, Weigel, and Arndt. Franckenberg became the first editor of Boehme's works, collected the biographical materials in *De Vita et Scriptis* and forged the popular but not quite accurate picture of Boehme.

In May, 1621, Boehme asked Christian Bernhard for a secret conference, requesting that Boehme's name be not mentioned (*Epist.* lxviii). On June 6, 1621, Boehme said that after the conference he had gone to Rudolf von Gersdorf's [1] manor where he found in von Gersdorf a "hearty desire for our talent." He asked Bernhard to get certain papers and send them to von Gersdorf who was on the right way, piously adding that "our angelical Kingdom is increasing." [2] In another letter of the same date he said,

I acquaint you that this writing . . . The *Aurora*, is sought and read by many learned . . . noble persons. . . .

Men very much, in all Silesia as also in many places in the Mark, Meissen, and Saxony, as letters come to my hand that are sent . . . ; also eminent people entreat that they be put into print; which to me at present, while Babel burns, is not acceptable or convenient. (*Epist.* xiii, 1)

Having been forbidden to write, Boehme was torn between two desires: to obey the Council or to expose his talent:

I thought that I wrote only for myself, and intended to have kept it by me . . .; yet now it is manifest, and come into men's hands without my knowledge and endeavor. (*Epist.* xvi, 9ff)

Boehme, with pardonable curiosity, was also interested in how his literary efforts were being received. Writing to Christian Bernhard, October 29, 1621, he said:

How goes it with your brother at Beuthen, to whom you have lent these writings, and what judgment does he make of them were very acceptable for me to know, for there are some more people at Beuthen . . . who also have some of them, and exceedingly desire the other; and you would show a service to your brother and others if you would lend them what they desire. . . . These writings are spread far and wide in many Countries; among high and low . . . I send you with directions three sacks for the corn, which Herr Rudolf [von Gersdorf] will send. . . . (*Epist.* xxi, 2ff)

Boehme was sending copies of his own works:

I send you the magical Globe, with the explanation thereof. . . . Send it back again as soon as you can, I will shortly send you something else . . . I thank you for sending the corn. I will . . . pay you for it. . . . If Herr M. Weigel would send my sack again, I should rest content, but I perceive . . . well how his heart is. I have discovered to him the Babylonish whore; and still friendly write to him, to try if he will be seeing. (*Epist.* xxx, 111)

Solicitous letters continued to come to Boehme. Dr. Adam Brux, of Strottau, wrote him for the third time asking for friendship and asking permission to borrow some of his writings. Since none were immediately available he copied something out for him (*Epist.* xxv, 5). But when Dr. Christian Steinberg requested further explanation of some terms in the *Aurora* Boehme refused, saying

> I give you to understand that at present it is not convenient to write . . . in letters seeing the time is dangerous, and the enemy of Christ horribly rages and raves; till a little time be past. (*Epist.*, xxviii, 7)

On July 9, 1622, Boehme sent a package by way of Christian Bernhard to Dr. Göllner of Troppau then in Breslau (*Epist.* lxx, 1). Dr. Friedrich Krause of Goldberg wrote Boehme for more explanations; Krause had been led to Boehme by Balthasar Walther (*Epist.* xxx, 6). Boehme thanked Krause for the "present I have received," (9) evidence that he was being remunerated by his friends for copies of his writings. That his industry was not without reward is clear from this letter to Christian Bernhard on November 12, 1622:

> I send you . . . two sacks, and pray you to take pains to fill them with corn, and take notice and seal it a little. In the sack there is a packet to Herr Rudolf von Gersdorf and to Herr Friedrich von Kregwitz; which should only be sent to Herr Gersdorf, he will send Herr Kregwitz's part . . . but pray take the pains to convey it to Herr Gersdorf. If you cannot light upon a messenger to your mind, then send it by a messenger on purpose. He will be well paid by Gersdorf, else I will pay him myself if he does not. Pray make the whole pack again, for I have left it unsealed for you. There is with each letter a treatise annexed, which is useful for you. You should do well to copy them out with the soonest conveniency, and then speedily without further delay, send it to the forementioned place. But pray pack each treatise with its proper . . . letter, and seal that by itself. . . . By Herr Kregwitz's letter you should only write out the bound or stitched sheets, the other two sheets that are loose, or unsewed, you may leave to Herr Gersdorf. Kregwitz has the beginning fair. Concerning the list of books from Herr Linder at Beuthen, I answer, that those mentioned books are mine, which were all made half a year ago, and part of them this summer. That which you have now received from Gers-

dorf is the one against the Methists, and here in Kregwitz's writing you may find also one of true Resignation. The others are partly great ones, especially the book *De Signatura Rerum*, the signature or impress of all things . . . Doctor Bruz also has one, and Doctor Gyller of Troppen. . . .

The expedient of smuggling out his writings in grain sacks was used to circumvent the ban on his works. He continued:

Concerning the Cossacks . . . they lie in Leutenmeritz in Bohemia, even to Lippe, and very much lay waste the country. It is said that they are to draw by us, and go towards Poland. But we have nothing certain . . . I suppose they will remain in Bohemia or Lusatia, and not see Poland, for we shall shortly have new times. The present peace is not firm, for the sickness is to death. (*Epist.* xxxii)

Balthasar Walther was, however, winning more admirers; Boehme mentioned a Mr. Nagel and a Mr. Teikmann (*Epist.*, xxxiv, 20). Also Boehme said that

I am continually exercised in writing; and therefore I have laid aside my trade to serve God and my brother in this calling, to receive my reward in heaven; albeit, I shall incur displeasure, and an ungrateful odium at the hands of Babel and the Anti-Christ. (19)

Times were bad. Boehme said to Ender that money could buy nothing. He also said that he had passed one of Ender's fields and seen the beets with which God had blessed him, and Boehme asked for three sacks of them (*Epist.* lxxiii, 3), adding greetings to Ender's sister and wife, and paying him for wheat and other foodstuffs. Ender sent Boehme fish and grain (*Epist.* lxxiv) which was duly acknowledged. Meanwhile, Boehme's writings were being copied; one copyist wrote three signatures a day (*Epist.* xxiii, 4). Ender was employing several copyists.

Thus did Boehme find religious fellowship outside of the institutional church, and his conviction deepened that the churches were incapable of building faith. He asked one of his correspondents, a Silesian nobleman, not to regard the loud cry, and pratings, where they promise to us the golden mantle of grace, and put them about us, and comfort, tickle, and flatter us with a strange pretence . . . All which will avail nothing. . . . There is great heed to be taken in respect of accepting and joining any of the supposed religions, for which men contend and fight; and not to assent with the conscience of faith to one party that gets the victory. . . .

Without the heretic's arrogated individualism, Boehme trusted his inward experience, believing that it was universally valid:

I pray . . . God . . . that He would . . . open His heart that his soul may see into the ground of my gifts; for truly I am a simple man, and I never either studied or learned this high mystery, neither sought I after it . . . I sought only the heart of Love . . . and when I had obtained that . . . then this treasure of divine and natural knowledge was opened and given unto me, wherewith I have not hitherto vaunted but . . . begged God whether the time were yet come that this knowledge might be revealed in the hearts of many. (*Epist.* xl, 14ff)

This claim was misunderstood; his "precious pearl" was despised by others and he hoped that his further writing would not scandalize his good name (*Epist.* xl, 19). Writing to Gottfried Freudenhamer he reasserted his claim:

I write not as one blind or dumb, without knowledge; I have myself found it by experience. I have been as deep in your opinions as yourself . . . I wish . . . that you might have an insight into my seeing, and that you might see with me out of my seeing. . . . I may come to see you myself if my affairs will permit, provided that it may conduce to God's honor and man's salvation; for I know many thirsty souls . . . with whom I might refresh myself, and they in me. (*Epist.* xlii, *passim*)

This circle, whether secret lodge of initiates or cautious group of half-heretics, was growing around Boehme, and he had an evangelical zeal to communicate, not a creed, but a religious experience.

This was enough to inflame Boehme's old antagonist, Gregory Richter. Boehme's fame, his association with nobility and physicians, his secret meetings with persons of quality, aroused the pastor's suspicions. Rumors spread. Yet since the *Aurora's* confiscation Boehme had to all appearances refrained from further writing; only his friends knew of the works after 1619.

So it must have come as a shock to Richter when on New Year's Day in 1624 several of Boehme's high-placed friends had the boldness to publish several of his tracts in a work entitled *Der Weg zu Christo.* Sponsored by von Schweinich, this work contained *Busse, Gelassen.,* and *Wiedergeburt.* Boehme had taken pains to maintain correct ecclesiastical relations; he had partaken of the communion regularly; he had worshiped with his family every Sunday; his sons had been baptized, catechized, and confirmed. Richter had no ecclesiastical grounds for complaint. What, then, was behind his anger? He seems to have been much annoyed by the secret meetings.

Richter stirred up trouble. He incited mobs to attack Boehme's house. Windows were smashed; Boehme was called vile names; Richter denounced him from the pulpit. Writing to Martin Moser on March 5, 1624,[3] Boehme said:

> The Devil is terrified . . . and . . . has raised up a great tempest. . . . The report . . . which came to you was nothing else but a pharisaical revilement . . . by means of a scandalous . . . lying pamphlet of one sheet of paper in . . . Latin . . . wherein Satan has plainly set forth . . . the pharisaical heart . . . And I confidently believe that the grossest Devil did dictate the pamphlet. (*Epist.* 1, *passim*)

Richter's broadside pamphlet, bearing the printed date of March 7, 1624, said that Boehme's work had as many errors as pages, that the work smelled of wax and shoe-blacking, that it was full of blasphemies, that God did not want His honor proclaimed by heretical shoemakers, tanners, tailors, wives, spiritualists, and doctors, that the old Arian heresy was not as bad as this new one, that Boehme denied God's infinity and taught quaternity instead of trinity.[4] Richter also charged that Boehme was an arrogant, presumptuous man pretending to a knowledge that he did not own,[5] and asserted that he was every day befuddled with brandy, beer, and "*Schnapps*," "all which," Boehme replied, "is untrue and he himself is a drunken man." (*Epist.* lii, 1) Richter wrote Pastor Fries in Liegnitz asking him to denounce Boehme from the pulpit and to the Görlitz Council, which he did.[6] Boehme probably was visiting at von Schweinich's near Liegnitz. Meanwhile Richter was demanding that the Görlitz Council[7] clap Boehme in jail.

The Görlitz Councillors had read Boehme's book and could find nothing offensive or heretical in it. The citizens liked it. They even said that Boehme's teachings were on the same ground as the Fathers (*Epist.* liii, 9). But the Council could not resist Richter's pressure and Boehme was clearly guilty of disobeying the order of 1613 forbidding him to write. So he was arraigned. The decree in the Minute Book reads:

Anno 1624, the 23rd of March. As regards the shoemaker of this city, named Jacob Boehme, it is decreed that, on account of manifold complaint respecting his alleged pernicious doctrine, he be summoned before the Council and enjoined to seek fortune elsewhere.[8]

On the 26th Richter's second *Judicum* appeared in which he called Boehme the Anti-Christ and vituperatively lampooned Boehme's claim to high knowledge.[9] On the same day Boehme was again arraigned. The Minutes again say:

Jacob Boehme, the shoemaker, and confused enthusiast or visionary, says that he composed the book, *The Eternal Life* [sic], though he did not have it printed, but that one of the nobility, Hans Sigmund von Schweinichen, had it printed. He was warned by the Council to seek fortune elsewhere, or in default of fair means this must be reported to the illustrious Prince Elector. Thereupon he declared that he would take his departure as soon as possible.[10]

(Boehme already had received summons to the Electoral Court and he was waiting for the Leipzig Fair before leaving.) Dr. Weisner's *Relation* gives the following fuller account of the examination:

When the magistrates were met . . . and sent for the falsely accused . . . they examined him, perceived no evil in him, they found no anger nor dislike in words or in deeds or behavior, to proceed from him; nor did they observe anything that was blamable; they asked him what hurt he had done the preacher? and therefore he intreated most submissively and earnestly: that their wisdoms would send for the complainant or preacher and cause him to say what he had done him.

Upon which the whole Council concluded that it was just that the preacher should be required to signify the . . . grievances, and thereupon sent two men . . . to the preacher, and intreat him to come to them . . . or . . . to relate those grievances. . . .

Whereupon he was enraged, and sent them word what had he to do with their judgment house . . ; what he had to say, that he shall speak in the place of God, from the pulpit . . ; what he had there said, they should follow that, and banish the vain, wicked reprobate heretic from the city. . . .

Accordingly the lords consulted, and could not find how they should justly help the master [shoemaker]; fearing the vehemency of their preacher . . ; and concluded to banish the innocent J.B. out of the city, in which conclusion some men of the Council would not consent, but rose and went their way, but the rest executed it, and . . . caused the uncondemned . . . citizen to be instantly banished out of the gates.

Which the patient blessed man disliked not; but answered in the name of God, my lords, I will do; but may I not go to my house first, and take mine along with me, or at least tell them my necessity? But they forbade it and he instantly was to be led . . . out of the city, with derision and scorn; then he said, Dear Sirs, let it be done seeing it cannot be otherwise. I am contented. So he was banished and gone away all night long.[10]

Next day, the twenty-seventh of March, Richter's third *Judicum* was published, in which he rejoiced that the city was rid of Boehme. He asked Boehme to leave quickly and to move far away so that no curse should descend upon Görlitz. The dirt which the shoemaker had spewed forth, he said, had contaminated the whole town, adding significantly, You have ignited all Silesia with your teachings! Weisner continued, saying,

But the next morning, when the Council were met together again, and had somewhat reconciled their disagreements, they made another conclusion, to hunt after the persecuted innocent man, and sent up and down about the country to seek him, and at length found him, and brought him solemnly and with honor into the city again, which was a wonder from God. . . .

Boehme returned home on the third of April and composed his answer to the Council. In this letter he defended himself against Richter's accusations in reasoned and temperate manner. Inasmuch as this letter is so revealing of his character and is otherwise unavailable in English it is here quoted in full:

Noble, Most Worthy, Esteemed, Very Learned, Most Kind, and Most Wise Gentlemen! I presently appear before my lords as a Christian and I am prepared to give account of my talents and knowledge which I have singly received from God's Grace only, as a gift.

As to my person, I know of nothing else to say except that I am a lay and simple man, and as a Christian [I] have become enamoured with my Savior's Love, and He has loved and betrothed Himself to my soul's inwardness, of which, since it is requested of me, I shall give account.

I have my knowledge and science out of such gifts, and certainly not from the Devil, as I am unjustly accused, to which a serious reckoning before Christ's judgment belongs, as is written: whosoever mocks the Holy Spirit eternally has no forgiveness, yet on my part I wish him God's heart-felt-compassion.

I wrote my first book in such knowledge, and only as a memorial for myself with intention to keep it only by myself and to show it to no person; but this, through divine intervention, was taken from me, and given to the *Primarius*, as the worthy Council well knows.

In this same book a philosophical and theosophical ground is described in such words as I at the time of my simplicity

could understand by myself and I did not intend that anyone else should read it. The *Primarius* has advertised this
same book for me with a wholly strange understanding contrary to my meaning and so scolded this whole time which
for the sake of Christ's Glory I have thus borne with patience.

When I defended myself against him before the *Minis-
terium* [11] and proved my ground I was then obligated by the
Primarius not to write more which I readily conceded. But
at that time I did not understand God's way, what He would
do with me. On the other hand the Lord *Primarius* as well
as the other preachers promised me to be silent in the pulpit
which has not taken place. But [he] has insultingly slandered
me the whole time and often ascribed things to me which I
am not guilty of, thus slandering and deceiving the entire
city so that I as well as my wife and children had to be a
spectacle, jest, and fool among them. Further at his command I left all my writing and speaking about such high
knowledge of divine things alone for many years, and hoped
that there would be an end to the slandering, which did
not happen, but became worse.

But the lord *Primarius* did not let it rest here, but loaned
out my book and answer to strange places, towns, and villages, and himself spread the same without my knowledge
and desire, where it has been copied out and viewed with
other eyes than he viewed it; through which it has gone from
one city to another, to many of the educated, both priests
and doctors, and many noble persons, also to the Duke of
Liegnitz, who wanted it, but wholly without my knowledge,
unknown to me.

Afterwards many educated persons or priests, doctors, also
noble and ducal as well as princely persons united themselves in writing and also a part in person, asking for more
of my gifts, knowledge, and confession; to whom I said in
the beginning that I dared not do it, it was forbidden of me
by the *Primarius*. But they produced Scripture with serious
threats of divine punishment, and demonstrated that each
one shall be prepared to give an accounting for his gifts and
faith, as well as his hope, and that God would take the
pound away from me and give it to him who accepts it; also
that one must obey God more than men, which I considered
and implored God that whatever such as did not redound to
honor His Name He would take it from me, and [I] gave

myself fully and completely to His Will, with prayer to Him and with petitioning day and night, until the divine noble gift was renewed for me and became enkindled with great heavenly light.

So in divine knowledge I began to answer the gentlemen's questions and upon request and desire to write some little books, among which also is this *Of True Repentance*, which now has been published.

For in this book my own process is shown through which I have gotten my gifts from God, which was written at the request of high and educated people and fell so deeply into the hearts of some that one of the nobility had it printed.

But since the Lord *Primarius* thunders so violently against it, condemning the same to the fire, also citing my person so insultingly, and setting the whole congregation on [my] neck, also proclaiming that I have poisoned the whole city of Görlitz as well as the principality of Liegnitz with it, and spread the same, and because of this the great clamor of the priests of Liegnitz arose about me, also that because of it the Honorable Council as well as the city of Görlitz stood in danger.

Therefore do I give answer, that such count for nothing and that such things are ascribed to me out of evil bias only by a few and perhaps even the aggravation of the Lord *Primarius* himself, since he observes that my innocence shall come to [the light of] day.

For in the first place I myself did not let the book be published. Secondly I did not circulate it in the principality of Liegnitz. Thirdly I know that his fears regarding such danger that the Duke of Liegnitz and the whole clergy would be annoyed do not hold up for I know this much that the Duke as well as some Counselors, also many of the clergy themselves, read [the book], who along with some of the high schools who are highly learned men love it; also it is beloved by some distinguished gentlemen in the Electoral courts in Dresden and Saxony, as also by some Prince Electors and gentlemen of Electoral cities, as I could demonstrate by many letters.

And [I] therefore fully consider that this is both from the Devil, directed for his kingdom, since he sees that his kingdom is revealed through it, and man is directed to repentance and Christian living.

Since the Lord *Primarius* condemns my books to the fire I

then ask and request that the Honorable Council, for God's will, shall command him that he show me my errors in this book item by item, allowing me to come to an answer or to a verbal conference in the presence of some gentlemen of the Council. Were he then to show me an error, I should gladly allow myself to be instructed and to follow him. But if not, since it is in print, he may also write against it, if it please the Honorable Council. There are surely learned people who will take my [cause] and answer him.

Finally he denounced me before the whole congregation, saying that I despised the church and the Holy Sacraments, often scolding me as a heretic, *Schwärmer*, and knave, and attacked me with regard to my honorably begotten good, honorable name [which has always been maintained] in good repute, and ascribed to me such things as are not true, saying that I continually drink myself full of brandy and other wines and beers like a hog, which is ascribed to me against God, honor, righteousness, and truth, out of bad feeling to make me hated by the congregation.

First, I do not despise the church because I myself go into it, much less the Holy Sacraments which I myself partake of. On the contrary I profess the temple of Christ Jesus in us, that we should hearken to Christ teaching us in our hearts according to Saint Stephen and the Apostles' teaching. Also I have written more clearly about the Holy Sacraments than I have ever heard from him in the pulpit, how they were to be explained.

So I am also no teacher nor preacher, and I do not preach nor teach, but I only give account of my gifts and knowledge, how I came thereto. And as far as I am concerned I dare not fear disciples for with my talent I do not associate with common people but with doctors, priests, and noblemen who are educated.

On this account [I] ask the one most worthy and wise Council to take me into proper protection against such slanders, insults, and untrue accusations for with such accusations, violence, and injustice are done me, and [I] live wholly soberly with prayer and mediation on God's gifts. I appeal to the whole city and know that there is no man who can show me to be so. But with the Herr *Primarius* one can often discover a drunken man! Yet I hardly go to one person's house, much less to beer-parlors or wine-cellars. But I dwell alone and quietly, as is well-known to the Council.

Boehme next wrote his answer to Richter himself which he completed on the tenth of April. It is known as *Apol. Richt.*[12] Gregory Richter's attack had spread Boehme's fame and had called civil and ecclesiastical attention to him. For orthodoxy then was zealously guarded by ecclesiastical watchdogs like Richter and by civil magistrates who under the provisions of the various treaties managed such affairs.

After the second brush with the Görlitz Council, Boehme prepared to go to Dresden, viewing the summons he had received before the Council's action as a chance to vindicate himself. On May 9 he started for Dresden by way of Löbau and Bautzen, arriving sometime before the fifteenth.

Dresden was in jubilee. The Saxons had news from Hungary that peace had been arranged between the Emperor and Bethlem Gabor. It was, of course, temporary. English and Scottish soldiers were around and the lull was prior to the storm.[13]

Boehme was not unknown there. Balthasar Walther, who had been director of the Elector's laboratory, had spread the word to his successor, Benedict Hinckelmann, with whom Boehme stayed. Here he was offered all Christian love and friendship, and his arrival was announced to courtiers and Boehme wrote that they read his little book and used it daily.[14]

Boehme wrote four letters home to Dr. Kober which describe his welcome and treatment. Courtiers sought him out for long talks. Joachim von Loss invited him to his castle for a visit, and Major Stahlmeister, the Elector's chief master of the horse, furthered his suit with the Elector. Some of his new friends gave him money. In Dresden he heard nothing of the tumults and uproars which had been his daily diet in Görlitz.

My printed book is already come into the hands of many officers and learned men, all of whom count it to be good, and a gift from God, and they labor and contrive how such things may be published. (*Epist.* lxi, 1)

And the *Primarius'* . . . libel is very wonderfully looked upon. . . . Some suppose that the . . . spiteful spirit has dictated it . . . He is despised by the priests . . . Herr Hincklemann has shown it to the Council and to the learned who wonder at the man's folly, that he dare vomit out his evil affections in public against a Christian book, some of the . . . councilors have signified . . . that . . . they will cause me to be invited to them for a Christian converse . . . with me. . . . My writings are copied out. . . .

This conference took place at Hincklemann's where Dr. Aegius Strauch and others talked about some misunderstood points in his book. Strauch commended Boehme's writings. Boehme nowhere mentioned an examination before the Elector himself, and the seventeenth-century writers (Calov, Spener, and Arnold) assumed that it took place for two reasons: Hegenicht asserted that it did, and Weisner gave an account of it. Others denied that Boehme had received Electoral vindication. Weisner's account, here given, is generally trustworthy. Boehme was

cited to Dresden and was examined in the presence of the illustrious prince Elector, by the chief doctors assembled together . . : Dr. Hoë, Dr. Meisner, Dr. Baldwine, Dr. Geryod, Dr. Leisler, and one Doctor more which I cannot name . . . and two professors . . . of mathematics . . . appointed to discourse about his writings; also in several ways to set about with all sorts of . . . questions but not overcome by any of them, but . . . rapidly and distinctly answered . . .

The illustrious prince Elector highly wondered at it and desired to know the final verdict; but they . . . excused themselves and entreated that . . . he would have patience until the spirit of the man should be more plainly clear to them . . .

Then the deeply-grounded . . . man asked them several questions . . . The simple man held forth . . . the truth plainly . . . and discoursed friendly with them. . . .

To the astrologers he said . . : Dear Sirs, thus far is the spirit of your mathematics right, exact, and grounded upon the mysteries of nature . . .

So they left him quietly . . . The illustrious prince Elector had great satisfaction in the answers. He required him to come apart by himself, and spoke with him . . . and admitted him to all favors, and gave him liberty to go to his house in Görlitz. . . .

The four letters which Boehme wrote to his good friend, Dr. Kober, back home in Görlitz, show his concern for his family. He asked Kober to

treat with my wife, and tell her she shall get patience, and give herself to quiet, and not be so fearful and dismayed at it, as I perceive she is, for it is very well with me and I am preserved with honor and love . . . I intend, God willing, to take care of her and my children. . . . There is a time coming wherein it will not be dishonorable to her; none know how to speak disgraceful things of us, but only one wicked man, who belies us. . . . Concerning my son Jacob, that he is come home, I rejoice, and desire . . . that he would stay in Görlitz till my coming, and not . . . dispute . . . with any. . . . Comfort my wife, that she may let go her fruitless care; there is no danger about me. I am at present well and better than in Görlitz. (*Epist.* xli.)

In the second of these letters he asked Kober to tell

my wife that she should not perplex herself by reason of me, but diligently pray that God would order it for the best, and if she wants anything, she knows very well where she may have it, she should only keep herself within, and a little submit herself; this stormy tempest will soon blow over. (*Epist.* lxii)

In the third of these letters Boehme asked Kober to

salute my wife and son, and let them read this, and exhort them to patience and prayer. I hope all will be well; they should have patience a little, who knows how the current may run? This persecution may serve for the best. I will within three weeks, if it may be, come home. . . . And exhort my son Jacob to wait, and that he should go often to Hans Berger and see what Elias learns, and that he behave himself with his schoolmaster in love, to whom he shall present my salutation, and not conceal my purpose, that he should look upon it, as if there were any cause to flee from [Richter], and for that cause Elias might be abused and evilly treated by the schoolmaster.[15] (*Epist.* lxiii)

In the fourth of these letters he said,

My wife need not cause any window shutters to be made; if they will break them they will, and then the fruits of the high priest will be seen; let her have a little patience. If she cannot get a place in Görlitz, I will get a place for her somewhere else, where she will have quiet enough; but let her stay at home and not go out except upon necessity, and let the enemy rage, but he will not eat her up. . . . By the bearer I send two reich-dollars to my wife for her occasions, if she want anything she knows well where she may have it; the key of the drawer lies in the parlor by the warming-pan on the shelf. . . . Salute my wife and two sons for me and exhort them to Christian patience and prayer, and to purpose no self-revenge. . . . My Jacob shall stay at Görlitz that his mother may have some comfort there until I can dispose it otherwise.

Boehme left Dresden only partly vindicated, neither justified legally nor branded an illuminated heretic. In comfort he went to his noble friends—to von Schweinichen, von Gersdorf, and von Franckenberg. From June to October he was at von Schweinichen's. Tales of his "hidden sight" were still being told [16] and he was still a sideshow freak to his Görlitz neighbors. The burghers said that he

frequented the company of the foremost enthusiasts, he often had his *raptus* and quakings, so that he sat in his corner writing, even though previously he could neither read nor write. He brought great books home . . . [and wrote some] that the theologians and professors could not contradict.[17]

Surely the sight of the short, high-browed, bent shoemaker lugging big books home, and his continuous writing, were enough for stories to grow on. During the last half-year he had been writing several things: two philosophical tracts, two mystical tracts, and one large but unfinished speculative work which might have become his greatest work.

In February, 1624 he wrote the *Table of the Three Principles* (*Taf.*),[18] showing that his final orientation towards the doctrine of God was still tinged with alchemical imagery although his nature philosophy had changed from the cruder ideas in the *Aurora*.

In March or April he wrote the *Clavis* [19] which was the

key to his works so much requested by his friends, a simplified glossary of the unusual terms which had appeared in his earlier writings. It does not represent a progressive step in his thought.

On March 25 he completed a lovely little work, *Dialogue Between an Enlightened and Unenlightened Soul,* (*Gespräch 2er Seel*),[20] the zenith of his mysticism, describing the psychological order of salvation as a dialogue between a regenerate and an unregenerate man.

Before the middle of June, while at Hinckelmann's in Dresden, he began *Of Divine Prayer* (*Gebet*), one of the towering monuments in the literature of devotion, an incomplete prayer book [21] which was to have had prayers for the week, at waking, rising, dressing, eating, working, et cetera—prayers for the Ten Commandments, and prayers on the Catechism. It remained unfinished.

In October he began *The Theosophical Questions* (*Theos. Frag.*),[22] a work which, had it been completed, would have become his deepest, clearest work. Who formulated these questions is not known, but there are hints that his Silesian friends propounded them. The work was planned to set forth a view of revelation, God, nature, creature, heaven, hell, and the world. But the same old problems, and the same mystical insight, here persist.

The reader is to know that in Yes and No all things consist. (iii, 2)

Abraham von Franckenberg recorded his last meeting with Boehme:

Having in the year 1624 been several weeks with us in Silesia . . . he was seized with a burning fever, and much swelled and bloated by an immoderate drinking of water, so that, at last by his own desire, he was brought in such condition to his own house in Görlitz.[23]

This was November 7, 1624.[24] Catharina was not at home, but Dr. Kober, his good friend, cared for him. But the end was near. Kober wrote

As we could find no satisfactory cure, I, along with Christoph Kütter of Sprottau, concluded that he should be buried without scandal.[25]

In the evening Kober asked Master Elias Dietrich to question Boehme on his faith, preparatory to final celebration of the Lord's Supper. Dietrich made the official reply. On the fifteenth of November, at eight in the morning, Boehme, growing weaker, was examined regarding his beliefs.[26]

Primarius Thomas, successor to Richter who had just died, granted Dietrich permission to administer the Supper, provided satisfactory answers were obtained. Dietrich's report [27] to the church authorities listed some of the questions put to Boehme.

Dietrich asked whether he believed that God was in essence and substance one and in person threefold. Boehme answered yes.

Dietrich asked whether he believed that in the beginning God had made man in His image, that man of his own self-will and beguiled by the Devil, had turned away from God and so fallen into temporal and eternal death and sin, that because of sin man must be punished eternally unless God took pity on him. Boehme answered yes.

Dietrich asked whether he believed that in the mediatorial person of Christ there were two distinct natures, that by divine nature He existed from eternity, equal in essence, honor, and glory to the Father and Holy Spirit. Boehme answered yes.

Dietrich asked whether he believed that the only mediator and the only way to salvation was Christ who must be seized through real faith which is a divine gift. Boehme answered yes.

Dietrich asked whether he believed a Christian ought to lead a holy, blameless life, according to God's command, as far as possible in this corrupt nature; yet with God he can gain nothing by this, but is saved by pure unmerited Grace. Boehme answered yes.

Dietrich now asked whether, if God prolonged his life, he would keep to Lutheranism. Boehme answered yes.

Dietrich reminded Boehme that he was to be content with

the revealed Word and not to dabble in revelations and visions. Boehme answered that he had read the New Testament and that diligently.

Dietrich exhorted him to combine Old and New as the Old referred to the New and the New to the Old. Further he was to write no more books. Boehme replied with an account of *occasionem scribendi* upon which Dietrich did not comment.

Dietrich asked whether he had partaken of the Supper lately. Boehme replied that the last time had been about three-quarters of a year before, with his wife and two sons in public church assembly. Catharina added that her husband had been several times absolved in Herr Andrea.

Dietrich asked whether his repentance and desire for the Supper was earnest. Boehme said yes.

Dietrich exhorted Boehme to watch what he was doing, for though he might deceive men, he could not deceive God, and he prepared to administer the Supper. But with a view to further defence against calumniators he proceeded further to ask whether Boehme felt that he was a sinner. Boehme answered yes.

Dietrich asked whether he sorrowed with all his heart for his sins. Boehme answered yes, and added, "*Manibus complicatis, oculis elevatis.*"

Dietrich asked whether he believed that Christ had died and shed His blood for his sake. Boehme answered, "Yes, for He Himself says, 'Come unto me all ye that are weary and heavy laden and I will give you rest.'"

Dietrich then asked whether he believed that God, for Christ's sake, would pardon and forgive all sins and be gracious and merciful, Boehme said, "Yes," firmly.

Dietrich asked whether with God's help he would mend his life and guard against sin. Boehme said, "Yes."

Dietrich asked whether he was ready to pardon and forgive everyone by whom he had been injured. Boehme said, "Yes, with my whole heart I forgive and desire of them like forgiveness."

Dietrich absolved Boehme in Christ's name, blessed the elements, and partook with Boehme of the Lord's last supper.

Boehme grew weaker. Saturday, the sixteenth,[28] he told

Hans Rothe and Michael Kurtz that in three days he would enter another world. Sunday, at two in the morning, he asked his son Tobias whether he also heard the sweet music. Tobias said that he did not. Then Jacob Boehme said, "Let the door be opened so as to hear the singing better." Later he asked, "What time is it?"

"Three o'clock."

"My time is not yet. O Thou strong God of Sabaoth, deliver me according to Thy Will! O Thou crucified Lord Jesus Christ, be merciful to me and take me into Thy Kingdom!"

At six in the morning, before the city gates were open,[29] he bade farewell to his wife and sons, murmured, and gasped, "Now I go hence to Paradise." [30]

The sun was rising on eternity.

NOTES TO CHAPTER ELEVEN

1. Zinzendorf's mother was a von Gersdorf.
2. Gichtel, editor of the 1682 edition, founded an "angelical brotherhood."
3. This letter's contents show that it was written after the *Judicum*. The letter's date is March 7. Probably the letter is incorrectly dated.
4. Cf. Jecht, *Böhme,* pp. 70–71.
5. Fechner, *Leben,* liii.
6. *Ibid.*
7. The Council consisted of Wolfgang Stolberger, Burgomaster; *Consules:* Fr. Schwettig, Barth. Jakobi, M. C. Staudt; *Scabini:* C. Cunrad, B. Hagendorn, Fr. Beyer, Nath. Scultetus, W. M. von Mollerstein; *Senatores:* F. Föster, Tob. Grautzke, S. Schnitler; *Syndikus:* N. Seb. Krebs. Of these M. C. Staudt (1580–1639) was patron of the arts and sciences, whose brother Daniel gave 100 marks to scholars and placed his fine library at their disposal. Materials from the archives of the Staude-Staudt-Stoudt family, c/o Don Ricardo W. Staudt, Buenos Aires.
8. Jecht, *Böhme,* p. 43. Was he still a shoemaker?
9. *Ibid.*
10. Weisner's *Wahrhaftiger Relation,* both passages.
11. No account of this meeting survives.

12. This survives in the autograph ms. Cf. Buddecke, *Verzeichnis*.
13. Peuckert, *Böhme*, p. 132.
14. *Ibid.*, pp. 136ff.
15. Elias, thirteen, was scholar in a church-controlled school.
16. Franckenberg, *De Vita*, #23. *Vide:* Freytag, *Bilder aus der deutschen Vergangenheit*, II, pp. 426ff.
17. *Ibid.*
18. Buddecke, *Verzeichnis*, p. xxi.
19. *Ibid.*
20. *Ibid.*
21. W. R. Garrison in a review of a translation of *Gebet* in *The Christian Century*.
22. Buddecke, *Verzeichnis*, p. xxi.
23. *De Vita*, #23.
24. Peuckert, *Böhme*, p. 140.
25. Kober, *Umständiger Bericht*.
26. Peuckert, *Böhme*, pp. 140–141.
27. Okeley, *Memoirs*, pp. 81–86.
28. The Knauthe ms dates it September 25, following references in Hans Emmerich's diary.
29. Boehme lived just outside the gates.
30. This account of the catechization and death is from Dr. Kober, #6. Kober, his physician, was with him when he died.

PART TWO

THE SCOPE OF BOEHME'S THEOLOGY

Although Jacob Boehme's thought, beginning in mystical experience, emerged out of the tensions of his age and region, it grew to become a mature organism as his day-star continued to rise. His theological metabolism was rapid and he quickly replaced old cells with new ones. He was ever rewriting, recasting, reformulating and his mature theology emerged as a body of positive thought only after he had firmly joined vision and life.

He struggled with the Yes and No in his own self. As long as he had only anticipated union he was schizoid, a divided self. His mature theology, result of final triumph over the bipolarity of his experience, united the two apparently contradictory sides of his personality. He struggled to join Renaissance nature philosophy with the usual subjectivity of Christian mysticism. In his earlier works connection was only sought, never found. Only in the works after 1623 did integration appear.

Our cross-section of Boehme's theology, then, is an attempted exposition of what we consider to be his integrated thought.

*Theogonies described the ori-
gin and development of the world
from obscure primordial impulses
to the clear and distinct variety-
in-unity of the organized kosmos.*
—ERWIN ROHDE: *Psyche*

CHAPTER TWELVE

GOD BEYOND NATURE AND CREATURE: THEOGONY

BOEHME's basic insight, gotten in the sunrise to eternity
and realized in life, was that in Yes and No all things
consist (*Theos. Frag.* iii, 2). To realize this he had to present
solution to the problem of being which explained the world's
generation, its "birth" and development. He had to postulate
a source which was both unthinkable and contradictory, the
origin of bifurcation and lying beyond necessity as the coincidence of contraries from which all finite realities proceed.

Like the Gnostics he had to give theogonic explanation of
how Yes and No arose from a basically indifferent dynamic
One. How did the one God become Yes and No, love and
wrath? How did the dialectical [1] world arise?

Boehme separates theogony from emanation. The former
explains how a trinitarian God arises, the latter how the
manifold things of the world come to be. He proposed two
schemes for solving these two problems: the "seven spirits
of God" and the seven natural principles. Many Boehme
students, including Hegel, have mistakenly identified these
two schemes, with confusing results.

The doctrine of the seven spirits of God had already appeared in the *Aurora* and persisted through his mature
thought.

The whole or total God stands in seven species or kinds, or

in a sevenfold form or generating; and if these births . . .
were not, then there would be neither God, nor life, nor
angel, nor any creature. And these births . . . have no beginning, but have generated themselves from eternity. . . .
These seven generations are none of them the first, the
second, or the third, or the last, but they all are seven. . . .
Yet I must set them down one after another, according to a
creaturely way . . , otherwise you could not understand it.
(*Aurora*, xxiii, 15ff)

To write otherwise would be to give the Deity imagined
form (*Aurora* xxiii, 46ff). These seven spirits were seven
ways of talking about a God and God was not to be restricted
to these forms. Each of Boehme's major works repeats this
warning: the Deity's immeasurable extent cannot be described (*Aurora* x, 26); external nature generates itself without beginning (*Princ.* iii, 3); the Deity has no beginning
(*Sig. Rer.* iii, 1) but is an eternally generating series (*Princ.*
vii, 14).

Boehme did not bother himself about the relationship of
this theogonic "myth" to reality: when God is mythologized,
is the mystery profaned? Schleiermacher held all mythologies
vain and ruinous mysticism [2] because in his view the complex divine genealogies, long emanations and procreations,
were not religious, as they aimed at breaking the highest
unity, the idea that all that moves us is One.[3] The impulse
behind theogony is the desire to solve the problem of evil:
"it is not easy to avoid the appearance of making God sus-
ceptible of evil."[4] Here did Boehme's problem begin because he tried to show God's self-manifestation without making him the source of evil.

Coleridge suggested that Boehme mistook the peculiari-
ties of his overwrought mind for realities and modes of
thought common to all minds.[5] He asked whether Boehme's
speculations were based on experience or upon fancy, suggesting that a second error is implied in that he confused
active natural powers with God.[6] This is really the question
of the validity of Boehme's symbolism.[7]

When Boehme wrote, modern subjective language had not
yet been created. And when he looked within he saw forces
and powers which he could not name, so his words bear

meanings which they do not now bear, meanings which were forged in the process of personal integration.[8]

From the time of pseudo-Dionysius the Areopagite the problem of the "names" of God has been more than the semantics of symbolism. In his theogony Boehme tried to describe how three persons came from One; in his doctrine of seven natural principles he tried to describe how the manifold world came from One. Here an antinomy appeared: the Source is no-thing, yet all, accessible to thought and yet irrational. Two roads present themselves: a positive way and a negative way. Two theologies result: apophatic and cataphatic. The former subordinates affirmation to negation; the latter subordinates negation to affirmation. If the Source is all then by affirming creation's multiplicity it may be reached; if the Source is no-thing then by denying created reality it may be reached. Boehme's significance was his combining of both theologies in one comprehending system of thought.

Boehme's final statement of his theogonic stages was presented in the *Tabula* appended to *Epist.* xlvii, addressed to Johann Huser. These stages are: 1) God as *Ungrund* with related descriptions; 2) God as primordial will, or God the Father as no-thing and all; 3) God as subjectivation of the will or Christ; 4) God as objectivation of the will, or Spirit, movement, life; 5) God as trinity; 6) God as Logos; 7) God as Wisdom.[9] However, Boehme cautions:

I exhort the reader not to understand in an earthly manner the high supernatural meaning. (*Gnad.* iii, 10)

The seven spirits of God also have psychological, or logical, connotations because they do describe according to a creaturely way and manner, that is, they reveal the logic of God-consciousness within man. They show also how man comes to a knowledge of God. Outer and objective parallel inner and subjective.

Boehme's God is no abstract, formal idea to be toyed with, reasoned, and seized outwardly "by selfish will and reason," but He is known only by him who achieves inward unity of will (*Myst. Mag.* xl, 54). Man finds himself seized by

God when he yields to God and becomes a willing instrument of God's desire (*Sig. Rer.* xv, 85).

Boehme's theogonic explanation was demanded by his taking St. John's Logos doctrine seriously. This is clear from the following:

For it is said (*John* i, 1-3): 'In the beginning was the Word, and the Word was with God, and the Word was God. The same was in the beginning with God. All things were made by Him and without Him was not anything made that was made.' In this brief statement we have the whole ground of the divine and natural revelation in the Being of all beings. For 'in the beginning' means the eternal beginning in the will of the Unground for a ground, that is, for the divine apprehension, since the will apprehends itself in the center for a foundation. . . . For the one will apprehends itself in the one power, wherein lies all hiddenness, and breathes itself forth through the power into an intuition, and this wisdom, or intuition, is the beginning of the eternal mind as the conspection of itself. This amounts to saying, the Word was in the beginning *with* God, and was God himself. The will is the beginning and is called God the Father, and He apprehends Himself in power, and is called the Son. . . . And in this connection it is said: The Word (i.e., the formed power) was in the beginning *with* God. For here two things are to be understood: namely, the unformed power, i.e., the *In;* and the formed power which is the *with,* for it has come into something and so into motion. The *In* is still, but the *with* is formed and compacted, and from this compaction and motion arise nature and creature, together with all being. (*Gnad.* ii, 7-11)

Here Boehme shows his dependence upon Christian theology.

Boehme's basic designation of God—the first of his seven theogonic spirits—is God the *Ungrund,* the no-thing and the all (*Epist.* xlvii, 37). He is first "hidden, unrevealed" (*Gnad.* ii, 20), or the hidden and the invisible (*Myst. Mag.* preface, 6).

God's transcendent unknowability has for him a twofold significance: first, it means God's transcendence, unknowability, irrationality. In Him all human antitheses are united, all irrational disunities resolved. So God is the dwelling of

the unity (*Theos. Frag.* i, 1), unapprehended of anything
(*Myst. Mag.* xxix, 1), on the other side of good and evil, of
Yes and No, of freedom and desire. Meonic, he is without
inclination and properties, deeper than thought.

But this unknowableness has another, profounder meaning. God is unknown to Himself as He has not yet won form
and knowable, comprehensible being for Himself; He is not
yet self-conscious. Already in the *Aurora*,

> God in Himself knows not what He is; for He knows no
> beginning of Himself, also He knows not anything that is
> like Himself, as also He knows no end of Himself. (*Aurora*
> xxiii, 17b)

So God is a nothing even to Himself (*Myst. Mag.* xxix).

God is unknown to creature for there is as yet no creature
to know Him; He is also unknown to Himself because He has
not yet won the formed image of His own self-consiousness.

The first word to describe this "spirit" comes from traditional Neoplatonic mysticism: God is the no-thing (*Nichts*).[10]
This stands in dialectical relation to creation but it is not the
negation of being.

> God is called the seeing and the finding of the nothing.
> And it is therefore called a nothing (though it is God Him-
> self) because it is inconceivable and inexpressible. (*Theos.
> Frag.* ii, 13)

The no-thing, Lord Sabaoth, is beyond nature and creature
(*Sig. Rer.* iii, 2) as the eternal one God (*Irrth. Stief.* 245).

The second word to describe this "spirit" is Boehme's own:
the *Ungrund*, Unground. Meister Eckhart had spoken of the
Abgrund, the Hindus have Brahman, but Boehme selects *Ungrund* as conscious antithesis to *Grund*. The *Nichts* seeks to
become an *Ich*, the *Ungrund* a *Grund*.

> In Eternity . . . there is nothing but a stillness without
> being; there is nothing either that can give anything; it is an
> eternal rest . . , a groundlessness without beginning and
> end. (*Menschw.* II, i, 8)

A dark craving lives in it which drives it towards a ground, towards nature and creature, towards revelation and self-knowledge.

> The nothing hungers after the something, and this hunger is the desire . . . For the desire has nothing that it is able to conceive. It conceives only itself, and draws itself to itself . . . and brings itself from Abyss to Byss (*vom Ungrunde in Grund*) . . . and yet remains a nothing. (*Myst. Mag.* iii, 5)

All visible and invisible things originate in the speaking of the Word, the finding of the ground (*Taufe* I, i, 1–7).

The third description has no clear origin: God in his transcendent unknowability is an eye that sees in a mrror:

> . . . we recognize it to be like a mirror, wherein one sees his own image: like a life, and yet it is no life, but a figure of life and of the image belonging to life. Thus we recognize the eternal unground out of nature to be like a mirror. For it is like an eye which sees and yet conducts nothing in the seeing wherewith it sees: for the seeing is without essence. . . . It is like . . . a mirror, and yet there is nothing which the eye or the mirror sees; but its seeing is in itself, for there is nothing before it that was deeper there. . . .(*Theos. Punkt.*, i, 7ff)

The fourth description is that God is the "all in unity" (*Alles*). This word came into prominence as his pantheism began to wane. Thus in his last major work he wrote:

> God is the eternal unity . . . which has nothing after nor before Him that can give Him or bring Him anything, or that can move Him; and He is devoid of all tendencies and properties. He is without origin in time and in Himself one only, as a mere purity without attingence. He has nowhere a place or position, nor requires such for His dwelling; but He is at the same time out of the world and in the world, and deeper than any thought can plunge. If the numbers of His greatness and depth should be uttered for a hundred thousand years together, his depth would not have begun to be expressed; for He is infinitude . . ; but the unity of God cannot be expressed, for it is through everything at the same time. (*Theos. Frag.* i, 1)

The fifth description is that God is the Mystery. This comes from alchemy.

> The *mysterium magnum* is the . . . hiddenness of the Deity, together with the Being of all beings, from which one *mysterium* proceeds after another, and each *mysterium* is the model of the other. . . . But you must understand this according to the properties of the mirror, according to all the forms of nature. . . . (*Myst. Punkt.* vi, 2–3)

The *Ungrund* is also the mystery hidden in all things, thus closely approximating the Hindu Atman.

The sixth description is that God is eternal mind, *das ewige Gemüth,* of the heart of God. This is unabashed idealism.

> As we men . . . rule over all things, that is the whole sphere of intelligibility, through the distinction of words, so does God, as the eternal mind of the one power, also work and rule through such image-like words. (*Theos. Frag.* xi, 1)

This description appeared in his earlier writings and gradually disappeared.

In this first spirit of God, described by these words, two cadences were aroused, one which led to self-consciousness and the other which led to self-revelation. For God is unknown to creature and to Himself. The dark Abyss's first movement is dual: a tendency to self-subjectivation which leads to self-knowledge and self-consciousness, and a tendency towards self-objectivation which leads to emanation and manifestation.[11] This is strange! An eternal no-thing desires to become a thing! It cannot remain eternal and become a something. The *Urwille* struggles to project itself into actuality. Freedom and desire, each negate the other. This is what Boehme means by the eternal love-play in God where the Abyss wrestles, sports, and plays with itself (*Myst. Mag.* v, 3). Thus begins Boehme's dialectical theology, a view *ex idea vitae deducta.*

Now a great step takes place. God the unknown—natureless, passionless, groundless, with no tendency to anything, but with a dark, unfathomable will towards a something—

strives to introduce Himself into a something so that He can find, feel, know, and behold Himself. (*Sig. Rer.* ii, 8)

For in the nothing the will would not be manifest to itself, wherefore we know that the will seeks itself, and its seeking is a desire (*Begierde*) and its finding is the essence of the desire, wherein the will finds itself. (*Sig. Rer.* ii, 8)

The *Ungrund's* dark craving is unfathomable, without essence, directed towards being where it can feel, will, know, love and be felt, willed, known, and loved.

Here we remind the reader that God in Himself . . . has no more than one desire, which is to give and bring forth Himself. (*Gnad.* i, 18)

This understanding is a free will, without source or cause, unapprehended and a nothing to itself (*Myst. Mag.* xxix, 1), a desire for a something (*Seel. Frag.* i, 13). The process of God's becoming self-conscious is described:

In this Chaos the eternal nothing comprehends itself in an eye or eternal power of seeing, for the beholding, feeling, and finding of itself. In such case it cannot be said that God has two wills, one to evil, and the other to good. For in the unnatural, uncreaturely deity there is nothing more than a single will, which is called also the one God; and He wills in Himself nothing more than just to seize and find Himself, go out from Himself, and with the outgoing bring Himself into intuition. . . . There is no cause of the divine power . . . save the one will, that is to say, the one God who brings Himself into a threefoldness as into an apprehensibility of Himself. This apprehensibility is the center . . . and is called the heart or seat of the eternal will of God, in which the *Ungrund* possesses itself in a ground. This heart . . . of the *Ungrund* is the eternal mind of the will, and yet has nothing before it that it can will, save only this one place of its self-discovery. The first will is therefore the father of its heart or the place of its discovery. . . . The unfathomable will . . . generates itself within itself into a place of apprehensibility. And the place is a ground and beginning of all beings, and possesses in turn the unfathomable will, which is God the Father. . . .(*Gnad.* i, 8ff)

All effort to probe beyond this will which gets a ground for itself produces confusion (*Menschw.* II, vii, 1ff).

> The first, unoriginated, single will . . . generates within itself the one eternal good as an apprehensible will. . . . The second will is the first will's eternal feeling and finding, for the nothing finds itself as a something. And the unfathomable will . . . goes forth, and brings itself into an eternal intuition of itself. (*Gnad.* i, 5)

In the depths of not-yet-being potential dialectic exists for the desire to self-subjectivation and self-knowledge contradicts the will towards self-objectivation, or emanation. These are fire and light. Fire consumes, light illuminates. In not-yet-being no will has yet arisen and so distinctions like that between good and evil are not yet (*Gnad.* ii, 37).

> For it cannot be said of God that He is this or that, evil or good, or that He has distinctions in Himself. For He is in Himself natureless, passionless, and creatureless. He has no tendency to anything, for there is nothing before Him to which He could tend, neither evil nor good. . . . There is no quality or pain in Him . . . [He] is a single will in which the world and the whole creation lies. . . . He is neither light nor darkness, neither love nor wrath, but the Eternal One. (*Gnad.* i, 3)

Knowledge comes after emanation, after the will has brought comprehensibility and form to itself. Previous to this act a gentle, harmonious "love" exists, but no essential tension. In *Ird. u. himl. Myst.* Boehme contrasted the formed will with the *Ungrund's* dark desire:

> The *Ungrund* . . . makes an eternal beginning as a craving (*Sucht*). For the nothing is a craving after something. But as there is nothing that can give anything . . . the craving itself is the giving of it, which yet also is a nothing . . . which makes within itself where there is nothing . . . though this craving is also a nothing, and there is nothing that can give it anything: neither has it any place where it can find or repose itself. (i)

This craving is self-centered and desirous; the eternal will is free (ii, 2) for it is

> free from the craving, but the craving is not free from the will. . . . The craving is indeed a movement of attraction or desire, but without understanding; it has a life but without knowledge. (iii, 1)

Desire, by realizing itself in and through the will, becomes an entity in the will's life, knowing what it is and does (iii, 2).

This process of making a formed will is pictured as the eternal speaking of the Word. The Logos, or spoken-forth Word, is the formed and found essence; the act of speaking is not that which has been spoken. The speaking has as yet no essence, for essentiality means for Boehme comprehensibility. The will is not yet the known Word. In the *Ungrund* then is the center of eternal nature where

> the eternal speaking word brings itself into a generation and also makes itself . . . a speaking Word. (*Myst. Mag.* ii, 7)

God was the Word which He spoke Himself. The act of speaking, *Verbum Fiat*, is also the spoken, *Verbum Domini*, the Word which creates where nothing was (*Myst. Mag.*, iii, 8). The formed Word is Christ; the speaking is the Father; and Boehme contrasts God's heavenly words with the halting momentary verbosity of man. Only prophets understand God's language (*Bedenk. Stief.* 84) and self-will prevents full understanding in ordinary men.

This eternal will is also designated as freedom, a drive to introduce the nothing into something so that the will may find, feel, and behold itself (*Sig. Rer.* ii, 6). The craving is not the freedom.

> The eternal divine understanding is a free will, not arisen from anything or by anything; it is its own peculiar seat, and dwells only and alone in itself, unapprehended of anything; for beyond and without it is the nothing, and that same nothing is only One; and yet it is also a nothing to itself. It is the one only will of the Abyss, and it is neither near nor far off, neither high nor low; but it is an all, and yet is nothing. (*Myst. Mag.* xxix, 1)

The eternal will is the first of two dialectical forces inherent in the *Ungrund,* the will-to-be, the *sich-in-sich-selbst-fassen.*

The second tendency latent in the *Ungrund* constitutes the third spirit of God—the tendency of the will to draw in upon itself in self-subjectivation, the yielding, propitiating, loving will which "tinctures" the harsh assertive Father will.[12] If the all were one then it could not be revealed for there would not be anything to which it might be revealed. (*Myst. Mag.* iv, 29)

The One, as the Yes, is pure power and life, and is the truth of God, or God Himself. He would in Himself be unknowable, and in Him would be no joy of elevation, nor feeling, without the No. The No is the counterstroke of the Yes, or the Truth, in order that the Truth may be manifest and a something, in which there may be a *contrarium,* in which the eternal love may be loving, feeling, willing, and such as can be loved. (*Theos. Frag.* iii, 2)

The process of begetting, imagining, seeing, speaking, mirroring (or however the Incomprehensible's self-discovery be named) results in the discovery of comprehensible forms; it is the discovery of consciousness.

The unfathomable will, i.e. the indiscoverable One, by its eternal discovery goes forth, and brings itself into an internal intuition of itself. Thus the unfathomable will is called Eternal Father, and the will that is found, grasped, and brought forth by the *Ungrund* is called His begotten or only Son, for it is the *Ens* of the *Ungrund,* whereby the *Ungrund* apprehends itself in a ground. (*Gnad.* i, 5–6)

This begetting is described by several images: mirroring, and eternal speaking:

It is the Father that speaks it, and the Word which is spoken out of the center of the Father is the Son thereof; and seeing the Father in His center calls Himself a consuming fire, and yet the Son (His Word) is a light of Love, Humility, Meekness, Purity, and Holiness. (*Dreyfach.* i, 40)

Three basic figures of speech are used: father-son, speaker-word, fire-light. These are not ultimate, however; Boehme is looking behind the images.

> The Father . . . generates out of Himself a second will, which in the first eternal will . . . opens the principle of light, in which the Father . . . becomes amiable, friendly, mild, pure, and gentle; and so the Father is not the source of darkness; for the recomprehended will which goes forth out of the center, and dispels the darkness, is His Heart, and dwells in itself, and enkindles the Father . . . and is rightly another person; for He dwells in the Father's essences in Himself, and is the Light of the Father; and His Word (or will) has created all things. (*Dreyfach.* i, 53)

The metaphor is immaterial. The Son has an illuminating function with regard to the Father's darkness.

Boehme's knowledge seems to go beyond the limits of language and his faltering use of metaphors attests to the failure of language to express his thought rather than to the paucity of his vision. He found words inadequate, especially the traditional terms of theology, and he forged new words to describe divine action:

> The Son is the first will's humility, and in His turn desires powerfully the Father's will, for without the Father He would be a nothing. And He is rightly called the Father's longing, or desire, for the manifestation of powers, viz. of the Father's taste, smell, feeling, and seeing. (*Gnad.* i, 23)

Here dialectic holds Father and Son together: a paternal will to be and a filial will to submit. (Cf. the fifth and sixth spirits of God, *infra*) The *Ungrund*, God unknown both to Himself and to creature, begets a will to be which begets the Son where the outgoing will turns back upon the Father. This is a picture of the divine self-consciousness. After this outgoing will finds itself in the Son it returns into the *Ungrund* of mysterious incomprehensibility to propitiate the wrath.

The Son is a person other than the Father, for He is the Light-world, yet dwells in the Father, and the Father begets Him in His will. He is truly the Father's Love, as well as wonder, counsel, and power (*Kraft*), for the Father begets

Him in His imagination, in Himself, and leads Him forth through His own fire, through the principle, through death, so that the Son makes and is in the Father another world or another principle than the fire-world in the darkness. (*Menschw.* II, iii, 11)

Here at the depths where the Trinity is generated the two embryonic forces of the *Ungrund* have divided into two forces leading to God's self-consciousness on the one hand and to His self-manifestation on the other. The Son as the instrument of divine self-consciousness returns to the Father's hidden depths, bringing light therein; as the instrument of self-manifestation, the center of being, He goes out to creation:

Accordingly, this outgoing is a ray of the power of God, as a moving life of the Deity, in which the unfathomable will has brought itself into a ground. (*Gnad.* i, 13)

The dialectic of Yes and No has thus produced a God of wrath and love, but the God who seeks to be known has not yet come to be. Nor is there a creature to know Him. He has become what we would call a personal God because He is now conscious of Himself, but to manifest His Power he has to go beyond self-consciousness. So the fourth spirit of God, or the third person in the usual Trinity, appears as the instrument of God's efflux (as Boehme says) or emanation. Already in the *Aurora* he had said:

The third diversity, or the third person in . . . God, is the moving Spirit, which exists for the rising of the terror or crack when life is generated, which now moves in all powers, and is the spirit of life. (xxiii, 25)

This was written before he had found the *Ungrund*.

Boehme's God, then, brims over into creativity for the *Ungrund's* driving will for a ground creates the instrumentality of its creativity, the Holy Spirit.

He is the Spirit . . . of God, and has not its original in nature, but is the first will to nature; yet he gets his sharpness in nature; and therefore He is the former and framer in nature . . . He is the bringer forth, the conductor, and the director; also the destroyer of malice and wickedness, and the opener of the hidden mysteries; he existed in the Father from eternity, without beginning: for the Father, without Him, would only be an eternal stillness, without essence. He is the essence of the will . . . out of which air rises. (*Dreyfach* iv, 77)

(This too was written before he had discovered the *Ungrund*.) Air is the first analogy of primitive minds.

God needs to become Spirit to manifest and realize Himself. So the Holy Spirit is the instrument but not the substance of creation, the tool that moves out into the void, creating, sustaining, fashioning, and forming. Spirit likens known with unknown, Source and End, Alpha and Omega. He is the work-master of the world's birth (*Aurora* xiii, 77), the creator of the all (*Dreyfach* viii, 72), the fashioner and former of all nature (*Dreyfach* iv, 77), the opener of nature's divinity (*Dreyfach* iv, 84). He dwells in man's soul (*Aurora*, preface 88) where He is born of will (*Menschw.* II, x, 11) and is responsible for the original, essential spirit of man. The Holy Spirit is also the creative force which drives man by anxiety to a new birth (*Menschw.* I, x, 1), leading to repentance (*Busse* i, 21), creating the courage to be humble and meek (*Complex.*). And at the end of time the Holy Spirit will move to fill the world, bringing it into conformity with God's will (*Seel. Frag.* xx, 11). All these figures are functions of God related to something beyond His self-conscious life.

The Father is the power . . . and the Son is the Light and the splendor of the Father and the Holy Spirit is the moving or exit (*Ausgang*) out of the powers of the Father, and of the Son, and forms, figures, and images all . . . and moves or acts, forms of frames, and images all that is in this world. (*Aurora*, vii, 42, 43)

This is the *Aurora*. In a mature work Boehme wrote:

The Holy Spirit is therefore called Holy and a flame of

Love, because He is the emanating power from the Father and the Son, viz., the moving life in the first will of the Father, and in the second will of the Son, in His Power; and because He is a shaper, worker, and leader in the emanated joy of the Father, and the Son in Wisdom. (*Gnad.* i, 24)

The Holy Spirit completes Boehme's trinity but three other "spirits" of God emerge in the process of generating the self-conscious, manifested God. His fifth spirit is the theogonic hypostatization of the tendency of the many to be encompassed within the One (*Taf. to Epist.* xlvii, 5). This is God's self-conscious transcendence and generally corresponds to the centripetal force of Plotinus,[13] the ἐπιστροφή, and it is the dialectical counterpart of the sixth spirit of God.

The *Ungrund* is the all and the no-thing. This is an antinomy, giving rise to dialectic. The *Ungrund* is "nothing and yet is everything" (*Gnad.* i, x). Now, the fifth spirit is the negating, self-appropriating, ingoing to the center which results in a God who from the creature's point of view acts in His own interests or as a "wrathful" God. This return is the Nay-saying, the wrath emerging from a self-conscious God, the darkness with Him.

And yet it cannot be said that Yes is separated from the No, and that they are two things. . . . Without these two, which are in perpetual conflict, all things would stand still without movement. This same is to be understood regarding the eternal unity of the divine power. . . . If receivability is to arise, there must be a special will to receivability which is not identical with nor wills with the one will. For the one will wills only the one good, which it . . . itself is; it wills only itself in similarity. But the emanated will wills dissimilarity, in order that it may be distinguished from similarity and be its own something, in order that there may be something in which the eternal seeing may see and feel. And from the special individual will arises the No, for it brings itself into ownness, that is, into receptivity of self. It desires to be a something, and does not make itself one with the unity. For the unity is an emanating Yes . . . being insentient; for it has nothing in which it can feel itself save in the receptivity of the differing will, as in the No which is a counterstroke of the Yes, in which the Yes is revealed, and in which it has a something that it can will. (*Theos. Frag.* iii, 3–5)

The Yes and No are not wills, that is persons, but tendencies and drives:

And the No is therefore called No, because it is a desire turned inwards, as shutting into negativity. And the Yes is therefore called Yes, because it is an eternal efflux or outgoing and the ground of all beings, that is, truth only. For it has no No before it; but the No first arises in the emanated will of receivability. (*Theos. Frag.* iii, 10)

This abiding-in-self, as Schleiermacher called it, is God's self-consciousness and is

Intrahent, and comprehends itself in itself, and from it come forms and properties. The first property is the sharpness, from which comes hardness, coldness, dryness, and darkness. . . . The second property is true feeling, as between the hardness and the motion, in which the will feels itself. . . . And in accordance therewith God is called an angry jealous God and a consuming fire; not according to what He is in Himself independent of all receivability, but in accordance with the eternal principle of fire. And in the darkness is understood the foundation of hell, as an oblivion of the Good; which darkness is entirely concealed in the Light, like night in the day, as may be read in John i, 58. (*Theos. Frag.* iii, 11)

The wrath is the No that returns from the found, discovered, and comprehended Son into the unknown hiddenness of the transcendent Father; it is God's self-consciousness, to draw His Self in again and contemplate in His mysterious self-interest. In *Beschau.* Boehme suggests Scriptural basis for this In and Out within God, his fifth and sixth spirits of God:

In John i, 11–13 it stands written: 'He [Jesus Christ] came to his own and his own received him not. But as many as received him, to them he gave power to become children of God, even to them that believe on his name; which were born, not of blood, nor of the will of the flesh, nor of the will of man, but of God.' The valuable ground of divine manifestation lies in these words—the eternal In and Out. For they speak of how the hidden, divine eternal Word—the divine mighty in unity—receded to its ownness out of the manifested, natural, creaturely Word. (iv, 1)

This "In" is the tendency to unity in the Godhead for in spite of his threeness He still is One:

When you are told about three persons in the Deity, and about the divine will, know that the Lord our God is one God only. (*Gnad.* i, 25)

One will therefore subsumes three persons and three functions, and the *Drang* to unity is Boehme's fifth spirit of God.

The sixth spirit of God, as already mentioned, is the movement of the unity towards manifoldness. Generally it corresponds to the Plotinian centrifugal force, πρόοδος,[14] and is the affirming, "loving" outgoing of the one will.

This outgoing is a ray of the power of God, as a moving life of the Deity, in which the unfathomable will has brought itself into a ground. (*Gnad.* i, 13)

This basic determination of the no-thing to become things, of a will to be, becomes the basis of creative activity.

From this holy fire has emanated the Yes, as a ray of the perceptible unity. This ray is the precious name *Jesus*, which had to redeem the poor soul from the wrath; and in assuming humanity, introduced itself into the soul, into the dissident central fire-wrath of God's anger, and kindled the soul again with the fire of love and united it with God. . . . In God there is no anger, there is pure Love alone. But the foundation, through which Love becomes mobile, is the fire of anger, though in God it is only a cause of joy and power. On the other hand, in the center of the wrath-fire it is the greatest and most terrible darkness, pain and torment. These two (the Yes and the No) are in one another like day and night, where neither can take hold of the other, but one dwells in the other. And they make two eternal beginnings. The first beginning is called the kingdom of God's wrath, or the foundation of hell wherein dwell the expelled spirits. The foundation of the Kingdom of God is pure Yes, as powers of the separable Word. And the foundation of the wrath of God is pure No, whence lies have their origin. . . . This emanated holy fire, when it was yet operative throughout the earth, was Paradise. And it is Paradise still, but man has been expelled from it. (*Theos. Frag.* iii, 6–7)

Yes is the movement out to manifestation in creation. This leads to Boehme's seventh spirit of God, which in many ways is his most characteristic idea—that of Wisdom, or as he called it, the Virgin Sophia.

When Boehme discovered his *Ungrund* as a dark deep of indeterminate Being he also came to understand that such a deep stood in dialectical contrast to the rich fullness on which all created things are mirrored.

Wisdom is the receptacle in which God's eternal will seeks, sees, and finds itself.

A one has nothing in itself that it can will, unless it double itself that it may be a two; neither can it feel itself in oneness, but in twoness it feels itself. (*Theos. Frag.* iii, 6–7)

One must become two before comprehensibility and consciousness are possible. The eye sees its image in the mirror —the mirror being the reflecting receptacle. Instead of having the One and nonbeing as the poles of his emanation, like Plotinus, Boehme's God had the *Ungrund* and Sophia, or Wisdom, co-operating to generate the world of things. The *Ungrund* makes a counterstroke so that the related dialectical processes of self-knowledge and self-projection may take place.

Boehme found the idea of Wisdom in the Wisdom literature of Scripture, in the Wisdom of Solomon [15] and Proverbs, and in the Cabala, although the ultimate source of the world-soul is Plato's *Timaeus* and the Plotinian world-soul.

Sophia is the image of God (*Seel. Frag.* i, 205) by which and in which the *Ungrund* can know itself; she is the body of God, the perceptibility of God in which the world's manifold differentiated powers are contained, the essential power of God's Love from which things get existence, the core of God's active Love, God's throne of Grace in man, the mediation between God and creature, the mirror in which the eternal will has seen a preview of all creation, the mother of all things (of Christ and of reborn souls), and the bride of man's soul. With Sophia man can enter into erotic union.

Sophia is the likeness of the Trinity (*Dreyfach.* v, 41), the likeness of God (*Ibid.*), a likeness according to the Deity and Eternity (*Menschw.* I, ix, 7), the image's framing of itself (*Gnad.* i, 16), the pattern of God's spirit (*I Apol. Tilk.*, 64), a figure in the mirror of God's Wisdom (*Menschw.* I, ix, 6).

Wisdom, as God's mirror, possesses the means by which He can come to self-consciousness. He sees His self projected against Himself. Seer, mirror, and image are God. The act of self-contemplation is also the act of self-revelation and differentiation, and He creates an antithetical counterstroke of His undifferentiated Deep to see Himself.

> The eternal wisdom . . . resembles the eternal eye without essence. . . . It is not essential, as in a mirror the brightness is not essential . . . for no seeing is without spirit; neither any spirit is without seeing. . . . Seeing shines forth from the spirit, and is its eye or mirror, wherein the will is revealed. . . . Seeing makes a will, as the *Ungrund* of the Deep without number knows to find no ground nor limit; hence its mirror goes into itself and makes a ground in itself. (*Theos. Punkt.* i, 11–12)

Again, the Father

> reveals the Word in the mirror of Wisdom, so that the three-fold nature of the Deity becomes manifest in Wisdom. (*Menschw.* II, ii, 12)

Secondly, wisdom is *Gegenwurf*, counterstroke (*Beschau.* iii, 6). Here Boehme's theory of knowledge is implied. God's image, created by His self-consciousness and self-projection, is the image of all things in which creatures know, revealing the fullness of His being, an instrument by which He unveils His inward depths and myriad forms to the world and to man.

Thirdly, Wisdom is the discovered (*das Gefundene*), that which is intuited. If the begetting of the Son is the comprehension of His being, then Wisdom is the comprehension of this veiled form in visible image.

Eternal Wisdom is the begotten being, as a mirror and ornament of the Holy Trinity, in which the powers, colors, and virtues of God become revealed, and in which the Spirit of God has seen all things from eternity. (*Bedenk. Stief.*, ii, 30)

Discovering His own dark nature God is born as a living image—that which has been born from within.

Wisdom is the emanated (*das Ausgeflossene*) which makes the hidden life visible, a matrix in which the Word has become formed.

Wisdom is the egressed (*das Ausgegangene*), the form in which the inner trinitarian life comprehends itself and then projects itself.

What has gone forth from the will, love, and life is the wisdom of God, that is the divine intuition and joy of the unity of God, whereby the love eternally introduces itself into powers, colors, wonders, and virtues. (*Theos. Frag.* ii, 1ff)

Wisdom is the exhaled (*das Ausgehauchte*), the breathed forth.

as an out-breathing or manifestation; and this egress from the will in the speaking or breathing is the spirit of the Deity, or the third person, as the ancients have called it. And that which is outbreathed is wisdom . . . which it . . . conceives to a life's center or heart, for its habitation. (*Myst. Mag.* vii, 8, 9)

Allied to this description is that of Wisdom as the articulated (*das Ausgesprochene*). The mute God strives to frame Himself as Word, the framed, spoken Word is the Son, the Word's articulation is the Spirit, and the articulated in which the hidden God comes from silence to hearable form is Wisdom.

The egress from the generation is the spirit of the formed Word and that which is spoken forth is the power, colors, and virtue of the Deity, viz. the Wisdom. (*Myst. Mag.* vii, 10)

Wisdom as the articulated is one of the commonest expressions in Boehme (*Princ.* xxii, 25; *Dreyfach* v, 40, 41)

Now how does the traditional trinity fit this scheme? Does Boehme have four "persons" as his critics claimed? His three-in-one God has a secretive life in Himself; but He also has a knowable life in which He steps out to form the world after His image and by which He may be known, for Wisdom is God's body (*II Apol. Tilke,* 57), the chest or container of God (*Kasten Gottes*) (*II Apol. Tilke,* 67), the receptacle (*Menschw.* II, i, 10). Wisdom

is not a genetrix, neither itself reveals anything. . . . It is the house of the Holy Trinity, the ornament of the divine angelic world. (*Theos. Punkt.* I, i, 10)

Clavis presents an excellent picture of Wisdom:

The Holy Scripture says . . . Wisdom is the breathing of the divine power . . ; it also says, God made all things by His Wisdom, which we understand as follows: the Wisdom is the outflown Word of the divine power, virtue, knowledge, and holiness; a subject and resemblance of the infinite and unsearchable unity; a substance wherein the Holy Ghost works, forms, and models; I mean, He forms and models the divine understanding in the Wisdom; for the Wisdom is . . . passive and the spirit of God is . . . active. . . . In her powers, colors, and virtues are made manifest; in her is the variation of the power and the virtue. . . . She is the divine vision wherein the unity is manifest. She is the true divine chaos wherein all things lie, . . a divine imagination. (19ff)[15]

Wisdom is the passive principle in the Godhead and so is feminine. But she is also "virgin" because she contains but does not beget (*Theos. Punkt.* I, i, 62). As the world of ideas she is far more vital than the Plotinian static νοῦς. The Plotinian emanation was not dialectical and the One was not a person, thus safeguarding theism at the price of a self-conscious, personal God. Boehme's Wisdom was needed to make God in Trinity self-conscious. Surely, some equivalent of Wisdom, or world-soul, is still today, as it was with Plato and Plotinus, the alternative to materialism.

Thus did Boehme think about God, seeking to maintain the active, personal considerate God of his experience. His idea of the seven spirits of God is Biblical, coming from Revelation i, 4 and commanding as much interest as Tertullian's legal conception of *persona*. Boehme elevates Plato's world-soul to the mystical theogony and it becomes the dialectical counterpart of Eckhart's *Abgrund* and of the Hindu Brahman. And Boehme maintains the overtones of Luther's distinction between the God of Revelation and the God of mystery.

Several problems emerge. First, the problem of the divine Being as such involving generation of a triune God from unity—theogony. Secondly, the relation of the triune God to creation—theodicy. Thirdly, the problem of life conceived as interplay of Yes and No—dialectic. By elevation of these problems to one plane in his seven spirits of God Boehme suggests a relationship.

On the trinitarian problem Boehme adds depth in that the *Ungrund* becomes separated from the Father; this saves him from pantheism. The problem of creation is that of the archetypes of finite beings, the world of forms. Boehme here is a full-blown Platonist. The problem of dialectics emerged from his sunrise to eternity and was the core of all his thought. By combining these in one comprehensive system Boehme achieved his greatness.

The doctrine of the Trinity has really two postulates: that within unity is trinity and within trinity is unity—one substance, three persons. Sophia is the "one substance," the consubstantiality within the Trinity and so must be distinct from the three persons although unable to exist apart from them. Sophia belongs in hypostatic being and is related to each of the persons. A curious prejudice associated Sophia only with the Son, but this is untrinitarian. Sophia's relation to the Father is that of revelation. She lets Him come to self-knowledge and self-consciousness, disclosing His depths. Her relation to the Logos is that she cannot exist apart from her connection with the Logos. Logos is in-going, a return and a propitiation; Sophia is outgoing to creation and to man. Sophia is the ὀυσία with which the Spirit works and out of which He makes the created world.

Boehme's whole idea of God is construed with a view towards maintaining two precious divine attributes: his personality and his tender concern for the world. The antinomies that result are due to his stubborn desire to hold on to both. A dialectical God results, a God of two modes, a God of love and a God of wrath.

Here begins to appear Boehme's solution to the problem of evil. Evil is related to self-consciousness, to nay-saying, to mystery. He distinguishes between the God in self-contemplation and the God in action. Two cadences, passive and active, give a God of these two modes. And for Boehme evil is the rebellion of self-centered activity against the passive, unyielding, mysterious power of the self-contemplating God.

NOTES TO CHAPTER TWELVE

1. On meaning of dialectic in this special sense, Cf. André Lalande, *Vocabulaire technique et critique de la Philosophie*, Paris 1951, p. 227, sense f.
2. *Speeches on Religion*, London, 1893, p. 49.
3. *Ibid.*, p. 134.
4. *Ibid.*
5. *Aids to Reflection*, London, n.d. p. 294.
6. Coleridge held this to be definitive for mysticism as a whole, for a man elevates his own experiences as typical of all mankind. Cf. *op. cit.* Cf. further: I. A. Richards, *Coleridge on Imagination*, New York, 1935, p. 71.
7. *Aids to Reflection*, p. 293.
8. Cf. C. G. Jung, *The Integration of the Personality*, and *Psychology and the Unconscious*.
9. Seven has a long history in folklore and other areas. *Vide:* W. H. Rascher, *Die Sieben- und Neunzehn in Kultus und Mythus der Griechen*, Leipzig, 1904.
10. The distinction between the divine nothing and the nothingness from which all has been made and of which nothing proceeds must be maintained. The latter is nonbeing, the former beyond being. Nonbeing is rational; superior being irrational.
11. Cf. Schleiermacher, *The Christian Faith*, p. 8: "Life is to be conceived as an alternation between an abiding-in-self (*In-*

sichbleiben) and a passing-beyond-self (*aussichheraustreten*) on the part of the subject."

12. Boehme's Christology has three modes: the eternal birth, the birth of the natural Logos, and the birth of Jesus from Mary. Only the first belongs to theogony. Boehme asserts that the first birth is unknowable (*Aurora* xviii, 23).

13. *Vide*: E. Zeller, *Die Philosophie der Griechen*, III, 2, Leipzig, 1881, p. 47ff.

14. *Ibid.*, p. 300ff.

15. The Scriptural passage is the seventh chapter of the Wisdom of Solomon which was included in the Lutheran Bible: "For she is a breath of the power of God, and a clear effluence of the glory of the Almighty; therefore can nothing defiled find entrance into her. For she is an effulgence from everlasting light, and an unspotted mirror of the working of God, and an image of His goodness. And she, being one, has power to do all things; and remaining in herself, renews all things; and from generation to generation passing into men's souls she makes men friends of God and prophets. For nothing does God love save that which dwells in wisdom. For she is fairer than the sun, and above all the constellations of the stars; being compared with light, she is found to be before it; for the light of day succeeds night, but against wisdom does not prevail."

Flower in the crannied wall,
I pluck you out of the crannies;—
Hold you here, root and all, in my hand.
Little Flower—but if I could understand
What you are, root and all, and all in all,
I should know what God and man is.

—TENNYSON

CHAPTER THIRTEEN

ETERNAL NATURE

WISDOM is the central aspect of God's self-manifestation in a threefold sense: first, theogonically, as His revelation of His self to Himself; secondly, theodocially, as His revelation of His self in creation; thirdly, regeneratively, as His revelation of His Self as Grace.

The second is Wisdom's creative function as a living being with a body having organic life. To escape pantheism, which holds that the world is God's body (thus implying the eternity of the world and making God responsible for the evil within it) one must give God His own body. Only with this idealism can materialism be avoided. A God having a life and body apart from the world transcends it. Here the opposite danger of deism appears and it is possible to shut Him up in impenetrable transcendence. Only an organic, creating, sustaining God with separate consciousness will be theistic, a πᾶν ἐν θεῷ.

Wisdom conceived as the instrumentality of God's self-manifestation is Boehme's solution to the problem of the relationship of God to the world. Wisdom is the revealeress (*die Offenbarin*) (*Menschw.* I, i, 12), the revelation of God's unity (*Taf.* 19), the revelation of life (*Menschw.* II, 1, 10), the unknown God's desire for revelation (*Gnad.* i, 9), and for self-manifestation (*Myst. Mag.*, vii, 6). She makes the triune God clear (*Menschw.* II, ii, 3), opening up the divine wonders (*Princ.* iv, 88), revealing the wonders of the divine element (*Princ.* xxii, 26), lighting up the Godhead's dark depths (*Dreyfach* xi, 15), becoming the figure in which God's wonders are known (*Dreyfach.* xi, 137), revealing the heavens and the divine wonders (*Princ.* xxii, 71).

These functions express Wisdom's functions; and, as Boehme conceived Sophia as feminine, his doctrine of God was therefore androgynous. Sophia, female divine principle, passively bears what the fatherly will seeks. This relationship is boldly expressed erotically in the old terms of bride mysticism:

Wisdom is the bride and the children of Christ are in Wisdom also God's brides. (*II Apol. Tilke* 73)

(In German soul is feminine; hence no difficulty arises.) He further says:

The Virgin is visible like a pure Spirit, and the Element is her body . . . the holy earth . . . and into this the invisible deity is entered . . . that the deity is in the pure element and the element is in the deity; for God and the element . . . are become one thing, not in spirit, but in substance. (*Princ.* xxii, 72ff)

The Father's love for Wisdom, for Himself, is His desire which brings self-realization, comprehensibility, and the ultimate embracing of the form thus revealed (*Gnad.* i, 9). Wisdom is the suffering, female, maternal, generating aspect in which the representation, revelation, and procreation of the Deity is perfected.

All things spring out of the eternal mother; and as she is in her own birth, so she has generated this world, and so every living creature is generated. (*Princ.* v, i, 2)

In this matrix God moves himself to creation (*Princ.* vi, 24).

In this first act of self-realization there is as yet no breaking of the unity. Opposition has not yet come, only self-knowledge. There is neither strife nor tension, only what Boehme called "love-play," harmony. So Wisdom is "virgin," a term often repeated. Virginity means that tension between God's active and passive principles has not yet produced creatures. There is dialectic, yes, but no procreation. Wisdom still mirrors God's image:

> She is a virgin and never generates anything, neither takes anything into her; her inclination stands in the Holy Spirit, which goes forth from God, and attracts nothing to Him, but moves before God. (*Princ.* xiv, 87)

The image is born without separation; she is God's image in which He glimpses Himself as spirit, seeing into the unfathomable deep (*Theos. Punkt.* I, i, 24).

Boehme was, of course, a vitalist and all creatures partook of a single vital center (*vis vitalis*) which alone accounts for their existence. An agent of separation is needed by which things were carved out. This is the Platonic demiourgos or, as Boehme called it, Archaeus (*Beschau.* ii, 11), or Separator (*Test.* II, 3, 19). When life's irreducible nature is granted and a vital center posited, this vital center can become identified with God. To avoid such pantheism the vital center is separated from divine being. God is spiritual, the world is partly material. Nor can the world simply be the object (*Gegenwurf*) of God. Boehme makes Wisdom the object both of God and of the world, thus avoiding pantheism in its true sense.

This is suggested from Boehme's anthropomorphic symbolism, the notion of macrocosm and microcosm. An androgynous God prefigures an androgynous man. The creative process is described in an important passage in *Menschw.*

> The nothing causalizes the will so that it becomes desireful, and the process of desire is a mode of imagination, as the will beholds itself in the mirror of Wisdom. . . . The mirror remains eternally a virgin without bringing forth, but the will becomes impregnate with the aspect of the mirror. . . . The will is Father, and the impregnation . . . is heart or Son . . . and proceeds from the will in the ground into the Virgin Wisdom. Thus the will's imagination, viz. the Father, draws the mirror's vision or form . . . into itself, and thus becomes pregnant with the splendor of wisdom . . .

This arises in the will and seizes itself in the center of the heart. . . . For the will . . . with the movement of the Spirit speaks forth power into the mirror of wisdom. . . . And with the speaking forth the spirit proceeds from the will, from the word . . . of God . . , into what is spoken forth, viz. into the mirror, and reveals the word of life in the mirror of wisdom, so that the threefold nature of the Deity becomes manifest in Wisdom. Thus, we recognize an eternal, unfathomable divine essence, and in its nature three persons, whereof one is not the other. (II, ii, 1–4)

These words partly describe Wisdom's revealing function. Revelation perfects itself not in the One's self-sufficiency in self-contemplation but in that the One leads itself into separate opposition to itself. First, Wisdom creates a fruitful self-realization of God's inner life; life's unity realizes itself in multiplicity; unity of knowing in multiplicity of knowing; voluntaristic unity in plurality of wills. As counterstroke Wisdom is beginning of separation, making fruitful manifestation of individual forms possible in God; she is the first principle of differentiation in which God glimpses potential variations of being.

This image makes the will of the Eternal One separable; it is the separability of the will from which powers and qualities arise. (*Beschau.* iii, 5)

Further unfoldings lead the One into ever new separations:

These powers are an efflux of themselves, each power bringing itself into individual wills. . . . From thence arises the multiplicity of wills, and from this also the creaturely life of eternity has taken its origin. . . . And yet it cannot be said that by this . . . a creation is understood, but the eternal imaged existence of the divine word and will . . . has . . . sported with himself in the formation of similitude. . . . The outgoing of the one will of God has . . . introduced itself into separability, and the separation has introduced itself into receptibility . . . passing out of the unity into plurality. Desire is the ground and beginning of the nature of the perceptibility of the particular will. For therein is the separability of the unity brought into the separability of self-hood. . . . For the will of the eternal One is imperceptible, without tendency towards anything; for it has nothing towards which it could tend, save only towards itself. Therefore it brings itself out of itself, and carries the efflux out of its unity into plurality, and into assumption of self-hood . . . from which qualities take their rise. For every quality has its own separator and maker within it, and is in itself entire, according to the quality of the eternal unity. Thus the separator of each will develops in turn qualities from itself, from which the infinite plurality arises, through which the eternal One makes itself perceptible, not according to the unity, but according to the efflux of the unity. (*Beschau.* iii, 7–11)

This first separation is not yet the beginning of dialectic but only God's discovery of His plurality. Structural dialectic appears only when free spiritual man has rebelled against God. The original separation comes through Wisdom and is the point of departure for the creation of separated representations of God's inner plurality in visible forms. The first Fall—Satan's altercation—disturbs the will's unity by self-hood. Only by this act in which a creature made in God's image seeks to put himself at being's center does dialectic arise.

Boehme's world is neither creature nor God's body nor the object of God. Nor is it cut off from life's center. Boehme avoided both pantheism and gnosticism. Life is a mystery, a paradoxical reality, the source of which is God.

God's self-knowledge and self-revelation perfect themselves in a *Blick*, a lightning-flash of divine imagination. This *Blick* is the central creative act unlocking the inner secrets of the great mystery.

The point of departure is the view that the *Ungrund* is an eye that "sees" itself in a mirror (*Theos. Punkt.* I, i, 7). The nonseeing divine darkness becomes seeing in a flashing glance of self-contemplation in which God sees himself. He simultaneously achieves self-consciousness and manifestation.

From such a revelation of powers, in which the will of the eternal One contemplates itself, flows the understanding and the knowledge of the something (*Ichts*), as the eternal contemplates itself in the something and in wisdom introduces itself into . . . a likeness and image. (*Beschau*. iii, 4)

Boehme's *Realdialektik* now begins to emerge, and one of his most startling ideographs appears, the view of the divine separation in fire which came to him from alchemy.

In the enkindling of the fire lies the entire ground of all mystery. . . . [In it] the spirit of God becomes moving, in the manner that air rises from fire.

Light is an old symbol which plays a large role in ancient metaphysics, especially Philo. God was light, and this separation was visualized as a breaking of the light into many rays. But Boehme's God is light only as far as He is spirit. Light demands fire, for fire is light's root (*Myst. Mag.* xxvi, 28). Light stands for the Son and the Son's begetter must be fire; indeed Scripture calls Him a consuming fire, a fire that never consumes itself nor exhausts itself. Like life fire synthesizes opposites:

Thus the two genetrixes, that of the wrath in fire and that of love in light, have brought their form into wisdom, where then the heart of God longed in the love to make this mirrored form into an angelic image, composed of the divine essence, so that they should be a likeness and an image of the Deity. (*Menschw.* I, ii, 4)

Fire produces light only when it is burning; to burn there must be matter, stuff. This primitive figure is Boehme's way of describing the burning, driving source at life's center comparable to the modern *libido*. Yet fire is not in itself ultimate.

Fire is the life of all principles—understand, the cause of life, not the life itself. (*Theos. Punkt.* ii, 10–12)

To burn fire needs fuel, something to consume.

Fire . . . cannot subsist without substance; therefore its hunger is after substance. (*Theos. Punkt.*, i, 27)

Wrathful fire engenders amiable light and destroys matter by changing it into spirit. This is the mystery. For Boehme fire was life.

When we consider what life is, we find that it consists mainly in three elements, viz. desire, the disposition, and the thinking. If we investigate further . . . we find the center of the essential wheel, which contains within it the fire-smith himself. (*Menschw.* II, iii, 7)

The results of this metaphor-symbol are many. If God has a burning center then He has matter which burns; fire needs fuel. Now where does God's fuel come from?

The principle of fire is the root, and it grows in the root. It has in its *proprium* sour, bitter, fierceness, and anguish, and these grow in the *proprium* in poison and death into the anguishable stern life, which in itself gives darkness, owing to the drawing in of the harshness. (*Theos. Punkt.* ii, 38)

Its properties are sulphur, mercury, and salt, symbols of alchemy's three principles. The dark matter, root, or *proprium*, is diaphanous and luminous in so far as it is penetrated by and "vanquished" by light. The burning matter is God's dark inchoate body; but the fire is filled by light.

In the eternal nature there are not more than two principles: . . the eternal burning fire, which is filled with light. . . . The fire takes to itself the fire's property, viz. life and self-discovery. And the second principle is understood in the light; but the essential substantiality from which the fire burns remains eternally a darkness and a source of wrath. . . . We see that fire is a thing other than that from which the fire burns. (*Menschw.* II, iii, 179)

Fire or burning the dark matter makes wrath and the wrath's propitiation. Here is destruction and birth, death and pro-creation.
So fire has a destructive calcinating force, a poisonous life (*das böse Leben, das giftige Leben*) opposed to pure being, to the amiable light before God. Like light the poisonous life is produced by fire sharing the source which is a *coinci-*

dentia oppositorum, a source which bifurcates into two principles.

In the end, however, fire is only an "illuminating" symbol
of life's source, of the deepest mystery. Boehme was no fire-
worshiper and the role he gave to fire went beyond anything
that the alchemists held.

The dark world and the light world, wrath and love, the
self-in-self-contemplation and the self-in-self-projection form
the Yes and No which become the bases of manifold forms.
The self-conscious God begets a hunger; the self-acting God
begets being in all its manifold variety. Here then are two
centers: a center of desire which makes a natural center and
a center of the will which produces God's trinity. In the
will there is a "birth" to desire and a "birth" to freedom.

So when Wisdom begins to manifest God's inner richness
the distinction between freedom and desire emerges. The
being of the Absolute (if such a formal word may be applied
to Boehme's God) forms itself into two contradictory centers, that of freedom and that of desire. Desire opposes will
in two ways. First, will in essence is movement and expan-
sion, a wanting to give itself. The will is then generous and
giving;

> The gentleness gives and the fire takes. The gentleness is
> emanent from itself, and gives a substance that is like itself
> . . . and the fire swallows this up, but out of it produces
> light. It gives something nobler than it has swallowed up—
> gives spirit for substance—for it swallows up the gentle
> beneficence. . . . Understand the meaning right: God the
> Father is in Himself the freedom out of nature, but makes
> Himself manifest by fire in nature. The nature of fire is His
> property, though He is in Himself the *Ungrund* where there
> is no feeling nor any pain . . . and draws for Himself . . .
> another will to go out . . . again into the freedom beyond
> pain. This other will is His Son. . . . It is this other will
> which breaks down death as the stern, dark source, which
> kindles fire and proceeds through fire . . . and fills the
> primal will which is called Father. . . . Therefore it can
> dwell in freedom, that is in the Father's will, and make the
> Father bright, clear, gracious, and friendly. . . . It is the
> Father's substantiality, it fills the Father everywhere.
> (*Menschw.* II, v, 6–7)

Desire, hunger for self, opposes the other will which is begotten in pain and suffering; it is hunger which seeks self-satisfaction, a thirst which seeks to be quenched, a sight that would be fulfilled—sensual images which for Boehme are indicative of a deeper meaning. The free will expands, desire draws in.

Desire has nothing that it is able to make or to conceive. It conceives only itself, and impresses itself, that is it coagulates itself, and draws itself to itself, and comprehends itself, and brings itself from Abyss to Byss, and overshadows itself with its magnetical attraction; so that the nothing is filled, and yet remains a nothing. (*Myst. Mag.* iii, 5)

Will is centrifugal, desire centripetal:

God . . . can desire nothing in Himself and therefore He brings Himself out of Himself into a divisibility, into a center, in order that a contrariety may arise in the emanation, viz. in that which has emanated, that good may in the evil become perceptible, effectual, and capable of will; namely, to will and separate itself from the evil and to re-will to enter into the one will of God. (*Ird. u. himl. Myst.* i, x, 14ff)

Desire

is the stern attraction, and yet has nothing but itself or the eternally without foundation. And it draws magically, viz., in its own desiring into a substance. (*Ird. u. himl. Myst.*, iv, 2)

The will tends to posit being in order to give itself to others, to manifest itself in them; desire seeks to possess others to nourish its own being. If the Absolute is the no-thing and the All then desire and freedom are but logical realizations of these ideas. There is one curious aspect, that while the will tends to posit being it is incapable of doing so, for the function of creation belongs to desire, as nature's all.

Desire's dialectical evolution corresponds to that of the will except that it is reversed. The evolutionary cycle is less pure and less rich because desire's life is frustrated. Will is spirit-vision; desire is passion (*Treib, Streben*) obscured by self-consciousness.

Desire is only an hungry will, and it is the natural spirit in its forms. . . . God is without desire as concerning His own essence . . . for He needs nothing. All is His, and He Himself is all. (*Sig. Rer.*, vi, 2)

Desire is the instinctive life which to reveal itself parts from itself and prolongs its life in the spirit. In spirit, not in itself, desire becomes self-conscious, or more exactly that spirit becomes conscious of its own desire. Spirit, however, reveals itself to itself. Both stand together, need each other, imply each other.

If there were but one will, then all essence would do but one thing: but in the counter will each exalts itself in itself to its victory and exaltation. And all life and vegetation stands in this context, and thereby the divine wisdom is made manifest, and comes into form to contemplation, and to the kingdom of joy; for in the conquest is joy (*in der Ueberwindung ist Freude*). But only one will is not manifest in itself, for there is neither evil nor good in it, neither joy nor sorrow; and if there were, yet the one, viz. the only will, must first in itself bring itself into a contrary, that it might manifest itself. (*Myst. Mag.* xl, 8)

Pure desire is incomplete and meaningless. Desire is always for something that can sustain it. Ever seeking to be something, it remains a nothing, perhaps even meonic. As it can find nothing it draws back into itself, tormenting itself. This is Boehme's *Angst*, a significant and powerful conception.

Each thing elevates itself, and would get out of the combat into the still rest . . . and only awakens the combat. . . . In the light of nature there is no better help and remedy for this opposition. . . . Now every taste desires only its like, and if it obtains it, then its hunger is satisfied, appeased, and eased, and it ceases to hunger, and rejoices in itself. (*Sig. Rer.*, ii, 4-5)

The self that aspires for itself kills itself: in willing itself the will limits itself; in desiring itself the will consumes itself. This is the heart of Boehme's dialectic. The ultimate threat is that desire, unless checked by freedom, brings death.

Real life is then struggle and, thankfully, victory. But the truth is that death is the root of life for the threat of death presses in upon life:

> Life proceeds out of death, and death must therefore be a cause of life. Else were there no such poisonous, fierce, fervent source fire could not be generated, and there could be no essence . . ; hence there would be no light, and also no finding of life. (*Theos. Punkt.* i, 68)

Sin is not death; rather, it results from desire, from self-will, from the death that is inherent in desire. Being is a continuing victory, and eternal life the final victory. The central fire is

> the only cause of life and motion of all powers; and without it all would be in the stillness without motion. (*Myst. Mag.* x, 43)

So death begets life.

Life and death, light and darkness, Yes and No, freedom and desire, good and evil! By opposing each other a third is produced, a generative process which reason cannot comprehend but which must be grasped by intuitive intelligence. Discursive reason (*Vernunft*) abstracts, and these abstractions are unreal because by abstracting the life-process is halted. Life is movement which must be grasped by an intuitive intelligence (*Verstand*) comprehending the entire process as well as the act of knowing. In intuitive intelligence no one phase opposes another; each implies the other.

> That cannot enter into particular existence which has no ground, which cannot be apprehended, which dwells in itself and possesses itself; but it proceeds out of itself, and manifests itself out of itself. (*Theos. Punkt.* vi, 7)

Divisibility, manifestation in particular existential forms— these cannot exist alone. Indeed, they need more (*Sig. Rer.*

xiv, 9). In fire all opposites coincide and it is *Verstand* which knows these while *Vernunft* can know only abstractions. True knowing is of the coincidence of opposites. Discovery of the eternal no-thing in which God beholds Himself is God's Wisdom or intuitive understanding (*Gnad.* i, 6), His self-conspection (*Gnad.* ii, 8).

Why does the Absolute thus develop itself? It emerges from the coincidentarious source to become spirit, master of nature and of life. From the primal separation in the *Blick* body results; body is life's concomitant (*Sig. Rer.* iii, 18). To escape death inherent in the fire, life is born as the realization of all the germinal possibilities within the *Ungrund.* (*Theos. Punkt.* i, 64)

> In fire there is death: the eternal nothing dies in the fire; and from the dying comes the holy life. Not that there is a dying, but that life as love arises in this way from the painfulness. The nothing or the unity thus takes an eternal life into itself, so that it becomes sentient, but proceeds again out of the fire into the nothing. (*Gnad.* ii, 32)

Whenever Boehme describes the generation of the supersensual life he must talk of it in cyclic terms. The free will desires; desire is an embryonic will. They oppose, and this opposition gives cyclic movement, life.

> We understand . . . how the light world fills the eternal freedom, or the primal will, which is called Father. . . . We understand also here earnestly and fundamentally how the natural life that wishes to dwell in the light-flaming world, must pass through death and be born out of death. (*Gnad.* iii, 6ff).

This life or movement from unconsciousness to full self-consciousness, a poised tension between life and death with final victory for life in Christ, takes place in man's mind and being.

This is drama, cosmic drama. The formless seeks form but in the movement to form there comes a moment when it is confronted with death. Then it struggles to avoid death by reconciling form (personality) with death. But in Christ, we shall later learn, life is victorious.

Spirit engenders itself in natural form. This proposition is important. In such engendering spirit finds that by getting a "body" it has introduced death into its being. All Boehme's images—from alchemy, folklore, mysticism, and the Bible— were meant to explain this vast struggle which he found in his world, in his self, and in his God.

Divine nature, or God's body, is what the dark unfathomable will is striving towards. Life can only be in body. Abstraction is not life. Life, the Unconditioned's search for conditioned form, the formless's effort to manifest its inherent potentialities, demands some body. This "body" is in Boehme's sense self-consciousness, form, personality, comprehensibility, and such as can be known, felt, willed, and loved. Apart from the chaotic *Ungrund* all essences are conditioned.

When the eternal will has found "bodily" form it has discovered a life of tension and dialectic. This cannot be endured. A new goal emerges—redemption, search for life in which death has been overcome. So another life-cycle begins, another birth is sought. The theogonic struggle is to get form; with it formal limitation is acquired. Now a life-cycle begins within a dialectical existence which looks forward to final removal of formal limitations, to a new birth in a new body.

Here Boehme's break with Neoplatonism is clear. He accepts emanation from the One. But he denies that return is regeneration. If the many were to return to the One salvation would be partial, for death would not have been overcome. Salvation is no retreat back into the primal ground of being, no escape back to *Nirvana,* thus dodging corporeal existence's meonic limitations, but it is, rather, full redemption by surmounting these limitations. His goal was individual form in which meonic trends have been destroyed. Oriental mystics, distrusting individuality, sought to surmount it in the abyss of being; they wanted a freedom from the self. Boehme advanced to a Kingdom where there is a first and a last, where spirits sat down to eat and drink with a risen Lord, where bodies were without death's darksome mystery, where Saint Cecilia plays her lute for the infant Jesus! Boehme, in distinction from Neoplatonic and oriental mystics and in full accord with Western cherishing of personality, sought freedom *for* the self to become a perfect self. He was one mystic who did not want to get rid of his self, only of his sinful self.

As he sat at his writing table he saw in the candle before him on its holder the cycle of all life. The candle had tallow, wax, and wick. Then there was the mysterious fire, the strange separator. Finally there was an unseen world of smoke, gas, air—tallow in a new birth! As the tallow burned it became liquid, then gas; this was life: congealed matter being changed into heavenly matter.

> See in a burning candle, when the fire . . . consumes. . . . There the substance dies, that is in the dying of the darkness it is transformed in the fire into a spirit and into another quality. . . . With the . . . fire the being of the candle passes into the consuming process, into a painful motion in life; and as the result . . . becomes light and shining in a large room. (*Gnad.* ii, 15)

Fire, agent of transformation, shows a process similar to alchemical transmutation which prefigures the redemptive life.

Within being there is hunger for manifestation, and, as no generation takes place without dialectic, Boehme creates his seven natural principles to explain this process. These seven natural principles are not the seven spirits of God (and this needs emphasis because so many Boehme students have mistakenly identified them):

> I have written . . . of the forms of nature. . . . It must not be understood as if the Deity were circumscribed . . . I write only of the properties, how God has manifested Himself through the internal, and through the external nature. . . . These seven properties can be found in all things; . . . In the internal world [they make] the Holy Element. (*Myst. Mag.* vii, 17–19)

These seven natural forms (*Gestalten*) show themselves as the breathing forth, circumscribing, forming, and bringing forth of the Deity into properties.

The circumscribing is the *Fiat*. . . . The desire is the beginning. . . . The whole ground is contained in the passage where it is said God created by the Word. The Word remains in God, and with the *scientia* or desire proceeds out of itself into division. . . . It is the beginning of nature. (*Gnad.* iii, 2)

How this comes about is described in a long and important passage from *Myst. Mag.* in which Boehme's nonconceptual imagery is clear. (Inasmuch as Boehme's views of the seven natural principles changed considerably as he matured, *Myst. Mag.* appears the best of his statements of this doctrine.)

The desire proceeding from the will . . . is the first form, and it is the *Fiat*, or *Let there be*. . . .
The first property is . . . astringent, harsh, impressing, self-conceiving, self-overshadowing; and it makes, first the great darkness . . ; secondly, it makes itself substantial in a spiritual manner, wholly rough, harsh, hard, thick, and is the cause of coldness, and all keenness and sharpness; also of all whatsoever is called essence; and it is the beginning of perceivancy . . . and introduces the contemplation into itself. But the desire in itself brings itself thereby into pain. . . .
The second form or property is the constringency or attraction of the desire; that is, a compunction stirring or motion. . . . Here arises the first enmity between the astringency or hardness . . . or sting of stirring; . . . The desire makes hard, thick, and congeals. . . . Thus the astringency is a mere cold rawness, and the compunction, viz. the attraction, is yet brought forth with the impression. It is even here as father and son; the father would be still; the son stirs the father and causes unquietness. . . .
The third property is the anguish . . . or welling forth, which the first two properties make. . . . In the contrition of the hardness the first sense of feeling does arise, and is the beginning of the essences; for it is the severation . . . in the word of the powers; each power becomes severable and sensible in itself. It is the origin of distinction, whereby the powers are, each in itself, mutually manifest; also the origin of the sense of the eternal mind. For the eternal mind is the all-essential power of the Deity; but the senses arise through nature with the motion in the division of the differentiation of the powers; where each power does perceive and feel

itself in itself. It is also the origin of taste and smell. . . .
Therefore the divine understanding brings itself into spiritual
properties, that it might be manifest to itself. . . . Now we
are to consider the working anguish in its own generation
and peculiar property; for just as there is a mind . . . in the
Word of the power of God, so likewise the first will to the
desire brings itself . . . into a mind. . . .

The fourth form of nature is the enkindling of the fire,
where the sensitive and intellective life does first arise, and
the hidden God manifests Himself: For without nature He is
hidden to all creatures, but in the eternal and temporal
nature He is perceived and manifest . . . by the awakening
of the powers. . . . The true life is first manifest in the
fourth form. (*Myst. Mag.* iii, 8ff)

Boehme warns us to

attend and mark aright! I understand here . . . the eternal
not the temporal nature. . . . Therefore do not foist in or
allege calves, cows, or oxen, as it is the course of irrational
reason to do. (*Myst. Mag.* iii, 20)

His point is that life is produced in trinitarian structure, that
matter, stars, and man are trichotomous.

These principles, acting dialectically, move to the separation in the fire, the purifier and the separator. Fire is the
source of all life (*Sig. Rer.* xiv, 23–34).

The fifth form is light, the triumphant kingdom of God's
great love (*Myst. Mag.* vi, 18):

The fifth form . . . is the true love-fire, which separates
itself in the light from the painful fire, and therein the
divine Love in being is understood. For the powers separate
in the fire terror, and become desirous in themselves. In this
form is also understood every characteristic of the first three
forms, yet no longer in pain, but in joy; and in their hunger
or desire. . . . The fifth form has all the powers of the
divine wisdom in it. It is the root-stalk of eternal life. . . .
It is called the power of the glory of God. . . . By means of
this power all things grow, blossom, and yield their fruit.
(*Gnad.* iii, 26ff)

The sixth form . . . is speech, namely the mouth of God,
the sound of the powers, where the Holy Spirit in the love

comprehension brings itself manifestly out of the comprehended powers . . . So there is a sensual effectual speaking
of the divine powers . . . by this is understood the five
senses, namely, spiritual hearing, seeing, smelling, tasting,
and feeling, where the manifestation of the powers work
together unitedly . . . as we see in a concert of music, how
all the melody . . . is united together. Further we understand in the sixth form the true meaning of the thoughts or
percipient senses. For when the spirit has brought itself out
of the (separated) qualities, it is in the temperament again.
(*Gnad.* iii, 31, 33)

The seventh form is . . . where the sound of the speaking word embodies itself in being, as an entity in which the
sound . . . embodies itself for manifest utterance. . . . This
seventh form is a comprehensibility of all the qualities, and
is properly called the whole of nature, or the formed, expressed Word. It is the inner, divine, uncreated heaven, but
stands connected with the divine active birth of the temperament; and is called Paradise, as a growing life of the comprehended working divine powers. (*Gnad.* iii, 37–38)

It is the sabbath within reality in

which the working power of the divine power rests. . . . It
is the true image of God, wherein God has perpetually fashioned Himself from eternity into an eternal being. (*Gnad.*
iii, 39)

Boehme's description of the life-cycle in terms of seven
natural powers came from the ancient astronomers who

have given names to the seven planets according to the
seven forms of nature; but they have understood thereby
another thing, not only the seven stars, but the sevenfold
properties in the generation of the essences. (*Sig. Rer.* ix, 8)

His reference is to the surviving Gnostic systems which
placed the planets in the following order: Jupiter, Saturn,
Mars, Sol, Venus, Mercury, Luna. Much of Boehme's abstruse
symbolism comes to clear light when this point is remembered. Furthermore, these seven forms are like the seven
days; the seventh is a day of rest (*Gnad.* iii, 39).

Each form contains the six others within it (*Myst. Mag.*

vi, 24) and all seven are found within all things (*Ibid.*, vii, 68), even in God's name ADONAI (*Theos. Frag.* ii, 10). Superimposed upon these seven forms of nature is another pattern: the first four together make the world's hellish principle while the last three form a divine element (*Dreyfach* ii, 50).

Here then is Boehme's life-cycle which moves through seven forms to a kind of being in which flesh has been transmuted. These forms are his life-cycle, but the shapes of individual beings are ruled by the angels. Boehme gave to angels a peculiar role, naively conceiving of them as having a beginning in the divine center and as arising with the Trinity's "birth" (*Myst. Mag.* viii, 1). They really are what we would call the formed individualized ideas of God in His wisdom. Originally they existed in two principles only and were created from the first principle (*Princ.* iv, 67), being of light's matrix.

They are the essence of both the inner internal fires. Their powers are the great emanating names of God. All have sprung from the Yes and have been led into the No, in order that powers might become manifest. (*Theos. Frag.* iv, 14)

Angels are the formed powers of God's Word, His outspeaking (*Theos. Frag.* vi, 5), His thoughts (*Theos. Frag.* vi, 5).

Now, what is angelic form?

As man is created to be the image and similitude of God, so also are the angels, for they are the brethren of men. (*Aurora*, v, 2)

Having human-like form

every angel is created in the seventh quality . . . out of which his body is compacted . . . for the body is the . . . compacted spirit of nature. (*Aurora* xiii, 33, 35)

They have hands, feet (*Aurora* xii, 78, 83), mouths and an aperture for breathing (*Aurora* vi, 10), no teeth or wings (*Aurora* vi, 17: xii, 84), nor limbs (*Aurora* vi, 12). They eat

paradisaical fruit (*Aurora* vi, 17) of the divine power (*Princ.* iv, 68) of God's Word (*Princ.* iv, 5).
Angels help God to rule the world.

God or the eternal unity rules all things through . . . angels. The power . . . is God's, but they are His instruments whereby He disports and moves Himself, and by and through which He reveals the eternal powers and wonders. (*Theos. Frag.* vi, 7)

Angels are God's wonder-workers, fashioners and shapers of His powers:

What angels will and desire is by their imagination brought into shape and form, which forms are pure ideas. . . . The divine powers have shaped themselves into such ideas before the creation of angels. (*Theos. Frag.* vi, 7)

Numbering a thousand times ten thousand (*Princ.* xv, 3), they are unequal in rank, ranged in three realms and seven dominions:

There are seven high dominions in three hierarchies . . . according to the seven properties of nature. Every form of . . . eternal nature has . . . a throne . . . wherein distinctions are understood as well as the will to obedience to the holder of the throne. This dominion they have under their administration as creatures of divine endowments. (*Gnad.* iv, 24–25)

Thrones are like the three principles. Each throne has seven princely hierarchies (*Gnad.* iv, 25). As free angels they have the possibility of falling. Before Lucifer's fall they were able to imagine themselves into the world of matter.

Each angelic realm is ruled by a prince: Lucifer, Michael, Uriel. Of these Lucifer was the most beautiful of all heavenly creatures (*Aurora* xiii, 31) ruling the second kingdom. Angels as such do not fall, but humble themselves before God's great majesty so that the eternal No may not get dominion over them.

Now, what is a principle—this idea that plays so large a

part in Boehme's views of eternal nature? In Boehme's view a principle is an abstraction which is conceivable only in terms of discursive reason. It does not appear to intuitive understanding.

A principle is a life (*Princ.* v, 9), an existence which has become what it was not, a thing which has sprung from a no-thing (*Menschw.* I, v, 9). For when life and movement appear where previously none existed, there is a principle (*Theos. Punkt.* ii, 1) which has only one spirit, one central life, one will (*Seel. Frag.* i, 30).

Boehme saw three principles, three worlds (*II Apol. Tilke,* 40). These three worlds make up the threefold emanation of divine being, deriving from three sources.

God is the essence of all essences, wherein there are two essences in one, . . the eternal light . . . and the eternal darkness. . . . These are the two principles, the original of which we know nothing of, only we know the birth, the indissoluble bond. (*Princ.* iv, 30)

From Lucifer's fall the third principle came.

These . . . three . . . are the one God in His wonderful works, who has manifested Himself by this world. . . . We are to understand a threefold being, of three worlds in one another. (*Theos. Punkt.* ii, 32)

These three principles are each other's cause. (*Gnad.* vi, 6)
The third principle which has come is the world of substance, matter, the world of men, of beasts, and of things (*Princ.* vii). It emerges from the first two principles.

The four elements are a principle of another property, and have another light . . . the sun. But in the pure element the things of this world are only as a figure. (*Dreyfach* v, 116)
The third principle comes from the power of the essences, and has its beginning from the power of fire and light . . . which is the *Mysterium Magnum* wherein all things lie. . . . And it is to be understood that the *Mysterium Magnum* is in itself good, and no trace of evil is to be found in it; but in its process of unfolding . . . it becomes a *contrarium* of qualities. (*Gnad.* viii, 7–8)

The great mystery has come out of wisdom; in it God has
seen the forms of the creatures (*Menschw.* I, i, 12), and He
created it so He might be manifested in matter (*Princ.* v, 16)
in seven days, giving angels dominion over it (*Gnad.* iv, 10).
This third principle is still growing

and therein are . . . created from what is inward the stars
and elements, which . . . together with the sun are called
the third principle. For the two inward worlds . . . the fire-
world and the light-world, have manifested themselves by
the third principle; and all is mixed together, good and evil,
love and enmity, life and death. To every life there is death
and fire; also, contrariwise, a desire of love, all according to
the property of the internal world. And two kinds of fruit
grow therefrom, evil and good; and each fruit has both
properties. They show themselves . . . in every life in this
world, so that wrath and . . . evil . . . are always fighting
against love, each property seeking and bearing fruit. What
the good makes, the evil destroys; what the evil makes, the
good destroys. For it is perpetual war and contention . . .
each bears and produces fruit . . . each will be lord. . . .
The external principle is . . . perpetual war and contention,
a building and a breaking. . . . In this struggle . . . growth
rises: . . one draws out of the earth its fruitfulness, the
other destroys . . . again. In all animals it causes . . .
strife; for all animals, and all the life of this world, except
man, is only a fruit of the third principle. . . . And all that
moves in the world, and man by his spirit and visible body
in flesh and blood, is only the fruit of the same essence, and
nothing else at all. (*Theos. Punkt.* i, 48ff)

Here, then, is Boehme's dynamic vision of a living, contending world in which all things are made up of Yes and
No. He saw that the world moved by this opposition and he
believed that only a surrendered humble understanding
could know eternal nature; rational reason could not do this
because, assertive and arrogant, it sought to resolve antinomies and paradoxes. His metaphysics and logic, if such it
may be called, were founded on paradox; he was a dialectical
idealist. Yes and No oppose each other and by opposition
define and condition one another, "bear" each other. The
Yes is strong affirmation, the No is suppression. God too has

Yes and No though from a creature's point of view He is
God only in His Love (*Theos. Frag.* ii, 12ff)

Dialectic, holding that one form implies another, that being moves by opposition, is Boehme's basic metaphysics. As
the formed Word is spoken forth four stages are to be understood: the unexpressed, unconscious ground, the act of speaking, the meaning, and the spoken Word. These are the four
steps in the process of spirit becoming flesh; the chaotic
source, the act of embodiment, the embodied self-consciousness, and the totality of manifested being or Wisdom.
Boehme's eternal nature was essential to his theology and it
saved him from materialist pantheism:

> God's love would not have been manifest without the
> eternal nature, that is, because the fire of love would not
> have been manifest without the fire of wrath. (*Gnad.* vii, 26)

Boehme's trinitarian structure which dominates his theology came from his mystical insight. Yet trinity was only
half of his idea of God. He held as firmly to God's unshatter-
able unity in His transcendence:

> We Christians say that God is threefold, but only one on
> essence. But that we generally say . . . that God is three-
> fold in person, the same is . . . wrongfully . . . understood
> by the ignorant, yea, by a great part of the learned. . . . He
> is threefold in His eternal generation. He begets Himself
> in trinity; and yet there is but one essence . . . to be under-
> stood in this eternal generation, neither Father, Son, nor
> Spirit, but one eternal life, of God. (*Myst. Mag.* vii, 5, 11, 2)

It became increasingly difficult for him to hold his doctrine
of three persons; he held that God is only person in Christ
(*Myst. Mag.* vii, 5). This vision is partly heterodox but must
be understood in the light of his conception of the meaning
of "person."

Here then is Boehme's threefold eternal nature, a world
of dialectic, manifested in a created world of strife and evil
which is, apart from the mysterious deep of God and from
the material world we know, an eternal nature.

Die Schöpfung, itzt am Ziel,
Harret, schweigt noch!—Ihr Gefühl
Wandelt in sich, und vermisst,
Was Geschöpf und Schöpfer ist;
Suchet einen, der mit Geist
Schmeckt und, was er ist, genuesst,
Suchet, der mit Gottesblick
Alle Schöpfung strahlt zurück!
                        —HERDER

CHAPTER FOURTEEN

TEMPORAL NATURE

BOEHME's understanding of creation, his entire cosmological speculation, found its start in Scripture's opening sentence: In the beginning God created heaven and earth. The key words are "heaven" and "earth" (*Myst. Mag.* x, 47). He had difficulty in conceiving of a world in which good struggles with evil as compatible with God's goodness. The act of world-creation was no problem for him: it happened when Lucifer fell (*Myst. Mag.* xii, 10). Heaven had existed even before the earth was. Basing his vision on the Biblical distinction between heaven and earth he postulated two creative acts: creation of heaven and its angels, creation of the earth and its beasts. Psalm civ gives Boehme the clue when it calls the angels flames of fire.

The term flames of fire denotes the central fire of the eternal nature, in which the creatures . . . stand, as the particular will of a being. But when God would realize his idea in the form of living creature, as in the form of self-will, He put in motion and separated the central fire in eternal nature. Thus the idea became manifest in the fire, which was accomplished through the breathing forth of the Yes. Thus the No, as the emanated will of self-receptiveness, took shape in the outbreathed Yes, in order that the creature might be

established in its own will. And thus its own will is understood in the central fire, that is, in the properties of the fire,
in which the creaturely life consists. For if this had not been,
then Lucifer could not in self-will have broken himself off
from the Good, and have fallen. If he had not possessed a
volition of his own, then God's power must have fallen. But
in this way the creature has broken off from the good and
willed to rule in the power and in the properties of the
central fire of nature, i.e. in the sphere of transmutation and
phantasy; to which the Devil likewise came. (*Theos. Frag.*
v, 2–6)

Creation began because the hidden God sought to manifest
Himself in all ways. The God who is a nothing which seeks
to become a something, who is known and who wants to be
known—this God has not yet gotten His will until a created
being loves Him. Only then does God come to completion,
become a God. So the created world represents a determined
(*sui generis*) mode of being which is essential to divine wisdom, to God's effective self-realization:

For all things are risen from the eternal spirit, as a likeness
of the eternal . . . which is God and the Eternity, has in its
own desire introduced itself into time, so that He is a life
in the time, and the time is in Him as it were dead. (*Sig. Rer.*
xiii, 2)

Commenting on the six days of creation, Boehme admits that
it is the

greatest mystery, wholly hidden from the external reason
. . . [for] there is neither night, morning, nor evening in the
deep above the moon; but a continued day from the beginning of the outward world even to the end of time.
(*Myst. Mag.* xii, 1)

Nevertheless, in six days God created the world's six categories (*Myst. Mag.* xii, 33).

We are to understand by creation . . . that the *Verbum
Fiat* has amassed the spiritual birth, and introduced itself
into a visible dominion and essence. (*Myst. Mag.* xii, 34)

The resulting world with its separate creatures is a figure-ment of the inner world. Internal characterizes external; spiritual manifests itself in body, clothes itself in form. (*Sig. Rer.* ix, 11)

Boehme was seeking to reconcile his religious intuitions with the metaphysics of his nature philosophy; he did this with his doctrine of signatures:

The whole outward, visible world with all its being is a signature or figure of the inward spiritual world; whatever is internally, and however its operation is, so likewise it has its outward character. (*Sig. Rer.* ix, 1)

What, then, is creation? For Boehme creation is *ex nihilo* but in a sense that is far from the traditional: the nothing is the no-thing, the *Ungrund.* Creation is a metaphysical separating.

It was the *mysterium magnum,* where all things stood in wisdom, in a spiritual form, in a wrestling spirit of love; not in the form of creaturely spirits, but in such a model that wisdom had thus . . . sported with itself. This model the one will has comprised in the Word, and suffered the attraction to work freely, so that every individual power . . . might be brought into a form according to its quality. Thus it is that the divine creative Word . . . has amassed into a compaction of powers. . . . As Moses says: in the beginning, i.e., in the inmassing of the *mysterium magnum,* God created the heavens and the earth, and said, let there arise all manner of creatures, each . . . according to his property. At the word *fiat* the great mystery became compacted into being, that is emerging out of the inward spiritual being into palpable tangible being, and in the compaction lay the attraction belonging to life, and that in two propria,[1] viz. a mental and an ental one. That is (1) a truly living proprium springing from the ground of eternity, and which is rooted in the wisdom of the Word, and (2) a proprium budding forth from the being's own desire as generated in itself, and which forms the growth wherein the vegetative life stands. Through this mysterium the *quinta essentia,* viz. the ens of the Word, originally became manifest and essential, and to it all the three principles were suspended. And here the ens has separated—what is spiritual passing into spiritual beings, and what is inert into inert senseless beings, as are earth, stones, metal, and the material matter. (*Gnad.* iv, 12–15.)

All things proceed from one "mother" and creation is separation (*Sig. Rer.* iv, 1) into mortal and immortal, life and death, spirit and body. At creation

the whole essence of eternity moved itself . . . and the whole form was enkindled and stirred, and that in the desire of manifestation; and there the generation divided itself into the flagrant of the enkindled fire into four parts, viz., fire, water, and earth, and the air is its moving, egressive spirit. (*Sig. Rer.* iv, 2)[2]

No new thing came from the earth's creation because God is not a maker in the objective sense (*Myst. Mag.* xix, 27).

Creation . . . is . . . a manifestation of the all-essential, unsearchable God; all whatever He is in His eternal unbeginning, generation, and dominion, of that is also the creation, but not in omnipotence and power, but like an apple which grows upon the tree, which is not the tree itself, but grows from the power of the tree; even so all things are sprung forth out of the divine desire, and created into an essence, where in the beginning there was no such essence present, but only the same mystery of the eternal generation, in which there has been an eternal perfection. . . . For God has not brought forth the creation that He should thereby be perfect but for His own manifestation, viz., for the great joy and glory. (*Sig. Rer.* iv, 1–2)

In Wisdom God imagined the world to show Himself and the product is the result of His self-desiring. Eternal nature generates rocks and hills and elements; creation is therefore indirect; God first imagined astral forces; these astral forces made the tangible world. Creation is therefore reproductive, self-continuing. God first created the heavenly world and after Lucifer's fall the earth; thus Boehme's fire-world and light-world combine to produce our world. Creation originates in God's desire for manifestation (*Irrth. Stief.* 43), a desire already formed in Wisdom. He created all things out of the no-thing which He Himself is (*Sig. Rer.* vi, 8) and creating the external world is the formulation of the seven natural powers.

Before the creation of creatures the "wonders and powers" were in an ideal world wherein the Spirit sported with himself (*Theos. Frag.* iv, 1). This was Wisdom, His image and counterstroke of the *Ungrund*. The two fires were as yet one fire with two principles in it and the third principle, matter, existing only as possibility. In creation the love-fire became the basis of heaven, and wrath fire of hell. At the word *fiat* substantial reality arose, yet before the *fiat* could take place an event had to happen, Lucifer's fall (*Dreyfach* v, 18; viii, 23):

When the central fire . . . moved itself, and brought itself into a more considerable desire . . . creation took place. This . . . God put into motion according to both fires. . . . In the course of this motion the hellish foundation of God's wrath broke forth, which God expelled from this working and shut up in darkness. There it remains . . . like a hungry maw full of craving after creation, and would also be creaturely and figurate. This is the cause . . . that Lucifer, the prince of a throne, turned away from God's Love to the central fire in God's wrath, in which he opined he was to rule over God's gentleness and Love. But on this account he was thrust from the central love fire . . . and now possesses hell. (*Theos. Frag.* iv, 3–5)

Lucifer's No, his receptivity to self-centeredness, which led him to put to proof the

property of eternal nature, and would not live in renunciation, but wished to rule in and with the Holy Name. . . . His creaturely will elevated itself . . . and abused the Holy Name in it. . . . He . . . broke off from the unity. He wished to rule over the Yes with the No, for the No had elevated itself in him and despised the Yes. (*Theos. Frag.* vii, 2–7)

Lucifer imagined himself into the dark matrix (*Dreyfach* ix, 38). He despised humility (*Gnad.* iv, 31) and, having a free will, became self-willed in fantasy (*Gnad.* iv, 29). He

fell because of his egocentric will (*Gnad.* iv, 32) which led
him to the fire's might (*Theos. Frag.* vii, 1–5) and, rebelling
against the meekness (*Myst. Mag.* x, 12), he wanted to
possess another principle (*Theos. Frag.* x, 3) and to act in
his own name.

So a new principle was made for him; he imagined himself into matter (*Gnad.* iv, 32). He was 'driven from heaven
into a new principle and the actual creation of this world
began (*Myst. Mag.* xiv, 17). He was locked out of the
first two principles (*Princ.* iv, 73) and a dwelling was made
in the darkness for him (*Menschw.* I, v, 21). Now he is the
prince of the world of fantasy (*Sig, Rer.* xvi, 15) and full of
pride, greed, envy, and wrath (*Aurora* xvi, 79ff). He lost his
bride, Wisdom (*Myst. Mag.* ix, 12), and he cannot become
an angel again (*Princ.* xvii, 66) because he lost the divine
names (*Theos. Frag.* viii, 9). From the loveliest of creatures
he became the most hideous.

These then are descriptions of Lucifer's rebellion and the
result—the first movement in nature (*Gnad.* vi, 12). God did
not plan the fall (*Myst. Mag.* ix, 3) but

created Lucifer for this harmony, to play with His Love-
spirit in Him, as upon the musical instrument of His manifested and formed Word; and this the self-will would not.
. . . How came that He would not? Yes, he knew well
enough; but he had no sensible perceivance of the Fall, but
only a bare knowledge. The fiery lubet, which was potent in
him, did egg him on, for it would . . . be manifest in the
essence of the wrath . . , in the root of fire. The darkness
also . . . desired to be creatural, which drew Lucifer. . . .
It drew him not from without. . . . The original of the Fall
was within the creature, and not without. . . . So it was
Adam also. Self-will was the beginning of pride. (*Myst. Mag.*
iv, 9ff)

Breaking away from God's unity

he was cast with his legions out of his throne, and immediately shut up by the darkness and had been grasped by
the fierce pride-wrath of the hellish foundation. (*Theos.
Frag.* xiii, 3)

Here the created world arose and on the first day of creation Lucifer was driven out (*Myst. Mag.* xii, 14) and on the third day he was locked in between time and eternity (*Myst. Mag.* xii, 35). This fall was followed by creation.

God spoke: *let there be light!* and there was light. And with this coming to be light, the Devil's might and strength was wholly withdrawn from him in the essence for here the light shone in the now awakened power, in the darkness; which light the prince of wrath could not comprehend: . . . It was the light of nature, which was useless to him. (*Myst. Mag.* xii, 14)

This Paracelsian light of nature was the quintessence of the other elements (*Princ.* vii, 7), the fiery tincture of the heavenly firmament (*Dreyfach* ix, 93). When God said *let there be light* the sun was created, the dialectical counterpart of Lucifer's darkness. Between Lucifer's darkness and this new light there was again a *contrarium* (*Gelassen.* ii, 10). So the first day's work separated light from darkness.

The darkness remained in the wrathful property, not only in the earth, but also in the whole deep; but in the light's nature the light of nature did arise . . . from the quintessence. (*Myst. Mag.* xii, 15ff)

All earthly materials were drawn together in one darkness and heavenly materials into one light. Between these natural dialectical forces life was produced.

Light is quintessence, the fifth element, source of the four natural elements (*Beschau.* iii, 21), the pure element (*Epist.* xx, 9). In it the Word became essentially manifest and in it all three principles were suspended (*Gnad.* iv, 15). This light of nature, from which the sun came, was in temperament, or in a state where love and wrath were mutually balanced (*Gnad.* viii, 29).

This natural light was freedom. Boehme understood that creation was more than making a planetary system; he also had to explain how freedom became impaled within the earth's four elements. The elemental earth came to be after Lucifer's fall as the by-product of the creating light (*Aurora* xvii, 9: xxi, 14). By making light he also made the dark. Earth is of no different essence than the stars; indeed, it is like the stars for whatever the natural light is spiritually, that the earth is in its coarseness (*Gnad.* v, 13). Earth became the third element, fire and light already existing. Boehme's four elements were created progressively: fire produced light, light air; fire also produced water and its ashes the earth.

The first day's work substantialized fire's polarities. Between these poles life was created. Freedom and desire thus were projected into the physical universe. Nature's light was made before earth. Here Boehme's solution—if such it be— to the problem of evil appears: the rough earth is a misdirection of freedom which permits light to be known. Goodness consists in order, in nature's subordination to spirit, of desire to will. Evil is the disorder, rebellion, perversion of making spirit nature's servant (*Sig. Rer.* xv, 14). Goodness is spirit victorious over earth's appetites.

On the second day of creation life and death were separated.

For there the light broke through the darkness, and made the dead body of nature to spring and flourish, and to be stirring and agile. (*Aurora* xix, 2)

The firmament which separates heavenly water from earthly waters was

the gulf between time and eternity, but that God called it heaven and makes a division of the waters, and gives us to understand that the heaven is in the world, and the world is not in heaven. (*Myst. Mag.* xii, 23)

The second day's work consisted in separating heaven from hell and separating the waters above the firmament from those below the firmament. God created

the firmament of heaven, viz. the strong enclosure to the darkness of the original matrix, that it might no more kindle itself, and generate earth and stones. And therefore He made the enclosure . . . out of the midst of the waters, which stays the might of the fire, and become the visible heaven, whence the creatures have proceeded, from whence now the elements fire, air, and water proceed. (*Princ.* viii, 9)

Boehme distinguishes internal, heavenly, sweet, spiritual water of life and light from elemental water. The water above the firmament is the water of eternal life (*I Apol. Tilke*, 259), akin to fire.

For light is also a fire, but a giving fire; for it gives itself to all things, and even in its giving there is life and being, i.e., air and spiritual water; and in this . . . water the love-fire of the light has its life, for it is the food of this light. (*Gnad.* ii, 29)

Spiritual water is the holy element from which the world and its four elements were brought into substantial form (*Myst. Mag.* vi, 5). In this spiritual water above the firmament God's spirit rules and reigns (*Myst. Mag.* x, 52), for it is Christ's body (*Myst. Mag.* x, 57). In this sweet, love-enkindling water (*Aurora* ix, 23) the Holy Spirit works in angels and men (*Myst. Mag.* xxii, 52; xxiv, 24). Through this spiritual water's power to break through death the new man and new world come (*Myst. Mag.* ix, 51).

The water below the firmament is an elemental earthy substance; a misty steam (*Sig. Rer.* iii, 23) which is a witness to the inner water's power (*Myst. Mag.* xiv, 70) and which came to be with Lucifer's fall (*Aurora* xiv, 21). Material water originates in the spiritual world (*Gnad.* iii, 24); without it fire cannot burn (*Myst. Mag.* xiv, 7) and within it the creatures live (*Princ.* xx, 53); from it bodies originate (*Aurora* i, 17). Holy water above the firmament is the dialectical counterpart of elemental water (*Myst. Mag.* xii, 24ff).

Outward water is the instrument of the inner . . . for the moving spirit in the Word is the water which rules the inner water of baptism. Dear Christians, let this be spoken unto you; this is the real ground. (*Myst. Mag.* xii, 26ff)

If the earth's regeneration is to follow, if the fallen elements are to be raised, the two waters must become separate in the final act of world-redemption; to do this they must have already been separated. So Boehme also has two heavens:

The outward heaven is passive, and the inward works through it, and draws forth an external fruit out of the outward; whereas the inward heaven lies hidden therein in the firmament, as God is hidden in time. (*Myst. Mag.* xii, 29)

On the third day God made life in the midst of death (*Aurora* xxiv, 41), by *fiat* dividing earthly waters so a dry place might emerge on which creatures might dwell. This dry earth grew verdant; life budded through dead matter; grass, herbs, trees, plants sprang forth.

Thus every essence became visible, and God manifested His manifold virtue with manifold herbs, plants, and trees, so that everyone that does look upon them, may see the external power, virtue, and wisdom of God therein. (*Princ.* viii, 9)

Paradise's verdant creation came as the originally perfect creation was distorted by Lucifer's fall.

For although many thousand . . . herbs stand one by another in one and the same meadow, and one of them is fairer . . . than the other, yet one of them does not grudge the form of another, but there is a pleasant refreshment in one another; so also there is a distinct variety in Paradise, where every creature has its greatest joy in the . . . beauty of another; and the eternal wisdom of God is without number and end. . . . You shall find no book wherein the divine wisdom may be more searched into . . . than when you walk in a flowery meadow, there you shall see, smell, and taste the wonderful power and virtue of God; though this be but a similitude, and the divine virtue in the third principle is become material, and God has manifested Himself in a similitude. But (this) is a loving schoolmaster to him that seeks. (*Princ.* viii, 12)

The third day's work was the moving life in the midst of the darksome earth's death.

Paradise meant for Boehme life sprouting from death

(*Menschw.* I, iv, 13). Paradise is budding through wrath, love coming from dead matter.

The holy element budded forth in the temperament through the four elements, and produced through the four elements heavenly fruit, which was pleasant to the sight and good for food, as Moses says. (*Gnad.* v, 9)

This Paradise, a holy fire which emanated from God (*Theos. Frag.* iii, 38), is a pleasurable, divine, joyous world without elemental strife, with no opposition and reaction, but only love-play (*I Apol. Tilke*, 131). The *Ungrund's* longing to be realized is fulfilled by Paradise which has no evil in it and is

where there is perfection, where there is . . . love, joy, and knowledge; where there is no misery; which . . . neither death nor the devil's touch, neither do they know it; and yet it has no wall of earth or stones about it, but there is a great gulf between paradise and this world. (*Princ.* ix, 7)

Paradise has its own peculiar substance and matter; it is transparent, glistening, composed of a bright, clear, visible substance (*Princ.* ix, 18).

The depth of this substance is without beginning or end, its breadth cannot be reached, there are neither years nor time, no cold nor heat, no moving of the air; no sun nor stars; no water nor fire; no sight of evil spirits; no knowledge nor apprehension of the affliction of this world; no stony rock nor earth; and yet a figured substance of all the creatures of this world. (*Princ.* ix, 21)

Before Lucifer's fall the world was all paradise (*Myst. Mag.* xxv, 16) but after this event it bloomed only in a small spot on earth (*Dreyfach* xi, 12), the Garden of Eden (*Myst. Mag.* xvii, 8). If nature is to be restored a small section of divine substance must remain within the otherwise corrupted earth.

On creation's fourth day God made the heavenly world of stars and planets. Already in 1612, two years after Kepler's views had been published, Boehme had revealed his Copernican views:

Some suppose that [the sun] runs about . . . the earth in a day and a night. . . . This . . . is not right. The earth rolls itself about; and runs with the other planets . . . around the sun. The earth does not remain . . . in one place, but in a year runs once about the sun. (*Aurora* xxv, 65ff).

With this fourth day the sidereal birth took place (*Aurora* xxii, 1). Boehme thus gave the world an external, sidereal, and internal birth (*Aurora,* xix, 32). Stars and planets were made from the light created on the third day (*Aurora* xxiv, 1), from the quintessence (*Princ.* viii, 8). Its source was the *Ungrund's* primitive fire, being realized in the natural center through the seven natural powers (*Dreyfach* vi, 44). Each planet had a special role in helping to sustain the created world (*Princ.* v, 10). The sun, though not nature's light (*Aurora* xviii, 125), is still the external world's ruling spirit (*Sig. Rer.* xii, 19) giving the stars their light (*Aurora* ii, 9), and taking Lucifer's place in energizing the world and so becoming the heart of the universe (*Dreyfach* ix, 25), the ruler and king of all nature (*Dreyfach* xl, 40), and the deity within the third principle (*Princ.* viii, 13–23):

Its rays kindle the . . . earth from which everything grows . . . whereby the magical fire is revealed. . . . Now as the power and rays disclose the mystery of the outer world, so that creatures and plants proceed from it; so, on the other hand, the mystery of the outer world is a cause by which the sun's rays are . . . enkindled. . . . But because the sun is nobler, and a degree deeper in nature, than the mystery of the outer world . . , it penetrates into the outer mystery and kindles it, and thus too kindles itself. (*Gnad.* ii, 23).

Being made of the quintessence of the sun helps to counter-act the earth's wrathful elements (*Princ.* xv, 9), enkindling sweet light in them and laying the foundation for eventual regeneration. The sun's vitality is also the universe's basic vitality (*Aurora* xxv, 38), originating the natural powers (*Aurora* xxvi, 12), propitiating wrath's fire and making all love and light (*Dreyfach* vi, 63). Through solar activity the

world's hidden mystery of forms and patterns becomes manifest within the substantial world (*Gnad.* viii, 13); from it things get life and substance; it is good to good things and evil to evil things (*Gnad.* viii, 13).
The sun generates the planets and stars which draw their vitality from it (*Gnad.* ii, 26).

We see . . . that the stars are so greedy and hungry for the sun's power that they introduce their desire . . . into the first three forms, and draw the sun's power into themselves. The sun . . . penetrates powerfully into the stars to receive their desire, so that they get their luster from the sun's power. (*Gnad.* ii, 26)

Each star has its own character (*Aurora* xxv, 25), and projects this individuality into the created world. By the stars good and evil become manifest (*Myst. Mag.* x, 6) in individual aspect (*Myst. Mag.* xiii, 8). As some stars are invisible, so many individual forms are not perceivable by the human mind (*Dreyfach* x, 38). Stars rule by the powers derived from the sun, from the quintessence which dominates the four elements. Stars awaken the dead elements and bring individuality into being (*Dreyfach* vii, 48).

Boehme gave special roles to the planets. His planets were Saturn, Jupiter, Mars, Venus, Mercury, Luna, and Sol. Each rules one of the seven natural powers, each planet being like its form. Saturn begets corporeality (*Aurora* xxvi, 2, 12) and has a dark wrathful quality; it is like the alchemist's lead (*Sig. Rer.* iv, 23). Jupiter is man's power to reason and to think (*Aurora* xxv, 107), begetting life in the divine vitality (*Aurora* xxvi, 17). It is the alchemist's tin (*Sig. Rer.* iv, 29). Mars is hunger, wrathfulness, anger (*Sig. Rer.* iv, 20), symbol of anxiety and gall, the alchemist's iron (*Sig. Rer.* iv, 37). Venus is mildness, humility, spiritual meekness (*Dreyfach* ix, 79), the propagative seed (*Sig. Rer.* iv, 21), the alchemist's copper (*Sig. Rer.* iv, 35, 36). Mercurius is God's active working Word which awakens the creature's life seed (*Clavis* 26); *Dreyfach* ix, 96), producing life and death and leading to the creative life-urge to spirit and essence (*Myst.*

Mag. xiv, 5). It is the active agent (*Sig. Rer.* iv, 30), the alchemist's quicksilver (*Sig. Rer.* iv, 30). Luna is the lustful (*Sig. Rer.* iv, 27) container of the created world's substances (*Sig. Rer.* iv, 27), the alchemist's silver. The sun is the world's perfection—pure gold.

By dominating their metals the planets rule the things which contain such metals, thus activating the earth and making it productive.

On the fifth day God commanded all manner of beasts to come forth, each after its own kind. Out of what were they to come forth? Out

of the matrix of the earth, that they might be of the essence of earth. . . . Now then if the beasts were merely out of a lump of earth, then they would eat earth, but seeing they are proceeded out of the matrix of the earth by the *Fiat*, therefore they also desire such food as the matrix affords out of its own essence; and that is not earth, but flesh. (*Princ.* viii, 38ff).

Each creature is a mode of divine revelation (*Irrth. Stief.,* 514) and

must remain in its place wherein it was apprehended in its creation and formed into an image, and not depart out of the same harmony. (*Sig. Rer.* xvi, 18)

Each creature is made after its own kind and

lives in its mother, whence it has taken its original. . . . It cannot live in another degree. As beasts upon the earth . . . therein they live; and thence they take their food and nourishment. . . . Birds were created in the sulphur of the air, therefore they fly in their mother; also the fishes in the sulphur of the water and the worms in the sulphur of the earth. Thus each thing lives in its mother whence it was taken, and the contrary is death. (*Myst. Mag.* iv, 19ff)

Individual characteristics come from the substantial origin, the outer emerges from the inner.

For we see that there are good and evil creatures, as

venomous beasts and worms . . . which desire to dwell only
in the dark and conceal themselves from the sun. In contrast
to them we find many creatures . . . fashioned from the
realm of phantasy, as . . . apes and such beasts and birds
as play monkey-tricks . . . We find . . . good friendly creatures. . . . By the food and dwelling of any animal we see
from whence it came; for every creature desires to dwell in
its mother and longs after her. (*Gnad.* v, 21ff)

What is this mother after which a creature longs? It is the
creature's formal character within the three principles. In the
first principle the mother is the fire's wrath; in the second
principle the mother is meek light; in the third principle
the mother is the sidereal world. For life each creature must
return to its mother, partake of its pure idea and become
attuned to its inner state of being.

Whatever idea dominates that is the mother to which the
creature must return. As each creature has a sidereal body
and an elemental body (*Myst. Mag.* xiv, 2) the sidereal
body's star is its mother. Not only does each earthly creature
come from this mother but it also seeks nourishment therefrom. This figure of speech means that creatures are nourished by their governing idea: a creature knows only the
mother that bore it (*Princ.* ii, 4); the mother only is eternal,
the creature temporal (*Aurora* xvi, 13).

The creatures, each made after its kind, are also in the
world of conflict, and the struggling, striving of creatures in
field and forest is witness to Lucifer's fall and to a corruption
within creation.

On the sixth day God, speaking the *Verbum Fiat*, said *Let
us make man!* From the mixture of elements and essences
already created God made an image to be like Himself to
have dominion over fish and fowl, over cattle and crawling
thing. God took of the heavenly element and of the earthly,
of all the constellations, degrees, and elements, and made a
twofold body for man—a spiritual and an elemental. The
spiritual body was God's image, clothed with the quintessence; the four elements were the corporeal body. Into these
God breathed a living soul, making a man of all three prin-

ciples (*Myst. Mag.* xv, 17) with a tripartite soul different
from that of Plato:

> And the soul . . . consists in three kingdoms: the first is
> . . . the dark and fire-world. . . . The second is the holy
> light world. . . . The third . . . is the outward astral and
> elemental kingdom. . . . (*Myst. Mag.* xv, 18ff).

Yet man does not have three souls, only one.

> And if this were not, then it could not be said, that the
> soul went to heaven or to hell, if it were not in it. . . . We
> are in no wise to think that the soul is God Himself. . . .
> But the soul is the . . . formed Word; it is the spirit and
> the life of the three principles of divine manifestation.
> (*Myst. Mag.* xv, 25)

The first man was the finest of God's creatures, creation's
secondary goal.

The first six days saw God creating all things. On the
seventh he gathered all the essences of the other six properties and made a seventh in which eternal day lies

> whence the days of time are proceeded; and the ancients
> have called it *Sonnabend;* but it is rightly called *Sönnabend*
> wherein God's Love does appear and atone the anger; as
> when the six properties . . . do enkindle themselves . . .
> they are atoned and reconciled in the seventh. . . . Thereof
> Moses speaks rightly, *God rested on the seventh day from
> all His works, and hallowed the seventh day.* (*Myst. Mag.*
> xvi, 20)

Rest has a special meaning. The divine vitality which entered
creation found itself conditioned by it. Each of the six powers
had come to be made up of contradictory manifestations.
This could not be tolerated; God drew contradictions back
into restful unity.

> This rest is the holy heaven . . . where time works in it-
> self, and sets forth for . . . the day of separation, where,
> at the end of the days of this world, evil shall be separated
> from the good, each thing shall possess its own heaven.
> (*Myst. Mag.* xvi, 25)

Departure into creaturely strife and disunity is not permanent; there is promise of a Sabbath at the end of time, a transparent glossy sea before God's throne (*Myst. Mag.* xvi, 27). This Sabbath is a promise of further divine activity when judgment shall be passed on all creation (*Seel. Frag.* xxx, 62).

Creation has proceeded from a *Quall,* which is Boehme's word for reality's dynamic center. A *Quall* is incomprehensible and irrational (*Seel. Frag.* i, 51), a particular source for each particular thing (*Myst. Mag.* viii, 20), the core of individuality (*Seel. Frag.* i, 52). Between this *Quall* and individual beings there lies a hierarchy, a pleroma which goes a long way towards answering but which does not finally solve the problem of creation. Like other theologians, including Plotinus, Boehme finds the gap between the One and the many unbridgeable. The two trends of his thought here emerge in basic conflict; his stubborn loyalty to God's goodness and his equally firm conviction of evil's recalcitrance. He could not admit that evil came from God; nor could he see how anything existed apart from God. His pleroma of causes only pushed his problem further into the background. God must realize Himself on all levels, yet some of the realized modes act contrary to His goodness. Boehme's solution, so characteristic of his mind, is the idea of the "divine within God," or "God so far as He is called God" (*Myst. Mag.* xxix, 9).

This is of course Boehme's permanent problem: why does God allow evil? His answer, the only seeming true answer, is to assert over and over again the goodness of God and the freedom of the human spirit (*Myst. Mag.* xxvi, 34). All his theology is founded on freedom; determined being is devilish (*Myst. Mag.* ix, 31). The only predestination he admits is the idea that all evil creatures within us are predestined to damnation.

Here then is Boehme's world which is at once the magical, organic manifestation of God as well as the object (*Gegenwurf*) of His kingdom of forms. This opposition cannot be tolerated. Tension must be released. The world and man, noblest of the creatures, must be redeemed.

NOTES TO CHAPTER FOURTEEN

1. The glossary in the 1730 edition gives *proprius* as meaning genius, the characteristic nature-spirit, the innate character.
2. This vision of the separation of fire into the elements is not too far from the modern view of the earth's origin.

CHAPTER FIFTEEN

MAN

THE KEY to Boehme's doctrine of man is Wisdom, especially his description of her as the image of God. Wisdom was the image (*Ebenbild*) or counter-image (*Gegenwurf*) of the unknown God; she was the mother-bride of
God and the mother-bride of man and thus the revealeress
of God in man and of man in God. She was also the form
of the God-image in man, the image binding man to God,
and the image revealing God's wonders in man.

This contiguity between man and God is consummated in
a flash, *Blick*. Not only does God see Himself in Wisdom
(*Princ.* xv, 14) but he also sees man (*Princ.* xvii, 12) through
her. In her the Holy Spirit discovers the human image
created in the *Verbum Fiat* (*Dreyfach* v, 44).

The *Blick* in which God knows man and man knows God
and in which man knows himself is the central act of divine
intuition, the act of self-contemplation in God, the divine
knowing of creatures, the creature's knowledge of the Creator, and the creature's knowledge of himself. In this creative
intuition the "eye" perceives all life's mysteries in Wisdom.

Wisdom is then man's heavenly corporeality (*Busse* i, 27),
man's highest essence and element.

That substantiality wherein the virgin of God consists,

Adam had on him; for the spirit of this world was given him, and breathed into him therein; but the essences were paradisaical, and sprung up through the one pure element, which the substantiality contains, and that substantiality the spirit of this world, in Adam, took into itself in its power. (*Dreyfach* xiii, 15)

Wisdom is man's heavenly pattern and image, his archetype,

the image of the heavenly world's substance in the soul's inner ground. (*Myst. Mag.* lvii, 9)

She is the love of Adam (*Gnad.* vii, 33) wherein God unites Himself with man. She is the heavenly Eve (*Myst. Mag.* lxvi, 52) who stands in heaven and paradise, mirroring herself in the soul's earthly qualities, as in the sun. Wisdom is the image of God both in the theogonic system and in man's soul.

And in this . . . is understood the angelic and soulic true image of God, whereof Moses says: God created man in His own image, that is, in the image of His divine imprint, according to the spirit; and in the image of God created He him. (*Gnad.* i, 15)

Boehme's description of Wisdom is philosophical idealism at its clearest:

She is the divine chaos wherein all things lie, viz. the divine imagination, in which the ideas of angels and souls have been set from eternity, in a divine type and resemblance; yet not then as creatures, but in resemblance, as when man beholds his face in a glass; therefore the angelical and human idea did flow forth from wisdom, and was formed into an image, as Moses says: God created him in His image; that is, breathed into it the breath of divine effluence, of divine knowledge, from all the three principles of the divine manifestation. (*Clavis* 19)

Just as Wisdom is God's bride so is she also man's. Here Boehme's androgynous views begin to appear inasmuch as he distinguishes between the female light-nature and the male fire-nature.

> The fire-soul must subsist in the fire of God, and be so pure as refined gold, for it is the husband of the noble Sophia, from the woman's seed; for it is the fire's tincture, and Sophia is the Light's tincture. If the tincture of the fire be wholly and thoroughly pure, then its Sophia will be given it; and so Adam received again to his arms his most precious and endeared bride . . . and it is not any longer man or woman, but a branch of Christ's pearl tree, which stands in the paradise of God. (*Myst. Mag.* xxv, 14)

This marriage of Wisdom with man's fire-soul forms the peculiar and in some ways primitive background for Boehme's androgynous man. Original man unites fire and light.

> Man should be the image and similitude of God, wherein God should dwell. Now God is a spirit, and all the three principles are in Him; and He would make such an image, as should have all the three principles in Him, and that is rightly a similitude of God. (*Princ.* x, 9)

Boehme gives various descriptions to this divine image in man: the angelical world in him, the idea, the lily-twig, Christ in him. In *Busse* he used the traditional image of German mysticism, *Füncklein;* he also calls it *glimmende Docht,* the glowing candle wick after the flame has been snuffed.

The point of departure for Boehme's idea of the *Urstand,* or the essential man before the fall, is the identification of the heavenly man with the resurrected Christ.

> I know the sophister will here cavil with me, and cry it down as a thing impossible for me to know, seeing I was not there and saw it myself. To him I say, that I, in the essence of my soul and body, when I was not yet I, but when I was in Adam's essence, was there, and did fool away my glory in Adam. But seeing Christ has restored it again to me, I see, in the spirit of Christ, what I was in

Paradise; and what I now am in sin; and what I shall be again. (*Myst. Mag.* xviii, 1)

In his soul man has all that God's spirit breathed into him at creation (*Bedenk. Stief.* i, 36), the image which was corrupted. In *Wiedergeburt* Boehme says that regeneration reverses the fall; primitive man and Christ are the same. All men are fundamentally one man; the Vine has branches which get vitality and produce fruit from the same root (*Myst. Mag.* xxiv, 15). Man's self-knowledge comes from the one God-man (*Myst. Mag.* xxiv, 15).

God made man in a pure element, a holy corporeality not of the earth's four elements (*Myst. Mag.* xvi, 6). Adam had a body wherein all the qualities stood in harmony (*Myst. Mag.* xvi, 5).

None lived in self-desire, but they all gave up their desire unto the soul. . . . They were all tinctured with sweet love so that there was nothing but mere pleasing relish and love-desire and delight between them. (*Myst. Mag.* xvi, 5)

Essential Adam had no strife, no war of opposites, no tension or disruptive dialectic; divine Love illuminated his inner parts as the sun lights the world (*Bedenk. Stief.* i, 36). This inner body was God's dwelling-place, an image of divine substantiality where the soul received God's meekness (*I Apol. Tilke* 233).

Thus . . . was the first man when he stood in paradise . . . in manner as time is before God, and God in time; and they are distinct, but not parted asunder. As the time is a play before God, so also the outward life of man was a play into the inward holy man, which was the real image of God. (*Myst. Mag.* xvi, 8)

Essential man's inner being, God's image, and his outer being, *limnus* [1] of earth, were not in conflict although the inner kept the outer imprisoned (*Myst. Mag.* xvi, 7) in perfect, undisturbed life in a body as clear as glass, penetrated by the sun's celestial light without darkness or death (*Sig. Rer.* xi, 51).

Essential man had a body because no spirit can subsist without a body, which is the spirit's mother (*Aurora* xxvi, 50). Boehme had no idealist antithesis between body and spirit; body was for him not flesh. It was rather form, definiteness, comprehensibility, that which can be known, willed, and loved, perhaps even personality. Inasmuch as only the *Ungrund* is incorporeal no spirit can exist without definitive form. Boehme's essential man was then no disembodied spirit but a man who eats, drinks, and reproduces.

Boehme develops essential man's physiology from Biblical descriptions of the risen Christ. The kingdom is not one of values and ideas but a joyous, majestic place where the redeemed sit down with a knowable Lord at banquet feast. Entrance into this kingdom is being reclothed in a new body. Adam's two essences

formed one body, wherein was the most holy tincture and divine fire and light, viz. the great joyful love-desire, which did inflame the essence, so that both essences did earnestly desire each other in love, desire, and love one another. . . . And yet they are not two bodies, but one; but of a twofold essence, viz., one inward, heavenly, holy and one from the essence of time; which were espoused and betrothed to each other, eternally. (*Myst. Mag.* xviii, 17, 18)

Androgynous essential man partook of all spiritual potentialities; man

is a little world out of the great world, and both the properties are in him. God said after the fall: 'Thou art earth, and unto earth shalt thou return.' (*Epist.* xii, 7)

In his outward being man is a little world of the great world and what the superior is that is also the inferior. Correspondence between the world and essential man implies that the world is like God; God is threefold; the world has three principles; man has body, soul, spirit.

Man was a mixed person. For he was to be an image of the outer and the inner world, and was to rule by the inner quality over the outer but as the symbol of God. (*Menschw.* I, iii, 13)

In God's power man was to be lord over creation (*Menschw.* I, iv, 7); his rule was to extend over heaven and earth, in all stars and elements (*Myst. Mag.* xvi, 2); he was innocent, childlike, unconscious of evil, without avarice, pride, envy or wrath (*Dreyfach* xi, 23):

> When God had created Adam thus, he was then in Paradise . . , and this clarified man was wholly beautiful and full of all knowledge; and there God brought all the beasts to him, that he should look upon them, and give every one its name, according to its essence. . . . And Adam knew what every creature was, and he gave to every one its name, according to the quality of its spirit. As God can see into the heart of all things, so could Adam do also, in which his perfection may very well be seen. And Adam and all men should have gone wholly naked, as he then went; his clothing was the clarity of virtue; no heat nor cold touched him; he saw day and night with open eyes; in him there was no sleep, and in his mind there was no night, for the divine virtue was in his eyes; and he was altogether perfect. . . . He was no man nor woman; as we in the resurrection shall be neither. Though indeed the knowledge of the marks of distinction shall remain in the figure, but the limbus and the matrix were not separated, as now. . . . Man was to dwell upon the earth as long as it would stand, . . manage the beasts, and have his delight and recreation therein. (*Princ.* x, 17–19)

He stood in heaven; his essences were in Paradise; his body was indestructible. He knew the divine angelic language and the language of nature (*Seel. Frag.* iv, 7); no fire burned in him, no water drowned him, no air suffocated him, no earth penetrated him—the elements stood in awe of him (*Dreyfach* xi, 23). Neither heat nor cold, sickness nor accident, terrified him. His body could pass through doors (*Menschw.* I, ii, 13). He lived a pure life like a burning oil flame. He had celestial perception and his intelligence passed and comprehended supernatural things (*Sig. Rer.* xii, 2).

Essential man, having no elemental body, needed no

bowels, belly, nor digestive organs. He ate spirit food, magically. The fruit he ate

> was pleasant to the sight, and good for food in a heavenly way; not to be taken into a worm-bag or miserable carcass as is done now in the awakened animal property. . . . In the mouth were the centers of separation. (*Gnad.* v, 34)

In this mouth he ate paradisaical food, which

> also was good. . . . Adam could eat of every fruit in the mouth, but not of the corruptibility, that must not be, for his body must subsist eternally but in Paradise. (*Princ.* xv, 16)

Likewise, essential man drank out of eternal life's source which lies hidden within earthly water (*Princ.* x, 20). This Boehme's general principle is clear, that a creature is nourished by that from which it originates. Animal man eats earth; but eternal man eats of the essential word of God (*Epist.* xlvi, 18). His mind is nourished from the star which is its original; the soul is nourished by the Logos (*Test.* I, i).

> And here we have the great *Arcanum* [2] of feeding spiritually, Dear Sons . . . you have the ground of all essentiality and the essences of all essences. And of this Christ has told us: He wanted to give you the water of eternal life, and would well up in you as a fountainhead (*John* iv, 14) not outwardly from the light-fire, but born inwardly from divine fire, whose image it is. (*Gnad.* ii, 30)

Essential man did not have an earthly body so his reproductive processes were not as now. Androgynous, no sexual act took place. Procreation and reproduction were asexual, without *partie honteuse*. The *Urmensch* or original man loved the divine image in himself. The first man

> was both man and woman before Eve, he had both . . . fire and water, . . soul and spirit, and he should have brought forth his similitude out of himself, as an image of himself by his own imagination and his own love; and that he was able to do without rending the body, for . . . the soul had power

to change the body into another form; and so also it had power to bring forth a twig out of itself, according to its property, if Adam had stood out the trial. (*Seel. Frag.* viii, 2)

Primitive Adam, in whom death was not yet real, really had no need of reproducing; he just lived on, for he was man, the species and individual together.

Boehme's originality appears best in his doctrine of fall and sin. Following his own ideas rather than churchly doctrine he rejected Adam's temptation as the first revolt against God; he understood that eating fruit was but logical result of a creature already fallen. He posited a fall before history and one in history. The transcendent fall happened when Adam slept.

Before he slept Adam had looked on God with a steady *Blick,* with open eyes his divine consciousness was not momentary—*Augenblick!* He was sleepless because the dialectic of sleep and wakefulness had not risen. Tired of unity, Adam slept and his imagination turned away from God. He broke consciousness away from God. He wanted

to contemplate . . . what evil and good was, how it would relish and be, in the unlikeness of the essence. (*Myst. Mag.* xviii, 28)

The knowledge of good and evil is of separateness and strife, and Adam

brought his will and desire from God into selfhood and vanity; and broke himself off from God, from His divine harmony. (*Myst. Mag.* xix, 3)

What Adam willed he got; when he contemplated plurality he got disharmony and dialectic. In his sleep this became possible.

Two things resulted from Adam's sleep: first he lost divine consciousness, the divine image; second he received a new kind of life—existence—which is marked by dialectical tension between opposing forces. This is where the *turba* [3] reigns. (*Bedenk. Stief.* 356a)

Adam was in the angelical form before the sleep; but after . . . he had flesh and blood; and he was . . . a lump of earth. . . . With his eyes he apprehended the light of the Sun and knew the first image no more. (*Princ.* 32, 33)

Sleep was succumbing to this world's powers, and Adam became a slave to just those powers which previously had served him. Now the elements ruled in him.

A further result of Adam's sleep was sexuality (*Bedenk. Stief.* 363). He was weakened and divided. Eve was made for him during his sleep. He was therefore guilty of adultery with regard to the Virgin Wisdom. In sleep he left Wisdom and got a new mistress. This suggests that he lost the original image of God (wisdom) and got an image of himself. He knew that he was alone; and God said it was not good for man to be alone; so another image was made (*Seel. Frag.* viii, 3):

When impotent Adam fell asleep the second creation of man began

for God took the tincture of the water, as a twig out of Adam's soul, and a rib out of Adam, and half of the cross that was Adam, and made woman of them. (*Seel. Frag.* viii, 5)

Adam fell asleep in eternity. He awoke in time. A new kingdom appeared, history began. Tensions grew, and Eve, who battled Adam's will and became the instrument of his temptation and of his fruitfulness, appeared. Man became sexual; he searched for the lost unity; his sexual eros was, however, a deceptive illusion.

The tincture is the longing, the great desire after the Virgin . . . but it is the divine inclination. . . . The masculine seeks her in the feminine, the feminine in the masculine. (*Princ.* xiii, 39; 46; 48)

Erotic love is illusion. In a memorable myth Boehme tells of its deceptiveness. The lover

supposes that he has gotten the virgin; he grasps with his

clutches, and will mingle his infection with the virgin, and he supposes that he has the prize, it shall not now run away from him; he supposes now he will find the Pearl well enough. But it is with him as with a thief, driven out of a fair garden of delight, when he has eaten his pleasant fruit, and wants to eat some more of the good fruit, and yet cannot get in, but must reach out with his hand, and yet cannot come at the fruit for all that; for the gardener comes and takes away the fruit; and thus he must go away empty, and his lust is changed into discontent. (*Princ.* xiii, 40)

The gardener is paradise, the fruit is the lost unity, the theft is the illusion of re-achievement in erotic experience. Adam's fall, then, did not result from sexual misuse; on the contrary, for Boehme, sex followed the fall. The original sin was that man broke away from the consciousness of God in sleep.

Sleep is, however, not punishment alone but also the promise of the future deliverance. In Adam disunity was possible—uncontested and undecided. When once contest has been invited and risk incurred then deliverance also becomes possible. Sleep points forward to Christ's rest in the grave (*Myst. Mag.*, xix, 5). Newborn man has to return back through Adam's sleep to awake in eternity, when the continuous *Blick* shall be restored.

The transcendent fall has repercussions. Adam lost divine unity, gained sexual disunity—a yes and no in life itself. Adam now ate the fruit that Eve presented to him. And with eating he changed. A new substance enters his being; a new mode, existence, is entered in upon. By eating earth he consumed the earth's dark death. He became part earth. He got the quality of inertia, decomposition, and death inherent in the earth. After the transcendent fall Adam's body

had not then such hard gristles and bones; O no, that came to pass first when mother Eve did bite the apple and also gave to Adam; only the infection and earthly death, with the fainting and mortal sickness, stuck in them; the bones and ribs were yet strength and virtue. (*Princ.* xiii, 13)

By eating earth he got a worm-carcass or *Madensack*. And

now in this body he is nature's child (*Aurora* xxvi, 78) and
now he belongs to Lucifer's kingdom (*Letzte. Zeit.* I, 74).

Man's consciousness of nakedness shows that he knows
that he has sinned and fallen. He is now ashamed of his
body. Other animals have coverings; only man is naked.

> When Adam and Eve . . . beheld themselves . . . they
> perceived the monstrous images and bestial form . . ; they
> took notice of the stomach and guts, into which they had
> stuffed the earthly fruit, which began to take effect, and they
> saw their bestial shame; and then they did lift up their minds
> towards Paradise, but they found it not; they ran trembling
> with fear, and crept behind the trees; the world has stirred
> their essences in the spirit with the earthly fruit. And then
> came the voice of God in the center of the gates of the Deep,
> and called Adam, and said: 'Adam, where art thou?' And he
> said: 'Here am I; and I am afraid, for I am naked.' And the
> Lord said, 'Who told thee that thou art naked? Hast thou
> eaten of the tree whereof I said unto thee that thou shouldest
> not eat thereof?' (*Princ.* xvii, 84)

Man's sense of nakedness is, then, a clue to his consciousness
of sin. Before the fall he had been transparent; his body
had been crystalline, pure; now he knows that he is naked.
Man loves and yet hates this coarse body. Man is captivated
by vanity for his body all the while that he is ashamed of it

> because it acquired such a monstrous form in its body. . . .
> From this has arisen human shame by which man is ashamed
> of his members and also of his naked form, so that he must
> borrow his clothing from earthly creatures. . . . This cloak
> is full proof to him that he is not at home with his soul in
> this aroused vanity. (*Wiedergeburt* ii, 19)

Adam and Eve sewed fig leaves together to cover their
shame, their coarse flesh and bones, the disease-ridden car-
cass. But nakedness is their sense of not-belonging in an
earth-body (*Princ.* x, 6–7).

> This borrowed clothing, together with the awakened earth-
> liness, and subjugation to the powers of heat and cold, is
> a plain and full proof that man is truly not at home in this

world. For all earthly appetites, cares, and fears, together with this false clothing, must perish and be severed from the soul again. (*Wiedergeburt* ii, 19)

Nakedness unlocks Boehme's atavism; man remembers his primitive, essential unity and his angelical form.

Another subjective clue by which man knows his alienation from this world is his anxiety (*Angst*)—a conception which Kierkegaard popularized but in another form. Anxiety is the tension between man's two wills. Man remembers his lost unity; he longs for his primordial freedom as he lives a life of torment and death (*Gnad.* iii, 5). Anxiety is the source-spring of hell-fire in a sensitive heart (*Tab. Princ.* 39), the cause of sadness and joy (*Aurora* xiii, 118). Without anxiety there would be eternal darkness (*Menschw.* II, iii, 13), an idle nothing (*II Apol. Tilke,* 141). Adam's fall made man sensitive to painful distinctions, basically the distinction between God and nature (*Gnad.* iii, 5); if man wants knowledge of God he must dwell in anxiety's house in his soul (*Menschw.* ii, vi, 12). Anxiety is

a root of feeling, the beginning . . . of mind, a root of . . . all painfulness . . , a manifestation of the eternal unfathomable will in the attraction . . , a cause of dying . . , the very root where God and nature are separated . . . [where] the manifest sensible life arises. (*Gnad.* iii, 5)

The fall was not because man was sensual; rather man became sensual because of the fall!

From the fall man also got his two forms of knowing—reason (*Vernunft*) and the understanding (*Verstand*). A new knowledge came with the fall which became separate from his divine knowledge—reason. Reason had an astral origin (*Menschw.* III, ii, 3) and is the world's spirit in man (*Sig. Rer.* viii, 3). Reason is a noble thing which is blind without God's spirit (*Menschw.* iii, v, 3). Inasmuch as reason comes from the stars it cannot search deeper than the stars (*Epist.* lv, 4) and however fine reason may become it still partakes of God's wrath (*Seel. Frag.* i, 84) and can know nothing about divine things (*Gnad.* ii, 2). Reason can know nothing of God's kingdom (*Dreyfach* xvi, 22), of the tree of faith (*Menschw.* III, viii, 7), and cannot come to certainty (*Sig. Rer.* xv, 22) but always stands in doubt (*Epist.* xii, 22). Reason breeds all disputation and strife (*Test.* II, i, 1–9) and runs around in circles (*Myst. Mag.* ii, 4) and becomes the tool of self-will and pride.

Understanding (*Verstand*) originates from the holy element (*Sig. Rer.* xiii, 8) and is the inner world's life, a free will (*Myst. Mag.* xxix, 1), and is Wisdom in her government of man (*Myst. Mag.* xxxv, 13).

God has appointed . . . one master . . . which can alone manage the soul of the great world . . . and appointed a type of its likeness as the reason over this officer, which represents . . . what he is to do and make; and this is the understanding, viz., God's own dominion wherewith he rules the officer. Now the understanding shows to the officer what . . . each thing is. (*Sig. Rer.* viii, 3)

In understanding man can search all things and even penetrate with it into God's Wisdom for by it God draws man (*Myst. Mag.* iii, 8). Understanding is man's inner life (*Clav.* 99) and comes from the inner light (*Myst. Mag.* xi, 25).

Finally, Adam's fall brought the great *turba*. The *turba magna* is the wrath and aroused vehemency of dumb nature, the poisonous source which produces freaks, sports, poisons, and other false expressions of the divine vitality.

Each form of nature . . . received its property in its hunger, and therein it is not annoyed or molested. . . . But if the will enters back again into the birth of the other properties . . . [then] is the abominate and *turba* born; for this will is entered contrary to the course of nature into a strange essence, which is not of its property. (*Sig. Rer.* xiv, 77)

When the *turba* was awakened fire and brimstone rained out of heaven (*Myst. Mag.*, xliv, 26); Lot's wife, by the *turba*, became a pillar of salt. The *turba* is the third principle's potential power to fall back into wrath again, the ultimate threat of existence.

These, then, are the preliminary results of Adam's fall; one other yet remains. With Adam sin appeared.

Although sin originates in Lucifer's fall (*Aurora* xiii, 116) it entered man after Adam's fall, proceeding from Adam's self-willed separation from God to the selfhood in all his Cain-like sons (*Gnad.* ix, 61):

Thus . . . may be known what sin is . . . Namely, when the human will separates itself from God into an existence of its own, and awakens its own self. . . . For all into which the will enters, and will have as its own, is something foreign to the one will of God. For all is God's and to man's own will belongs nothing. But if it be God's, then all is its also. Thus we recognize that desire is sin. For it is a lusting out of one into many and introduces many into one. The will possesses, and yet should be will-less. (*Myst. Punkt.* iii, 16ff)

Before the fall there had been but one man with one will—now many men had many wills.

Each particular fire burns in accordance with the character of its own being; and here separation and enmity are born. . . . Covetousness is sin, for it is a desire to be out of God. . . . Pride is sin, for it will be a thing of its own, and separate itself from God. . . . Seeing . . . we are in God but one in many members, it is against God when one member draws itself away from the other, and makes a Lord of itself. . . . Pride will be lord and God alone is Lord. Thus there are two lords, and one separates from the other. All therefore is sin . . . that desire possesses as its own, be it meat or drink. (*Myst. Punkt.,* iv, 9ff)

In a remarkable figure of speech Boehme says that the Devil strewed sugar upon Adam (*Princ.* xvii, 93)

and that sugar he shall eat eternally, and frame his will continually therein to get other sugar. . . . And hereby it is signified to the ungodly, that they shall also eat the same sugar eternally, which they have continually baked here, with their blasphemies, cursing, robbing, and taking the sweat of the needy and miserable to maintain their haughty pride. (*Princ.* xvii, 94)

Instead of seven sins Boehme has but four: arrogance, avarice, envy, and wrath (*Aurora* xiv, 47). Arrogance longs to be mighty, powerful, and great; avarice wants to draw everything to itself and to possess it; envy seeks to kill what avarice does not appropriate; and wrath seeks to subject all to pride. In its pure, unfallen state the soul had possessed the principle of eternal nature and had been capable of good and evil (*Gnad.* viii, 46) but in its fallen state it was rigorously imprisoned by sin.

For here lurks original sin in the center of nature. . . . Here too are the inherited sins of parents and grandparents, like an evil poison. (*Gnad.* viii, 46)

No one is sinless for the great *turba* is in the earth he eats and infects all beings who partake of the earth. It holds men captive and as long as he has a body of earth so long will he be held by sin.

And, although our soul goes forth and becomes new-born in God, yet it possesses the outward body still, and consumes it. (*Seel. Frag.* xiv, 7)

Man needs not only the soul's new birth but a new body in which the *turba* has been overcome (*Princ.* xix, 33).

These then are the results of Adam's fall. When he ate fruit he got earth and its curse. This now begets sin. To gain final victory he must get a new body too.

Boehme's three principles produce a man of spirit, fire-soul, and earthly body (*Aurora* iii, 18, 19). This is how Boehme rejects Greek dualism and accepts Paul's spirit, soul, and body. Yet Boehme gives these his own meanings:

Man is an image of the Being of all beings . . . Namely, 1) the soul is the eternal central fire of self-will, for out of it creatures have come and not from the pure Deity. And 2) the spirit . . . is the central fire of light, sprung from the eternal idea, from the power of God . . . But 3) the outer body is from the outer world, from the four elements and the stars. (*Theos. Frag.* xii, 15–17)

Man participates in each of the three principles, sharing in the constituent totality of the human image.

The first and most inward ground in man is Christ, not according to the nature of man, but according to the divine property of the heavenly nature, which He had begotten anew. The second ground of nature of the soul, understand the eternal nature, and in it Christ manifested Himself and assumed the same. The third ground is the created man . . . of . . . earth, with stars and elements. (*Gnad.* vii, 37)

Without the dialectical interaction of these three worlds the redemptive and regenerative processes could not proceed. (*Myst. Mag.* xxxii, 6). By associating these three worlds with the three alchemical substances Boehme saw them as longing, willing, and desiring.

Longing is a hunger, or an infecting of the desiring, and the will is a retention in the desiring; and now if the desiring must retain the will, then it must be comprehensible, and there must not be only one thing alone in the will, but two; now, then, seeing there are two, therefore the attraction must be the third, which draws that which is comprehensible into the will. (*Princ.* xiv, 62)

From these three Adam was made, a full complete image of the triune God (*Theos. Punkt.* ii, 29). And without this trichotomous psychology man could not be restored to wholeness. Here the real reason for the three principles appears.

The first ground, which is Christ, is the working life of the divine Love; . . the second ground is the natural fire-life of the creaturely soul, wherein God calls Himself a jealous God; in the third ground is the created world which in Adam was in equipoise, and fell asunder in the Fall. (*Gnad.* vii, 7ff)

These dominate man's life; whichever ground he serves enslaves him (*Princ.* xvi, 37). Only in man are all three principles manifest (*Dreyfach* iv, 58).

The doctrine of the indwelling Christ gives Boehme's trichotomous psychology importance. Christ lives in man's heart (*Dreyfach* xi, 68) as the second principle (*Menschw.* I, xii, 19) because He is the second principle in man.

This name Jesus, as the purpose of His Love, God has

inspoken into the mother of all men and as a living power embodied it in the eternal covenant, and has fulfilled the covenant by introducing the Divine Being into human quality. (*Gnad.* viii, 23)

From eternity Christ has been eternal love in man (*Gnad.* vii, 31), coming to us for our salvation and as long as the soul loves He is in man's heart (*Gnad.* ix, 63). He is never extinguished. He thrives on the trials of unbelief and is like a glowing wick after the candle has been snuffed. He is the inward light, *Fünklein,* which can become fanned into the flames of consuming Love.

Boehme's psychology, by insisting that this divine spark is essential for the creation of human nature, departs from that of Sebastian Franck and Hans Denck. Boehme's Christ is redeemer and sperminal Logos (*Irrth. Stief.* 25); He is restorer of unity as well as indwelling Word. All men share in the Christ within: not all choose to unveil Him fully. All beings share the eternally spoken Word; not all share the Word made flesh, that is, the Word projected into the third principle.

Here Boehme's refusal to identify his second principle with the second person of the Trinity makes sense. The Christ of history reawakens and rekindles the soul's innermost ground. His drawing power, or tincturing, attracts the inner Word. Like cures like—this is the old formula.

Boehme's doctrine of the soul is complicated. Like Plato, Plotinus, and Schelling he held that the world had a soul, an oversoul, which the eternal essences have made from the divine vitality (*Seel. Frag.* iii, 4). This world-soul participates in all three principles (*Dreyfach* ii, 5) and binds them, giving them unity. The soul's task was to keep all in balance, in harmony. The soul, not deriving from the four elements, has been

breathed into man . . . by the moving spirit. Which original is before the light of life . . . out of which the light of God is enkindled . . ; therefore the soul is God's own essence or substance. (*Princ.* iv, 20)

The soul is begotten by the interaction of the first two principles, wrath and love.

> The soul . . . is the roughest thing in men; for it is the original of the other substances or things. It is fiery, harsh, bitter, and strong, and resembles a great and mighty power, its essences are like brimstone; its gate or seat out of the eternal original is between the fourth and fifth forms in the eternal birth. (*Princ.* xiii, 30)

Man's soul lives in his heart but dominates his brain (*Seel. Frag.* viii, 7, 8). Wherever man is influenced by divine vitality, there is soul (*Seel. Frag.* vii, 9); in man the soul hovers between hell and this world (*Princ.* xvii, 7), capable of being swayed by either. It is demonic in the sense that it can be good or evil (*Princ.* x, 14).

After Adam's fall the soul's imagination became external (*Irrth. Stief.* 346), losing its holy divine *Ens*, its holy substance and spiritual qualities (*Gnad.* vii, 11), becoming blind to God (*Test.* I, i, 21). It is bound by three strong chains (*Princ.* xxv, 8) which infect it with worldliness (*Dreyfach* xiii, 8). It has self-will, possessing a light of its own, and stands in the sun's light (*Princ.* xiv, 11), surrounded by love, wrath, and this world's spirit (*Bedenk. Stief.* 71).

Man's spirit derives from God and the constellations (*Aurora*, preface, 98), ruling and dominating man's mind (*Aurora*, v, 39), and helping him to search the divine deep (*Aurora* xi, 71). Each element has its spirit: fire-spirit, water-spirit, air-spirit, and earth-spirit (*Princ.* vii, 35). Each spirit "eats" of the mother that bore it, seeking the maternal substance as fulfillment for its longing (*Epist.* xxxi, 20). Not all external world spirits are of the Holy Spirit (*Myst. Mag.* viii, 19); some have fallen through self-will.

Boehme's man is threefold and he has fallen on each of the three aspects: his body is corrupt earth, his soul has a burning hunger, his spirit has led itself into world dominion. He needs total regeneration.

The four elements produce four complexions (*Theos. Frag.* xii, 17). Fire governs the choleric, air the sanguine, water the phlegmatic, earth the melancholic.

Fire's choleric complexion makes courage, sudden wrath, aroused pride, and arrogant self-centeredness. Air's sanguinity is subtle, friendly, joyous, of uncertain courage, changeable, easily persuaded, witty. Water's phlegm is fleshly, coarse, feminine, frugal, stubborn, dull. Earth's melancholy lives in the tension between light and darkness, good and evil, dominated by tragedy and anxiety (*Complex.* 3ff). In as much as the melancholy complexion comes from earth it shows its dark chamber of death and puts man on the boundary between life and death, waiting for permanent release (*Complex.* 40).

Boehme's anthropology with its distinction between essential man and existential man explains man's present situation on the boundary between life and death, Yes and No, as son of God and child of earth (*Princ.* xx, 82). Man

has two worlds in him. The property to which he turns himself, to that world he is introduced, and of that world's property will he eternally be, and enjoy the same; either a source of light-world gentleness, or a hostile source from the dark world. Here he buds and grows in the middle world between the light-world and the dark-world; he may give himself to which he pleases. The essence which obtains the dominion in him, whether fierceness or gentleness, the same embraces him, and it hangs unto him and leads him; it gives him morals and will, and unites itself wholly with him. (*Theos. Punkt.* iv, 22–23)

External man was created a tool and instrument of the internal (*Sig. Rer.* xv, 18), and the gross, corporeal man was not God's image but a horrible monster (*Myst. Mag.* xvi, 1),

a house or husk of the spiritual man, in which the spiritual man grows. . . . The outward gross body . . . shall not inherit the Kingdom of God (*Clavis* 14ff).

Christ came to help redeem man's inner spirit (*Theos. Frag.* xii, 17) and this inner man is Christ's loyal and obedient servant (*Myst. Mag.* lxxi, 55).

Natural man, standing on the "limit between life and death," as Boehme called it, has two properties, both of which draw him and desire to have him. . . . Man is drawn and held of both; but the center stands in him, and he has the balance between the two wills (*Princ.* xxi, 20).

That kingdom to which he gives himself, to that does he become subservient (*Princ.* vii, 2). God has produced in man a creature of two wills (*Dreyfach* vi, 66) who is both good and evil (*Aurora,* ii, 9), alive and dead. In man the name Jesus fights the dragon in combat between typical wrath and typical love (*Theos. Frag.* xi, 13ff). Whoever wins, wins forever (*Princ.* xvi, 42). Before the fall Yes was manifest in man's essence; afterwards it was concealed (*Gnad.* xiii, 37). Yet

Man is not so altogether corrupt that there should not be any possibility at all left in him. (*Epist.* xlii, 49)

He still can be redeemed (*Menschw.* I, xiv, 19) and redemptive action is grounded in the divine image within his own being; he is capable of comprehending everything in his heart (*Princ.,* preface, 2; xvi, 32) because he has a free will (*Princ.* xxii, 15; *Dreyfach* vi, 68). He can live in health (*Sig. Rer.* ix, 69) because he can release the curse laid within the earth (*Sig. Rer.* xi, 85).

Since man is also created of earth and of astral spirits (*Princ.* xvi, 24), and since the rule of earth and stars has made him a hypocrite and sinner (*Princ.* xvi, 28), he tends towards being a devil. God said that He would put enmity between the woman's and the serpent's seed. This enmity is powerful within man, not outside of him. Man seeks an earthly kingdom (*Myst. Mag.* lv, 43) and remains blind to God's works (*Epist.* xlviii).

Great theological systems usually meet in trying to define man's role in the world. Boehme's man is the key to his world for he is an individual and personal image of God (*Sig. Rer.* x, 3) and an image of the world itself (*Myst. Mag.* ii, 5). Though man is God's image by natural right, he is not so in fact; the image has become obscured by rebellion against God's will. Man, impaled in existence, is deeply moved by life's inadequacy. He longs for a better world.

This longing establishes his superiority to the beasts (*Gnad.* v, 26). Man also desires earth, but differs from the animals in wanting a better earth. The perception of animals is circumscribed by desire and instinct; they do not ask concerning either their origins or their destiny. Man does. Man surpasses the beasts because he can go beyond himself. This is his true freedom.

Boehme's man is in some ways the signature of all things, who by understanding the language of nature knows God's formed words. When Adam walked through the garden he named the things he saw into reality. But Adam fell. Now he no longer understands nature's words. A principle of distortion has entered reality and man longs now for wholeness. He lives in the hope of the restoration of the totality of that lost image; this totality which is the New Man in Christ, restorer of the fallen, distorted image.

NOTES TO CHAPTER FIFTEEN

1. *Limnus* is the purest earth-essence.
2. *Arcanum* is mystery.
3. *Turba* is the aroused wrath in nature, a poisonous source, which destroys everything.

Wirt als ein kint,
Wirt toup und blint,
Din selbes iht
Muoz werden niht;
Al iht, al niht trib über bor.
—FROM THE *Dreifaltigkeitslied*

CHAPTER SIXTEEN

REDEMPTION

THE DOCTRINE of Wisdom defines Boehme's exposition of Incarnation and redemption for if Wisdom is the form through which and in which God completes Himself then Wisdom is finally the form by which He restores a fallen world. To maintain his realism (theologically considered) Boehme refused to identify Mary with Wisdom. If the incarnation was not in a real person, if Christ did not become man in Mary, if He did not put on the corrupt earth, then He could not have helped man. What Christ did not adopt as His own He could not redeem.

Many have taken upon themselves to write of the Virgin Mary, and have believed that she was not a daughter of the earth. To them . . . has been presented a reflection of the eternal virginity, but they have come short of the true mark. Some have simply supposed that she was not the daughter of Joachim and Anne, for Christ is called the seed of the woman, and indeed is, and He Himself attests that He came from above, from Heaven; He must therefore, according to them, be wholly born of a heavenly virgin. But this would profit little to us poor children of Eve, who have become earthly and carry our souls in an earthly vessel. Where was our soul, if the Word of Eternal Life had not taken it to itself? If Christ had brought a soul from heaven, where was our soul and the Covenant with Adam and Eve, by which the woman's seed was to bruise the serpent's head? If Christ had willed to come and to be born wholly from Heaven, He would not have needed to be born a man on earth. (*Menschw.* I, viii, 1)

Wisdom, the hidden God's instrument of self-manifestation, assumes her role as revealeress also in the Incarnation.

Mary's body is the receptacle of her soul, her soul is the receptacle of Wisdom, and Wisdom is the receptacle of the divine Logos. Each corporeal form is the receptacle of the higher spirit which is produced and realized within it. Wisdom is God's body (*Epist.* xxxi, 48) and so bears the Son, the eternal will's first manifestation. Mary unites the divine and human nature which was disrupted in Adam. In her betrothal between Wisdom and man is again possible, making the second Adam historically present in the *Benedictus* when wisdom reunited herself with Mary.

Christ has truly, in the body of the Virgin Mary, attracted to Him our human essences, and is become our brother; yet these human essences cannot comprehend the eternal Deity, only the new man, born of God, comprehends the Deity. (*Princ.* xiii, 41)

When the Holy Spirit announced the conception Mary had the total God within her.

And for this cause God became man, that He might in Himself generate anew the soul of man again, and might redeem it from the chains of fierceness of anger, and not at all for the bestial's body's sake, which must melt into the four elements, and come to nothing; out of which nothing will remain. . . . But in the new man (which we attract on to our souls in the bosom of the virgin) we shall spring forth and flourish again; and therein is no necessity nor death. (*Princ.* xxii, 22ff)

The Incarnation's purpose is ultimate resolution of the tension between life and death. How does wisdom enter Mary? Here Boehme allegorizes:

God said to Adam and Eve: the seed of the woman shall bruise the serpent's head, and thou, serpent, shall sting him in the heel (*Gen.* iii, 15); that is, in the wrath of God thou shalt slay him, but he will bud forth out of death and bruise thy head, that is, will take away your power and overcome your wrath with love. . . . In this same sign the highly precious Virgin of the wisdom of God, in which Christ, as the breaker down of death, was to become a true man, deprive death of its power, and destroy the devil's sting; he was to tread the winepress of the fierceness and wrath, and enter into the wrath as into the center of fire and extinguish the fire with His heavenly blood. (*Menschw.* I, vii, 10)

In Mary Wisdom brings the Logos to a new form; Christ is eternal but in Mary He became man. No new God has thereby been created; He merely became man (*Dreyfach* vi, 79). Wisdom's reunion with humanity is no abrupt inbreak but rather realizes a theogonic act. Unity was broken by Lucifer and Adam; the image of union restores the lost unity, yet this image—or better, this remembrance—of union has been present in man as prophecy and judgment. When Adam broke unity God directly gave a new promise:

God spoke again into our poor fallen soul in Paradise, immediately after the fall, the Covenant and root of His highest Love and Grace, through the Word, as the center of Grace to corruption, and to the new generation. (*Myst. Mag.* lvi, 25)

This has been continued in history by the carriers of the covenant, a spiritual lineage by which Abraham's faith was invested in Isaac according to the inward ground (*Myst. Mag.* lvi, 28). There was difference between the image in the line of the covenant and the restoration in Mary:

The works of the law were before God in the mirror, till the life was born again from the covenant and the fulfillment came. Then the works of the mirror ceased, and the works of the fulfillment of flesh and blood . . . began again; for in Mary was the beginning. (*Menschw.* I, ix, 16)

In the Incarnation Christ again brought the improperly compounded, disunited essences into full harmony.

Boehme's Christology was dialectical; his Christ was androgynous. If the fall resulted in the loss of unity, then the Savior (whole-maker) restores the image to fullness and makes that image available for all men.

The new birth in sum is this: that the angelical image must be born again which God created in Adam. God formed Adam in the image of God, and though He knew that he would not stand, yet he appointed Him the Savior who could bring him again into the first image, and therein establish him forever. (*Myst. Mag.* xix, 21)

As the fallen Adam was androgynous, so also the second Adam, for He restores unity to the fallen image:

And when Christ on the cross had again accomplished this redemption of our virgin-like image from the divided sex of male and female . . . he said: *it is finished* . . . Christ turned back Adam into his sleep from the vanity, and from the man and woman, again into the angelical image. (*Myst. Mag.* xix, 7)

Male and female, having parted in Adam's sleep, reunite themselves in Jesus. The male and female principles

were indeed united in the incarnation . . . so that they were inseparable, but the true ens of the soul, which the Word assumed in the name JESUS, was of us men from the female tincture . . . which was severed from Adam (and put into the woman) that this property in the light might transmute . . . the fiery masculine property again into the live and divine humility, and that the masculine and feminine property might be quite changed into one image again: As Adam was before his Eve, when he was neither man nor woman, but a masculine virgin. (*Myst. Mag.* lvi, 20)

Here the incarnation gets special meaning. Christ became man in the woman but He was born male. Manhood comes from the Father, womanhood from Mary.

Christ was born of a virgin, that He might sanctify the woman's tincture again, and change it into the man's tincture, that the man and the woman might be one image of God, and no more man and woman, but masculine virgins. (*Myst. Mag.* lvi, 46)

Here even in the incarnation a manifestation of Boehme's Yes and No is apparent, the conflict between the hidden God of wrath and the known God of Love. Let man

ascribe the male to God the Father, viz., to the first principle, where God's Word does manifest itself in the fire-world, which is the first center of the creature; and the female let him ascribe to God the Son, viz. the second principle, where the divine eternal Word does manifest itself in the light of Love. . . . In this manner fire produces light. (*Myst. Mag.* xxiii, 45)

As expected reunion follows the process of division. Fire and light had separated (*Gnad.* vii, 17ff); in the fall Adam got fire and Eve light (*Myst. Mag.* xix, 17; xxii, 43, 44); In Christ both were again united.

When an androgynous Christ is thus posited the traditional bride-mysticism makes more sense. In Christ each sex finds what it lacks to be whole. Boehme sees in sex a shadowy, vague, incomplete prototype of final unification.

We understand, then, the incarnation of Christ in a natural way, like that of all men. . . . Christ in nine months became a perfect man and at the same time remained a true God, and was born into this world in the manner and mode of all Adam's children, by the same way as all men. And that, not that He needed it—He could have been born magically—but He desired and was destined to remedy our impure, animal birth and entrance into this life. He was to enter into this world by our entrance, and lead us out of the earthly quality. For if He had been born magically in a divine manner, then He would not by nature have been of this world. . . . How then would He have willed to suffer death, and enter into death and break it to pieces? . . . He is truly the woman's seed, and He entered into this world in the natural way, like all men; but went out by death in the divine way, in the divine power and essentiality. . . . For the earthly part, which He received from His mother Mary into Himself, into the divine nature, died on the Cross to earthly nature. The soul was thus in the essentiality of God, and descended as a conqueror into the hell of the Devil, that is, into the fierce wrath of God, and quenched it with God's love and gentleness that characterize the divine love-essentiality. . . . And this was the reason that God became man, in order that He might lead us out of death into the life eternal, and quench with His Love the wrath which burned within us. (*Menschw.* I, x, 9ff)

So Christ became man in the woman's seed (*Myst. Mag.* xxvii, 26), conceived of Mary's will naturally (*Princ.* xviii, 96), yet sinless (*Princ.* xxii, 36), drawing human flesh, soul, and spirit to Himself in Mary (*Dreyfach* xi, 26)

Christ cannot be known from the letter of Scripture (*Buchstaben*) or reason (*Menschw.* I, i, 10). Only the regenerate man who has put on Christ's God-manhood as his own can know His person (*Myst. Mag.* xxxvii, 30). Boehme has a divine and human nature in Christ (*Irrth. Stief.* 420, 438) but not in the traditional sense; he sees that all men partake of the formative Word (*Irrth. Stief.* 131), but only the faithful partake of the formed Word. In Adam the formative Word was made, but He had not yet taken on flesh (*Epist.* xii, 58). In Jesus this happened, so Christ is the formed Word.

Boehme's Christology was also dualistic: his Christ had two natures, a formative Word beyond corporeal existence and a formed Word in Jesus. In Jesus Christ the judgment implied in man's consciousness of his nakedness—man's knowledge of losing the *imago dei*, the image of God,—is altered. Nakedness is poignantly revealed in Christ's nakedness. However, Christ is not just the restoration of the lost image, not merely sentimental reminder of a lost ideal; He is a new being, partaking of both human tragedy and of eschatological hope. In Him the new birth gets its new body.

Why did God become man? Boehme has some new answers to Anselm's old question. God sent Jesus to open the gate of the birth in man's life so he might be reunited with God (*Princ.* iv, 39). He sent His Son to overpower the dragon-source and wrath in man and so to redeem man from the No (*Theos. Frag.* xii, 12). He had to take on all three principles or else His saving, redeeming work would have been incomplete (*Taufe* I, iii, 5, 6). Moreover, Christ had to take on human form so God could create an androgynous man:

> Only the male kind was circumcised, and in the same member that is an abomination before God and a shame of the soul, for impregnation was not destined to be bestial. Circumcision is thus a sign and figure, intimating that this member should be cut from man and not appear with him in eternity. And Christ had to take on the form of a man, though inwardly He stood in a virgin image, that the purpose of God might stand. For the man's or the fire's property must rule, and the woman's or the light's property must soften his fire and bring it into a gentle image of God. (*Menschw.* I, vii, 13)

In the incarnation Christ also sanctified the female principle:

> In Eve . . . God established His Covenant and brought His Word thereinto, that the woman's seed (i.e. the heavenly seed which the Word was to reintroduce, and in which God and man were to be again one person) should bruise the head of the power of the serpent's spawn and the Devil's will, and destroy the Devil's works. (*Gnad.* vii, 19, 20)

In Boehme's view Christ's work was victory over darkness and No, over the wrath.

> In man the name Jesus fights against the dragon. This combat is not a creaturely thing . . . It is a combat between Yes and No, between the typical wrath and the typical love, between the first and second principles. (*Theos. Frag.* xi, 14, 15)

Why was combat necessary? Why did Christ have to suffer and die? Because

> the human will must be broken and slain, and through death be introduced again into the holy name. Christ, accordingly, had to die and bring the human will through death, through hell, and through this foundation, because the self-assumption of a will cannot subsist in God. If a will is to subsist in God, it must be impatible and non-suffering, so that it may

be able to dwell in fire and yet not be laid hold of by the fire. (*Theos. Frag.* xi, 19)

In this connection Boehme repeats an image as old as Origen, which is, perhaps, the heart of his theology:

As the sun in the elements presses through everything, and kindles itself in the elements, and yet its light remains free; or as fire through-heats iron, and yet becomes not iron, but the iron is only an object in which the fire elevates and inflames itself; so pure also must the will be which is to possess God's unity; no assuming may be in it. (*Theos. Frag.* xi, 20)

Christ is the tincture that transmutes God's wrath into Love. Boehme says that He was the guiltless Lamb (*Irrth. Stief.* 436) but He did not pay the price in sacrifice for man's enormous sin. Boehme understands that the inner Christ never did die (*Princ.* xxii, 54), as the legalist view of the atonement demands:

When Christ died on the Cross, the name JESUS did not also die. . . . No, it cannot be, the Eternity does not die, only the spoken Word. . . . The anger of God was set on fire and did wholly die. (*Sig. Rer.* xii, 3ff)

Only by conquering the third principle could He conquer self-will.

Why did He have to die? In order to rise again in a new form of life (*Princ.* xxv, 13). He entered death and brought man out of darkness into the freedom of the divine life.

Therefore Christ had to die, and with the soul's spirit pass through the fire of eternal nature, that is, through the wrath and hell of the eternal nature . . . and make our soul a way through death and wrath, in which we might with Him and in Him enter through death into the eternal divine life. (*Menschw.* I, iii, 7)

He had to take the four congealed elements back into nature's fire, reheat them, and pour them out in a new form without the dark wrath (*Dreyfach* v, 142). Through His

death the cherub's sword was broken (*Menschw.* I, vii, 3)
and the serpent's head bruised (*Sig. Rer.* vii, 24). The Devil
was vanquished (*Princ.* xxiii, 9) and man released from
bondage, death, and corruption (*Sig. Rer.* vii, 44). Christ destroyed our death in His (*Menschw.* I, vi, 4), tinged humanity with His blood (*Epist.* xxxviii, 14), opened up a gate
for all (*Dreyfach* vi, 95), restoring the image corrupted in
Adam (*Gnad.* ix, 87).

The resurrected Christ symbolizes the original and the
final perfection of man, the first-born after death (*Myst.
Mag.* xli, 11). Christ has incorruptible flesh, and in Him sin
has been removed as possibility by forgiveness. What Adam
lost Christ restored.

For by human works sin had come into the world, and so
also it had to be slain by human works. (*Gnad.* ix, 59)

This refutes the premise of Anselm's view by claiming that,
though the sin be great, it was not great enough to demand
a God as payment. Originating with man, sin had to be
appeased by man. God cannot undo what man has done.

If it will enter then it must do it in the manner and form
as it went out, for it brought itself into false desire and lust.
Even so likewise it must introduce itself again by returning
into a sorrow and conversion, and in the sorrow of repentance again introduce itself into a divine desire which is called
faith. (*Myst. Mag.* xxvii, 35)

In a lovely reapplication of the parable of the good Samaritan, Boehme said,

The fair image fell among murderers, that is, among the
harsh spirits of nature . . . These held the image captive
and drew off from it the robe of Paradise and left it lying
half-dead. Now there was need of the Samaritan, Christ. And
that was the cause that God became man. If the harm could
have been healed through the speaking of a Word or a word
of forgiveness, God would not have become man. (*Menschw.*
III, vi, 2)

By forgiveness and reconciliation Christ restored man's

original unity. The new man is also androgynous, neither marrying nor giving in marriage. He enters a real kingdom, with a new spiritual body, to sit down to a banquet of sacramental food—Christ's new body and blood. All his horrible memories have been removed. Nakedness and anxiety are gone. The *turba* has been removed. Profane love has been changed into holy love (*Bedenk. Stief.* 325) and wedded people now love spiritually. This is a far cry, indeed, from the oriental dream of *Nirvana.*

As the living Word of life the resurrected Christ dwells in man's heart (*Dreyfach* xi, 88). This becomes the basis of redemption.

Therefore it is said: watch, pray, be sober, lead a temperate life, for the Devil . . . walks about as a roaring lion, seeking whom he may devour (*I Peter*, v, 8). Follow then not after covetousness, money, goods, power, and honor, for in Christ we are not of this world. For therefore it was that Christ went to the Father . . . in order that we should follow Him with our hearts, minds, and wills; and hence He says that He will be with us all the days, even to the end of the world (*Matth.* xxviii, 20). . . . We must force a way out of this world, out of the earthly man, and give up our will to His Will, and introduce our imagination and desire into Him; then we become pregnant in His virginity . . . and we are new-born in Christ in ourselves. For as death passed upon us all by Adam, so the Word of life passes upon us all from Christ . . . Christ need not first leave His place and enter into us, when we are new-born in Him; for the divine being, in which He was born, contains everywhere the second principle. Wherever it may be said that God is present, there it also may be said that the Incarnation in Christ is present too; for it has been revealed in Mary and thus inqualifies backwards to Adam and forwards to even the last man. (*Menschw.* xii, 19)

If Christ in the second principle is in everything, why must man turn to Him? Indeed, Jesus lives within all as unchangeable Love and to this indwelling Christ man turns.

In every man . . . the word of promise . . . must become . . . a being, and this is accomplished in repentance and conversion. God says in Isaiah (1, 18): Though your sins be as red as scarlet, if ye turn, ye shall be white as snow. This takes place when the kingdom of Grace is manifested in the kingdom of nature. . . . When the poor sinner repents, God comes in Christ's spirit and brings forth a new son out of Christ's flesh and blood in him . . . And thus commences the gestation of the new man. (*Gnad.* x, 4ff)

Christ speaks His Being into all men but not all want to hear His Words (*Gnad.* xiii, 4) nor do all respond by comprehending His essence within them.

Man's foremost response to Christ's work is repentance, departing from the sin of pride and from the pride of sin (*Irrth. Stief.* 297). Repentance is the quieting of man's false imagination (*Gnad.* xiii, 7) for

no longer to be doing is the . . . best repentance. This . . . is when . . . the soul begins to be still from imagining. . . . There is no judgment from without upon it, but only in its own judgment. . . . For imputed Grace from without is of no effect. . . . The imputed Grace . . . must be manifested in us, in the inward ground of the soul, and be our life. . . . Repentance should not be put off till the end, for an old tree takes root badly. If Christ is not in the soul, there is no Grace nor forgiveness of sins. Christ Himself is the forgiveness of sins who with His Blood transmutes in our soul the introduced abominations. (*Gnad.* xiii, 7ff)

Repentance leads to prayer, man's second response to Christ's work.

Real prayer is not the habit of repeating the words of prayer; no, such verbalizing without heartfelt devotion and divine desire is merely an outward act, an external word-carving. (*Gebet* i)

There is true prayer and false prayer, the latter dependent upon the nature of him who prays. Prayer is a discipline in which the will is transformed and can enter into the divine will and become saturated with divine Love (*Dreyfach* xii, 25). Prayer without Love is unavailing (*Dreyfach* viii, 13) because it is the soul's hunger for God's primordial will

(*Dreyfach* xvi, 47). Man must not come before God with naked breath and idle words; he must come converted from his false way of life:

We must want to depart from all arrogance, falsity, wrath, envy, and stubbornness. We must want to yield our whole heart and soul to God, the Holy Spirit, so that He is our repentant activity and our desire in prayer. He shall enclose our will and desire in Himself, leading them to God, so that we may die to our false vanity and desire in the Death of Christ, which has been declared to us all, being born in the spirit of Christ to a new will, mind, and loyalty to God. And we shall henceforth come before God with our new will and birth in such a power of righteousness and purity, like His children which He has dearly bought through the Blood and Death of His dear Son, regenerating them in His Spirit. (*Gebet* 10)

Through such prayer the inner Christ is awakened and God's enkindled fire-wrath is quenched (*Aurora* xvi, 11, 12).

Man's third response is true faith. In a fine passage Boehme describes what he means by true faith.

Now, faith is not an historical knowledge, that man should frame articles to himself and depend on them alone, and force his mind into the works of his reason; but faith is one spirit with God, for the Holy Spirit moves in the spirit of faith. True faith is the power of God, one spirit with God. It works in and with God. It is free and bound to no article, save only to the true love, in which it gathers the power and strength of its life; human delusion and conjecture are of no consequence. For as God is free . . . in such a sense that He does whatever He wills, and needs give no account about it; so also is the true faith in the spirit of God. It has no more than one inclination, viz., to the Love and Mercy of God . . ; it seeks not itself in carnal reason, but in God's Love . . . It regards the earthly life as nothing . . . It gives itself up in humility to the will of God . . . It makes where there is nothing, and takes where nothing is made. It is operative, and no one sees its being. It is mighty, and yet is the lowest humility. It possesses all, and yet embraces nothing more than gentleness. It is thus free from all iniquity and has no law, for the fierce wrath of nature has no influence upon it. It exists from eternity, for it is comprehended in no ground. (*Menschw.* III, i, 2–4)

Faith, one of the powers of God (*Princ.* vii, 3), is born in a resigned man's will (*Menschw.* I, xi, 8). It is the essential Word in men from which the incorruptible flesh is made (*Gnad.* ix, 98). Where faith is absent the Word has no essence (*Test.* I, ix, 42).

Persecuted by his church, Boehme bore little love for the outward heap of stones which could neither save nor redeem (*Menschw.* I, xii, 3). But he cared with all his heart for the mystical seed in the believer's heart (*Myst. Mag.* xxxvi, 60).

.The whole titular Christendom is turned into mere sects and orders, where one sect despises and brands another as unrighteous. And thus they have made of Christendom a mere murdering den, full of blasphemies about Christ's person; and have bound the spirit of Christ . . . to the forms and orders of disputation. (*Myst. Mag.* xl, 94)

In the churches self-seeking rules; each wants to be master.

In the stone-houses of the churches, cathedrals, and cloisters . . . they do counterfeit somewhat of Christ, seeing that they there read the writings which the Apostles left behind them; but afterwards in their preaching . . . they foist in the kingdom of nature, with brawling and disputing; and spend their time with disputing, confuting, and contending about sects (and different mental idols and opinions), in so much that one party is brought wholly to condemn the other, and the ears (and hearts) of the hearers are so infected with gall and bitterness that one sect wilfully opposes another, and cries it down for devilish; whence nothing but wars and disdainful provocations do arise, to the desolation of countries and cities. (*Myst. Mag.* xl, 98)

A Christian has Christ on the inward ground (*Gnad.* x, 37) and so has the church in his heart (*Myst. Mag.* xxxvi, 60). The real church is Christ and He dwells in us (*Menschw.* I, xiii, 3). To go into a world-church without the inward Christ can make no one good (*Test.* I, preface, 6) as Satan often leads penitents to church believing it is a real church when it is only a bawdy-house (*Myst. Mag.* lxii, 45, 36) for God's concubines.

This hard word was compensated for by Boehme's description of the inner church of the spirit which is Christ's image on earth (*Sig. Rer.* xi, 54) and His mother (*Sig. Rer.* xi, 35). There are two churches, Cain's and Abel's (*Myst. Mag.* xxvi, 25; xxvii, xxviii); Cain's rides high; Abel's dwells within it. The true temple is Divine Love (*Myst. Mag.* lxxiv, 26) and where Love becomes visible the Church of Jesus Christ is.

Boehme's order of salvation is within and the means of Grace are subjectively adopted. External forms are unnecessary. Since Christ lives essentially within the regenerated soul (*Myst. Mag.* xxxix, 9) He nourished and sustains him by means of His sacraments. A Christian hungers for Christ's members (*Myst. Mag.* lviii, 52), wanting Christ's sustaining nourishing food.

The testaments of Christ are nothing else but a loving bond . . . wherewith God in Christ binds Himself to us and us to Him. (*Wiedergeburt* viii, 2)

Boehme's metaphysics, with its earthly and heavenly substances, determines his sacramentarian views:

The outward heaven is the . . . conception of . . . water. . . . The holy water is yet continually separated from water under the firmament. This holy water is that of which Christ told us, that He would give us it to drink; that should spring up in us to a fountain of eternal life. The holy heavenly corporeality does not consist therein; it is the body of Christ which He brought from heaven, and by the same, introduced heavenly, paradisaical essentiality into our dead . . . body; and quickened ours in his. . . . In this heavenly essence the Testaments of Christ consist (*Myst. Mag.* x, 56)

This holy essence is eaten by the soul and the earthly mouth does not chew it with its teeth (*Seel. Frag.* viii, 3ff). The outward meal is a remembrance of the inner (*Seel. Frag.* viii, 3). Sacraments are not sin offerings or sacrifices (*Myst. Mag.* xxvii, 43) but a feeding on God's essence.

Boehme, the Protestant, held two sacraments: baptism and

the supper. While Schwenkfeldian ideas are sometimes expressed by Lutheran phrases like *Unwürdig, Taufbund,* Boehme's words really are superficial.

Circumcision and baptism are one act (*Myst. Mag.* xl, 10) and baptism is made with the heavenly water in which God's flaming Love-word has incorporated itself. The body is baptized with elemental water, the spirit with heavenly water (*Sig. Rer.* vii, 67) by means of the Holy Spirit (*Test.* I, ii, 39). The minister baptizes with outward water while the Holy Spirit baptizes with the water of eternal life (*Princ.* xxiii, 37). Boehme does not distinguish infant or adult baptism; he says that all sinners need continuous baptism (*Theos. Punkt.* viii, 9).

The Supper is the sacramental meal by which Christ's body is fed to man's soul (*Dreyfach* xi, 75). It was instituted by Jesus in the upper room.

When they met together and made known the wonders of the Lord, and sat together with a fervent spirit; then, after exhortation one of another, they distributed the Lord's Last Supper, as He had commanded them: They took bread and brake it, and ate of it, and thereby and therewith have commemorated the Lord's Death; in like manner also they took the cup, and drank of it, and commemorated the shedding of His Blood; saying one to another, Take and eat the Lord's Body, which was given for us on the Cross. So also they did with the cup; they took it in their hand, and drank of it; for the uppermost of the congregation began, and said to the other, Take the cup and drink the Blood of Christ our Lord, which He has shed for us on the Cross for the remission of sins. . . .

Here Boehme sets forth a democratic supper without priestcraft; there is no sacrificial thanksgiving:

He gave not . . . the earthly substance . . . which was despised, buffeted, spit upon, scourged, and slain. . . . He gave them His holy body, His holy flesh . . . whereby the Disciples were capable of receiving Christ, and became members of His Body. (*Dreyfach* xiii, 10ff)

In the Supper man is nourished by light, drowning the wrath

and so becoming incorporated in the Love which is Christ. He draws Christ to and within Himself.

The reborn man, in a new body, the production of which is the aim of Boehme's soteriology, again achieves the total human image foretold in Scripture and promised in faith. He gets again what Adam lost, a body of harmonious elements and equivalent Love. This is eschatological man. To achieve this total human image by restoring Adam's pristine essence to man was the second covenant's purpose.

God has decreed a day, in which He will bring the essence of the old and first Adam through the fire, when it shall be released from vanity, from the craving of the Devil and from the wrath of eternal nature. We understand further how God has brought again into us His holy being . . . in the true pure Love, and has rekindled His Love . . . and generated a new image. (*Menschw.* I, xii, 10ff)

Salvation is thus healing us, making us whole. Our earth body puts on Christ's essence only after death; but our soul can put on His heavenly flesh and blood here and now (*Gnad.* viii, 97ff). External flesh cannot be regenerated until after the general resurrection on the last day; but the inner man's new birth begins with his faith and proceeds through a process of repentance, resignation, ethical regeneration to expectant hope (*Princ.* xvi, 48). The new birth is acquirement of a new will (*Myst. Punkt.* iii, 25) which is the expressed name JESUS (*Tab. Princ.* 72). When the soul leaves the third principle and goes into the second it stands in Jesus' heart (*Dreyfach* iii, 49); man, therefore, departs from his animal nature (*Princ.* xxi, 70), enduring suffering, trial, and tribulation (*Menschw.* II, vi, 12) as Christ did, for to be newly born we must follow Christ (*Gnad.* ix, 116). The newly born person is wisdom's child and has become whole again (*Myst. Mag.* lxvi, 47).

The redemptive struggle continues in man. Christ has opened up a gate (*Gebet* 31) but not all men enter in. Christ offers a new birth in a new body but the earth is ever yet present.

So long as the earthly man lives, the soul is . . . in dan-

ger, for the Devil has enmity with it . . . and reaches . . .
after the fire of the soul; here fighting is required.
(*Menschw.* II, vi, 11)

The world is full of the Devil's snares set to catch men
(*Dreyfach* xiv, 20). The elemental earthly life is still at
enmity with the newborn man; death is still present (*Myst.
Mag.* lii, 13–14).

The noble image must always be in strife against the outer
reason-life, and the more it strives, the greater grows the fair
tree, for the image co-operates with God. (*Menschw.* III,
viii, 7)

The crown of victory is set upon the revived soul which,
however,

as soon as it transpires, is immediately laid aside as a crown,
just as one crowns a king—afterwards the coronation must
be proven by trial. So it happens with the soul since she is
still surrounded with the house of sin, for, if she were to fall
again, then her crown would be defiled. (*Busse* 27)

Believing man is regenerated only in his inner nature; in his
external body the struggle continues (*Bedenk. Stief.* 50ff).
Sin still cleaves to flesh and many, like David, become so
strong that they fall again (*Gnad.* vi, 33). No one is excluded for there was no ordaining regarding any individual
soul, merely a general predestination in Grace (*Gnad.* xii,
9). Man is free. His life is a battlefield of two wills, a fateful
duel.

As a twig grows out of the earth, and the essence flees
from the earth, and is drawn up by the sun till a stalk . . .
is produced out of it, so also does God's sun in His power
always draw man's lily, i.e., the new man, from the evil
essence. (*Menschw.* II, vii, 12)

There is no dodging or avoiding this struggle; it takes place
in all men; none are free of it. This inner Christ

shines for all peoples, for one as well as another: for one

people in His revealed Name, and for another in the name of the one God. He draws them all. (*Gnad.* xiii, 18)

At this dawning those heathen Christians who have true knowledge shall be judged more vigorously, especially those who conceal and hide the Light by false interpretations; who persecute one another. Christians live just as selfishly as the heathen.

Why then will we wrangle here about a knowledge of the gifts? In Christ are all the treasures of wisdom. If we have Him we have all; but if we lose Him, then we have lost all, and ourselves too. The one ground of our religion is, that we love Christ in us, and love one another as Christ has loved us. . . . But this love is not manifest in us unless Christ become man and be manifested in us. He gives His Love to us so that we love one another in Him. (*Gnad.* xii, 21ff)

The end shall come again to the beginning. Life's wheel shall revolve. To live in Love is to live in Eternity (*Dreyfach* xviii, 21) and to live in Love is to dwell in God (*Seel. Frag.* i, 46). Here is freedom beyond existential dialectic, a true rest, a sabbath beyond selfhood's iniquity and worldly evil (*Myst. Mag.* xl, 32).

Man now still lives in time and temporal evil shall continue until the golden age (*Seel. Frag.* iii, 21) when all secrets shall be manifest (*Myst. Mag.* xxxv, 2), all desires known. This is Enoch's time.

Boehme, like so many great Christians, felt that this age was near. His own time was that of the seventh seal—six already had been broken—but soon the new day's dawn— which he had seen in vision—would become actualized and hell's horrors would stand revealed (*Dreyfach* xv, 2, 3). Then will come the thousand years of God's peace (*Seel. Frag.* i, 4), ending the distinctions in time and history. Then will the disharmony of the third principle be removed; the *magna turba* in the earth will pass. Sin's power will be broken. The sleepers will be awakened (*Dreyfach* v, 130), wrath will be changed into Love.

The last judgment is . . . an ingathering by the Father of

all beings and of all that He has brought forth through His Word. Into whatever anything in free will has separated itself, into that will it enter. (*Gnad.* vi, 86)

When this youngest day comes wars will cease, elemental strife will pass. Life no longer will be made up of Yes and No in conflict. Yes and No will be melted, fused into one wonderful joyous harmony. As Boehme wrote in the copybook of a friend:

> *Weme Zeit ist wie Ewigkeit,*
> *Und Ewigkeit wie die Zeit,*
> *Der ist befreyt*
> *Von allem Streit.*

Ach Gott, wo soll ich weiter fragen!
Er ist bei keiner Kreatur.
Wer führt mich über die Natur?
Wer schafft ein Ende meinem Klagen?
Ich muss mich über alles schwingen,
Muss mich erheben über mich:
Dann, hoff ich, wird mirs wohl gelingen,
Dass ich, o Jesu, finde dich.

—ANGELUS SILESIUS

EPILOGUE

JACOB BOEHME had seen eternity's dawn. This red-flaming vision of a new spiritual world lit up the darksome shadows of his age and of his heart. He saw Yes and bitter No in all things—in his war-torn Lausitz homeland, in his sin-buffeted self, and in his riven church. This was the one pole of his vision.

The other pole was never quite projected in full perspective into his temporal consciousness but it persisted with a stubbornness which Gregory Richter could not comprehend. Boehme's dawn was no mist-shrouded breaking of a worldly day; it was sunrise to *eternity*. His ultimate vision, never really expressed in his writings but ever implicit, was of universal spiritual unity in the bonds of peace. The Yes and No which he saw were provisional, passing prelude to a world ultimately at peace with itself. Although he never formulated this part of his vision in the utopian terms which some of his contemporaries employed, still this sabbath was the heart of his sight.

His sun had dawned! But what a Sun it was! As his follower, poet Angelus Silesius, wrote:

Jesus, ew'ge Sonne,
Aller Engel Wonne,
Was für Freude muss es sein
Wenn du kommst ins Herz hinein.

Jesus, Sun of Righteousness and Prince of Peace, had dawned in Boehme's heart to a new eternity. This was a dawning to a new age and a new world.

Boehme—and now, perhaps, we may want to call him the "blessed Jacob"—was a Christian mystic on whom the gracious Spirit had descended. However maligned by Gregory Richter, he stood in the line of prophets who, without benefit of priestly ordination, had seen the mystery unfold itself. Boehme, though, was neither classical nor oriental mystic; he had climbed no ladders nor escaped the wheel of reincarnative births. Closing his eyes and mouth—as mysticism originally suggests, perceiving the great mystery, he was led to penetrate beyond the breach between man and woman, between creed and creed, and between God and the world. Plotinus, typical classical mystic, had been four times transported into ecstasy. Not Boehme, however. He claimed, on the contrary, that God had come down into him. Thus did he reject classical mysticism's ascending Gothic, the mysticism of hierarchies, fashioning instead a properly Protestant mystical genre of descending Agapé. He wanted nothing of ladders, pilgrimages, levels, stages, degrees, hierarchies— the ascending steps of an ambitious faith seeking to seize and to know the Godhead. For between medieval mysticism and Boehme there towered Luther and his *simul iustus et peccator*, for the reformer had centered the attention on the psychology rather than the mechanics of repentance, as Boehme's tracts on *Busse* show.

Some insist that mysticism implies *Nirvana*, that is, that the self must be destroyed by being lost in the abyss of pure being. This is posited on a view which sees selfhood as evil. Boehme was aware of this danger for he wrote:

> But her [Sophia's] marriage to the Soul is not immediately consummated nor is that image which was distorted in Paradise immediately restored. Here is dangerous ground for man, since both Lucifer and Adam fell at this point, which may happen again because man is still firmly bound by vanity. (*Busse* 32)

Not only did Boehme disclaim *Nirvana;* he asserted that it was man's chiefest sin.

Nirvana is the necessary religious goal of monism. It appears only within those metaphysical systems which consider the self's finitude evil *per se*. What this means, in short, is that the doctrine of sin defines the dualism which the mystic seeks to resolve. And the solution to the problem of evil *is* mediated to the mystic by the metaphysical environment in which he happens to dwell.

The Greeks had formulated the problem of evil by assuming that matter was evil; this made them seek, therefore, to become fleshless. Buddhism, identifying evil with suffering selfhood, had sought to void the self in apophatic pantheism. Orphic deliverance had been by transcending individuality in esoteric orgiasm, a holy bestiality. Stoicism had sought to harmonize individual reason with the universal mind. The Neoplatonists had sought deliverance by intellect through supra-rational apprehension of Truth. Each way had been determined by its view of evil which issued from the metaphysical climate which surrounded it.

It is, perhaps, clear that the prevailing metaphysical climate conditions the view of evil which in turn determines the religious quest. Flesh, self, matter, ignorance, suffering—each has been exorcised. But this is negative, for these goals are obtained by some scheme of negation, a point of view which was clearly expressed by Pseudo-Dionysius:

We shall obtain ecstasy by denying or removing all things that are—like as men, who, carving a statue out of marble, remove all the impediments that hinder the clear perception of the latent image and by this mere removal display the hidden statue itself in its hidden beauty.[1]

In contrast to this negative mysticism, Boehme sought a new man who was a regenerated son of God. Selfhood, individuality, conditioned existence were for him not evil *per se*. So he did not seek to remove these "impediments" because he did not believe that they impeded. He knew that his lily could become a perfect lily only because it welcomed the energies of earth, air, and sun, only if it grew to full individual perfection from within. To be a lily was not in itself evil. What Boehme wanted for himself and for his world was not to get rid of the multiplicity of finite forms but simply to remove the great curse within reality which prevented the multiplicity of God's wisdom from becoming expressed in forms. His was a world-redeeming not a world-escaping faith!

This mystical revolution—and that is what it really was—was wrought when Boehme, freed from a medievalism which had been shackled by Greek metaphysics, sought to combine the new cosmology of the Renaissance with his Lutheran Bible. The medieval church had sought to get man to heaven. But Boehme's Bible told him that Christ had commanded us to love! Now, *love is a this-world ethic!* It is not an ethic of renunciation. It takes place within time and we do not wait for death to become lovers. Wrath and love—his temporal Yes and No—were both present judgments within a world of time, and their resolution could be accomplished within history without ecstatic transcendence.

Boehme's mind, surrounded by a theological climate almost as dry as the Sahara, knew that religion was more than creed-hawking, system-building, and confessional apologetic; it was love! He approached the task of externalizing this faith, which is basically an irrational one, with bold, fresh, and uninhibited mind, one that was not trained in the schools and knew neither the Lombard's *Sentences* nor the Philippist *Loci Communes.* And as a consequence he fashioned a theology whose images and terms were in full rebellion against the usual theological categories, thus pointing forward towards the future liberation of theology by the subjective language of romantics like Schleiermacher. This fresh, bold, venturing spirit brought Boehme much pain and discomfort—but it is also the index of his greatness.

Boehme's Yes and No were within his self, too. He was indeed the first significant voluntarist because he sought removal of the divided wills within his being. The Neoplatonists had understood the place of will in the processes of ideation and knowing; Augustine had known that the achievement of consciousness was an act of will; Duns Scotus and Occam had given will prominence in their epistemologies. But Boehme saw in his divided self both fire and light, both egocentric libido and yielding love, and he knew, not that one will was necessary for consciousness, but that two wills were wanted.

Without dialectic no thing can become manifest to itself. If nothing resists it, then it continually proceeds from itself; it does not return to itself again. . . . If the natural life had no dialectic . . . then it would never ask for the ground from which it came. (*Beschau.* i, 8–9)

With Eckhart will had been a means of knowing God, and in the late sixteenth century will had meant knowledge for control; the unity sought in Counter-Reformation mysticism was unity of control, implying the new psychology of Loyola's *Spiritual Exercises.* This voluntaristic monism could not produce self-consciousness and Boehme's problem with regard to the Trinity, posited for the first time in Christian history, was to produce a self-contemplating God known by a God-contemplating self.

The traditional trinitarian view describes how God acts *vis-à-vis* His creation; it does not show how He knows Himself. Boehme's theogony is therefore an unusual attempt to show how both a self-contemplating God comes to know Himself and then, after creation, how He knows and is known by His creatures. To do this Boehme had to conceive of God's inner life as both conscious and beyond consciousness; he had to postulate his nonrational *Ungrund,* an idea—if so it may be called—which follows from the difference between the *deus occultus* and the *deus absconditus.*

The *deus occultus* grew from the union of Dionysian mysticism and nominalism as in Gerson's *Considerationes de mystica theologica,* holding that God is hidden from man, and man, knowing only that God is, can know positively only what God is not. The Lutheran-Boehmist *deus absconditus,* however, posits not so much a God hidden *from* man as a God whose mysterious depth is unknown both to Himself and to His creature—a God who is to some degree a mystery.[2] Boehme's formulation of his fundamental problem is put in language as clear as that of any philosophical theologian; he wrote:

Had the hidden God, who is merely one Essence and Will, not led Himself by His Will out of Himself, had He not brought Himself out of eternal comprehension in the *temperamenta* [3] into a differentiation of wills, and had He not led the same differentiation into a subjectivation of natural and creaturely life, and did this same differentiation not stand in strife in life, how then would the hidden Will of God, which in itself is single, become manifest to itself. (*Beschau.* 1, 10)

Boehme, then, sought to explain how a self-conscious God and a self-conscious creature came to be.

By thus postulating a dark mysterious point of identity behind God's consciousness Boehme raised an aspect of God which is neither nature nor spirit, subject nor object, thought nor being, but the unity of all contradictions. When once a *coincidentia oppositorum* is thus postulated then two basic laws of thought are abnegated: the law of contradiction and the law of the excluded third. A new logic appears. Aristotle had asserted that where there is disparity there can be no love.[4] But Boehme saw deeper. He understood that where there is no disparity there can be neither love nor self-consciousness. To love one needs both a lover and a beloved. Love implies, nay demands, separate persons—lovers, selves. If love be man's chief end then selfhood cannot be evil *per se* nor is self-consciousness evil *per se*, as classical and oriental religions hold. This was Boehme's fundamental insight for he saw that love demanded two self-conscious beings who were capable of freely directing their own loves beyond themselves. Oriental and classical religions denied the validity of finitude and personality and they considered limitation and differentiated existence as evil. Not so Christianity, however much it may have been formulated in Aristotelian terms. Boehme's vision of a loving kingdom where there was a first and a last, where perfected selves sat down to eat heavenly manna with their risen Lord, while not unique with him, was, however, unfamiliar ground for oriental and classical mystics. Boehme, by validating self-conscious personality, also validated the Christian ethic of love. Surely this achievement, while shared with other great spirits within Christendom, is great enough for so simple a man, the humble and meek little cobbler of Görlitz.

Boehme has been victimized by a false reputation. Surely we have quoted enough from his pen—however inadequate translation may be—to dispose of the popular notion that he had an "apocalyptic obscurity" in his style. He wrote clear German, sometimes a German of more-than-average merit, and whatever obscurity there was issued from the inadequacy of language rather than from paucity of vision or littleness of mind. His vocabulary, as has already been said, was not the usual verbiage of theology; herein, however, lies its value. Writing before man had acquired precision in describing subjective states, writing with little allegory, he yet managed to convey his profoundly inwardized vision of the nature of consciousness and of the world.

Perhaps, when the ultimate sunrise dawns to final eternity, Boehme's vision that all things consist of Yes and No will prove to have been close to the ultimate truth. Our physicists, immersed in their tables and formulae, working their slide-rules and calculating their logarithms, know that an atom is the dynamic equipoise of plus and minus and when the *temperamentum* is disturbed by the flaming fire-flash —a truly cosmic *Blick* and *Blitz*—chaos ensues. Stripped of its nonessentials Boehme's vision is proven each time an atom is split.

Not only were atoms made up of Yes and No, plus and minus, but our human society also was split into affirmation and negation. Boehme lived his earthly course on the banks of the Neisse river in eastern Germany, and today the fateful Neisse-Oder line splits two worlds apart. Living thus on the boundary of East and West his vision of binding Love may yet prove capable of bridging the chasm of our riven world. It yet may prove a *sunrise to eternity*. As he would have said,

"To this end may God help us all!"

NOTES TO EPILOGUE

1. *Myst. Theol.* tr. Rolt., 194–195.
2. Hinc Verbum factum est et sapientia dei abscondita et exinanita, ut nostram quoque hanc pessimam sapientam absconderet et examiniret, quae est plena vanitate errore et peccata. Luther in *Werke*, Weimar edition, I, 34.
3. This is harmony without dialectic or contrary wills.
4. *Eth. Nic.* 1165. b.17

BIBLIOGRAPHICAL NOTE

BIOGRAPHICAL MATERIALS about Boehme are for the most part confused and untrustworthy, especially the earlier materials. The first critical analysis was Will-Erich Peuckert's *Das Leben Jakob Böhmes*, Jena, 1924. Here the early materials were scanned and the background well integrated, although full use was not made of Boehme's own letters. Richard Jecht's *Jakob Böhme—Gedenkgabe der Stadt Görlitz*, 1924, presented the new materials from various sources in the Görlitz Archives. There are at least eighteen references to Boehme in the official records, and we know as much about him, in the objective sense, as we do about his slightly older contemporary, William Shakespeare. The best source, however, is Boehme's own writings.

The several collected editions of Boehme's writings contain seven tracts which deal with biographical materials. These have been translated and published by Francis Okeley, *Memoirs of the Life of Jacob Behmen*, Northampton, 1780. The first of these tracts is von Franckenberg's *De Vita et Scriptis*, which has been often cited in our work. Dr. Peuckert has traced all of Franckenberg's materials back to even more remote sources, except of course those materials which he made up. The second of these tracts is Dr. Weisner's *Wahrhaftiger Relation*, the account by a Breslau physician which was sent to the Boehmist groups in Amsterdam in 1651. It is trustworthy, although limited. The third tract, and the most reliable, is Dr. Kober's *Umständiger Bericht*, a longish account by Boehme's personal physician which was written in November, 1624, the month of Boehme's death, and therefore the earliest work we have. It is fully trustworthy and contains detailed descriptions of Boehme's illness, his last hours, and eight supplementary documents as follows: a) Dietrich's letter to Kober, b) Dietrich's Questions to Boehme which we have paraphrased in our work; c) the eulogy given at Boehme's funeral; d) Boehme's widow's petition to the Council; f) Michael Kurtz's account of the funeral; g) Michael Kurtz's eulogy; and h) specification of certain questions prior to absolution.

The text of Boehme's writings, although the product of much labor by the early editors, still presents major problems.

The printed versions are clear enough, but the problem arises from the relationships of these versions to the several manuscripts. Variants exist in the manuscripts. Furthermore, the British translations made by the commonwealth-period Boehmists were most likely made from printed Holland-Dutch versions and so were not direct translations from Boehme's German.

When Franckenberg first listed Boehme's writings his chronology was not fully correct. And we are not sure that all Boehme's works have survived. In 1675, Beets, publisher of the German versions, inserted an advertisement in the back of one of Franckenberg's books saying that a tract, *Der Krauter der Natur*, was known to have existed. What a find this would be to discover that Boehme was also an early botanist! Boehme himself says in *Apol. Richter* something about his book on the noble Sophia which he also mentions in *Letzte Zeit* I, 1, 2. He also refers to several small treatises which he had given here and there and kept no copy of.

Werner Buddecke has found most of the manuscripts that were available to the early editors and he has catalogued them in his *Verzeichnis*. Also he has collated these with the early printed editions.

The manuscripts were originally gathered by a wealthy Amsterdam merchant, van Beyerland, who, after much trouble and with considerable luck, finally got these writings to Holland where he proceeded to translate them into Dutch. All of Boehme's works except *Irrth. Stief.* and *Aurora*, along with *Sig. Rer.* and *Myst. Mag.*—works of his maturity—first appeared in Dutch. The last three appeared in German editions. The manuscripts were handed down to Beyerland's heirs, and Franckenberg brought out an edition in succeeding years. In 1682 Gichtel brought out his famous edition, erroneously called the first, which was reset and brought out under Glusing's editorship in 1715. Then Johann Wilhelm Ueberfeld re-edited the works, compared them with the manuscripts, modernized the spelling, and brought out the 1730 edition in ten volumes which is the standard. We have used it, and it is now in process of being made available in a modern German edition. The Schiebler reprints of the 1682 edition are not critical.

Of the vast literature on Boehme Koyré's is the only work of comprehensive scope and Benz's the most penetrating. The best interpretations still are the lectures which Franz von Baader made on Boehme, especially on *Gnad.*, the work of his deep maturity.

In our opinion—and the reader may take it for what it is worth—most interpreters have made two mistakes: first, they have failed to see his growth, his ability to discard ideas when they no longer suited him; and secondly, they have failed to appreciate Boehme's own understanding of his categories, of the "joints" in his system. The fatal mistake, made by Hegel and so many others, is to identify the seven spirits of God with the seven natural powers.

INDEX

CPSIA information can be obtained at www.ICGtesting.com
Printed in the USA
LVOW130553060712

288826LV00002B/63/P